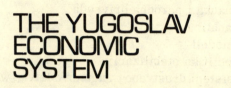

THE YUGOSLAV ECONOMIC SYSTEM

By the same author:

Towards a Theory of Planned Economy
An Essay on Yugoslav Society
Business Cycles in Yugoslavia
Yugoslav Economic Policy in the Post-War Period
Self-governing Socialism (with M. Marković and R. Supek)
Ekonomika naftne privrede
Medjusektorska analiza
Ekonomska nauka i narodna privreda
Ekonomska analiza
Ekonomski modeli
Ekonomska politika stabilizacije
Integrirani sistem društvenog računovodstva (with
    Z. Popov, D. Dimitrijević, and I. Vinski)

THE YUGOSLAV ECONOMIC SYSTEM

THE FIRST LABOR-MANAGED
ECONOMY IN THE MAKING

BRANKO HORVAT

 International Arts and Sciences Press, Inc., White Plains, N.Y.

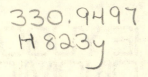

© 1976 by International Arts and Sciences Press, Inc.

This book is an expansion and revision of Yugoslav Economic
Policy in the Post-War Period: Problems, Ideas, Institutional
Developments by Branko Horvat, first published as a supplement
to Volume LXI, Number 5 of The American Economic Review.
Copyright American Economic Association 1971.

Library of Congress Catalog Card Number: 75-46111

International Standard Book Number: 0-87332-074-3

Printed in the United States of America

CONTENTS

PREFACE
TO THE SECOND ENGLISH EDITION

The first edition of this book covered the period up to the end of 1969 and was published as a supplement to the American Economic Review in 1971, under the title Yugoslav Economic Policy in the Post-War Period: Problems, Ideas, Institutional Developments. This edition was soon sold out, and frequent references in professional journals indicated that there was substantial interest in a text of this kind. Instead of reprinting this edition, however, I decided to wait a few years and then prepare a revised and enlarged version. The present edition is almost twice as long as the original one. It is brought up to date through the end of 1974. It also fills two major lacunae of the first edition by adding chapters on regional development and agriculture. The latter was given particular attention, since agriculture is generally considered the weakest link in socialist development.

The book thus covers the entire period of existence of the new Yugoslavia — that is, the thirty years between the end of the Second World War in 1945 and the beginning of 1975. These years represent one of the longest peaceful periods in the turbulent thousand-year history of the five Yugoslav nations. They are also the most productive historical period, in the sense that these Balkan peoples have been able to introduce true social innovations — perhaps for the first time — in the general course of world development. During these thirty years, Yugoslavia has been a busy social laboratory. The results — not always desirable or expected — are well worth studying.

In analyzing economic and social processes, I tried to achieve complete coverage of all relevant written sources. I hope that no important book or article is missing from the list of references. As for interpretation of facts, I relied on my own experience as an active participant in these processes, from the days of the Revolution, when I was active in underground youth groups and later in the Partisan Liberation War, up to more recent times, when I served as a member of the Federal Planning Board and participated in various economic committees of the federal government. In order to understand the process of development, one must become familiar with the facts, compare policy proclamations with the achieved results, study the theories and ideas which led to a certain policy, distinguish the economic and political ingredients in decision making, and analyze carefully the causes of both successes and failures. This is roughly what I tried to do in the present book. The text itself is kept as brief as possible, and every important statement is referenced with some source where a more complete argument can be found.

It is my pleasant duty to acknowledge with thanks the collaboration and help of several persons and institutions. My colleague Dr. Marta Bazler-Madžar wrote Chapter 7 on regional development. Dr. Helen Kramer translated Chapters 8-12 from Serbo-Croatian into English and provided me with valuable linguistic assistance and helpful comments. The American Economic Association kindly granted the permission to use the text of the first edition. The Institute of Economic Sciences in Belgrade provided me with necessary facilities for the completion of this study.

Branko Horvat

Belgrade, February 1975

THE YUGOSLAV ECONOMIC SYSTEM

INTRODUCTION

Yugoslavia may be described as one country with two alphabets, three religions, four languages, five nations, six federal states called republics, seven neighbors, and eight national banks. The country has a population of 21 million and lies in the heart of the Balkans, with all that this connotes historically. For centuries the Balkans have been a meeting place of three world cultures, with their three powerful religions: the Catholic West, the Greek Orthodox East, and the Moslem South. In the contemporary era, these cultures are associated with three types of economic organization — capitalism in the West, central planning in the East, and underdevelopment in the South.

All these influences have been felt. A rather turbulent history was to be expected in a country with such a geographic location and such characteristics. The present generation of Yugoslavia has experienced all three known modern economic systems: capitalism before the war, centrally planned economy after the war, and self-governing socialism in more recent years. The last-mentioned system is Yugoslavia's own innovation, and so far the only one of its kind in existence. The same generation has also experienced all four modern political regimes: bourgeois democracy (in the form of a constitutional monarchy and multiparty system) before the war, fascism during the war, one-party state immediately after the war, and self-governing democracy, which is now in the process of development. It has also lived through a partisan national liberation war and a revolution. After the war, a centralized kingdom was replaced by a federal republic, and in three decades the country had four constitutions. Finally, the same generation has experienced three different economic epochs: a preindustrial stage before the war, rapid industrialization in the two decades after the war, and the recently begun stage of a modern industrial economy

The Yugoslav Economic System

Table 1

Selected Indicators of Development

	Prewar		Yugoslavia, 1968
	Yugo-slavia	Western Europe[a]	
Production per capita:			
Electric energy (kilowatt-hours)	80	500-1300	1000
Crude steel (kilograms)	17	150-300	96
Cement (kilograms)	60	100-190	190
Cotton yarn (kilograms)	1.3	5-11	5
Consumption per capita:			
Energy (kilograms of coal equivalent)	180	2100-4300	1030
Fertilizers (kilograms)	3	20-65	96
Sugar (kilograms)	5	24-47	25
Stocks per 1000 population:			
Radio sets	9	110-200	160
Automobiles	1	17-50	20

Sources: SGJ-1969; UN Statistical Yearbook, 1956.
a. France, Germany, Sweden, United Kingdom.

approaching the Western European level. Before the war, 77 percent of the population were peasants and 40 percent were illiterate. A few economic indicators will suffice to show the economic development that has taken place since then (see Table 1).

Since 1968, the further increase in the level of living has been rapid. In 1973 three-quarters of nonagricultural households had television sets and 27 percent (in Slovenia, 39 percent) owned automobiles. On the other hand, large discrepancies have not yet been overcome. Illiterates still constitute one-sixth of the adult population — one-third in the most backward region of Kosovo; but, at the same time, with 15 university and college students per 1000 population, the country has moved close to the very top on the world list for this indicator.

Such a tremendous pace of change virtually destroyed all traditions; but it also created a new one — a tradition of no tradition, a tradition of change. In line with this, the 1958 Program of the League of Communists — the heir of the Yugoslav Communist Party — ends with the words: "Nothing that has been created must be so sacred for us that it cannot be surpassed and cede its place to what is still more progressive, more free, more human."

In such circumstances, economic discussion displayed certain unusual features that make formal presentation somewhat difficult. Until about 1960, most of the discussion was not put down on paper, or at least was not published. Further, professional articles made practically no use of references. There was the feeling that a complete break with the past had been made, and so there was nothing to which to refer. In the same period, professional literature was almost completely descriptive. This was due partly to the fact that the first university departments in economics were established only after the war. It is said that 90 percent of all the scientists who have ever lived are alive today. As far as Yugoslav economists are concerned, this percentage is virtually 100.

The second reason for the lack of analytical literature is to be found in the fact that there was hardly any time left for analysis. Economists were busy changing organization, institutions, and policies, and keeping themselves informed about all these changes. Unless one had the inclinations of an economic historian, it did not make much sense to engage in a long-term research project. Before the book came off the press, the system would already have been changed. Thus for quite some time professional economists were just describing what was happening. Description always precedes analysis.

Finally, until recently, attention was focused mainly on what Yugoslav economists call the "economic system." Economic policy in the traditional sense — the use of a set of instruments to achieve desired results in a given framework — hardly existed. Problems encountered were generally solved by changing the institutional framework itself. For a long time, and to a certain extent even today, economic policy consisted of an endless series of reorganizations. The search for an appropriate economic system was the main preoccupation of economic policy.

After 1960, economic organization began to assume a more permanent shape and economic discussion began to take a more familiar form. Since then, articles have begun to make use of references, ties with the past and with the rest of the world have been established, economic debates have become frequent and lively, professional competence has increased, and a specifically Yugoslav theory of economic policy is now beginning to emerge.

THREE SOCIOECONOMIC REFORMS

1. CENTRALLY PLANNED ECONOMY

Institutional Development

Of all the European countries occupied by the fascist invaders, Yugoslavia was the only one to liberate itself by its own forces. The National Liberation War coincided with a genuine social revolution. This meant two things: an unbelievably high morale — the readiness to assault the heavens, as a poet said — and also an almost unimaginable degree of devastation of the country. About 1.7 million people were killed in battles, in concentration camps, by penal expeditions, and by domestic quislings. One in every nine inhabitants disappeared in this way. Almost two-fifths of the manufacturing industry was destroyed or seriously damaged. About 3.5 million out of 15 million people were left without shelter. The loss of national wealth amounted to 17 percent of the total war damage suffered by eighteen countries represented at the Paris Reparations Conference in 1945 [1, pp. 27-29]. Apart from all this, the financial system of the country was in chaos; divided and occupied by various aggressive neighbors, the country was left with seven kinds of currency (German marks, Italian lire, Hungarian pöngos, Bulgarian leva, Albanian francs, Serbian dinars, and Croation kunas).

The first task of the new government was to repair war damages as fast as possible and to organize the economy on what were considered to be socialist principles. For this purpose, all available human and material resources were centralized, and by 1947, with enormous efforts and great enthusiasm, the prewar output was again matched. The program of socialist reconstruction was carried out by means of legislative and political activities.

Yugoslavia was a peasant country. Peasants participated in the National Liberation War en masse. Agrarian reform, initiated after the First World War, had never been fully implemented because of the opposition of the ruling classes. No wonder that one of the first moves of the new state was to undertake a radical agrarian reform. The land was to be given to those who tilled it. Less than three months after the end of the war, a law was passed that took away arable land in excess of 87 acres from farmers, and in excess of 12 acres from nonfarmers. Big landowners lost their land without compensation. The land that was acquired in this way was distributed among poor peasants, who received about one-half of the total land, cooperatives, and state farms [4, pp. 53-54].

The next crucial move, undertaken in 1946, was nationalization of private capital in industry, mining, transport, banking, and wholesale trade establishments. In 1948, nationalization was extended to retail trade and catering and in 1958 to residential buildings with more than three apartments. About one-half of the Yugoslav economy, outside agriculture, had been owned by foreign capital. Of the remainder, a sizable part had belonged to the Royal Government, which had owned coal and iron ore mines, forests, and the largest agricultural estates; had enjoyed a monopoly in retail trade of tobacco, salt, matches, and kerosene; and was the largest wholesale trader, transporter, importer and exporter, banker, construction entrepreneur, and real estate owner [2, p. 78]. Since a number of private businessmen collaborated with the fascist invaders and quisling governments, their property was confiscated. Those who took part in the Resistance — and Communist Party members did so as a matter of course — very often gave away their property without asking for compensation. In addition, as was noted earlier, many business establishments were destroyed or damaged. In such circumstances, complete nationalization was practically possible and relatively easy to carry out, and did not represent an excessive financial burden.

The next move was to introduce planning by law in June 1946. Plans were prepared by the Federal Planning Commission, responsible directly to the federal government.

Everything was now ready for the new Constitution, which was adopted in 1946. Article 15 read: "In order to protect the essential interests of the people, increase national welfare and make proper use of all economic potentials, the state directs economic life and development through a general economic plan, relying on the state and cooperative sector and exercising general control over the private sector in the economy." This paragraph may be considered as both the definition and the inauguration of a specific socioeconomic system, later to be known as administrative socialism or etatism.

The year 1947 brought the First Five-Year Plan, which was to lay the foundation for the future industrialized and developed Yugoslavia. The Plan was extremely ambitious — national income was to be doubled as compared with the prewar level — but in the first eighteen months it was quite successfully carried out. It appeared that the period of violent revolutionary upheavals was over and that the country was settled on a well-defined and predictable course of economic and social development.

For Yugoslavia, however, history had always had surprises in store. This time the surprise was more than unexpected: it was a complete shock. In the first half of 1948, Stalin accused Yugoslav Party leaders of revisionism and antisovietism. Yugoslavs rejected the accusation, and soon afterward the Cominform countries launched a full-scale political and economic attack. The Yugoslav Communist Party was excommunicated from the "family of brotherly parties," various treaties were abrogated unilaterally, development loans were canceled, trade with Yugoslavia (amounting to about one-half of her total foreign trade) was reduced to virtually nothing by the middle of 1949, and a complete economic boycott was established.

The first reaction on the Yugoslav side was a somewhat naive but understandable attempt to prove that Stalin and others must have been misinformed, that no one questioned orthodoxy in organizing a socialist economy, that state ownership and central planning were keystones of the system. Motivated by considerations of this sort, in January 1949 the Central Committee of the Party decided to accelerate the collectivization of agriculture. An income tax law passed in August 1948 had already stated that "the rate of taxation should be such as to foster peasants' work cooperatives by means of lower taxes." A law on cooperatives passed in June 1949 provided a legal framework for various types of cooperatives. Individual peasants were free not to join cooperatives if they chose. But by political propaganda and various administrative and financial devices, the authorities exerted strong pressure on them to join, and they did so in great numbers.

Meanwhile, the organization of the economy was modeled after the Soviet pattern. The state budget absorbed the greater part of national income. The state apparatus was running the economy directly by means of ministries and directorates. By 1950, organizational development had so advanced that the Yugoslav economy could be considered as a model of an administratively run or centrally planned economy [3, pp. 126-70]. This was also the climax. As early as 1950, a new development occurred. The following year a complete overhauling of the economic system was in full swing. And by the end of 1951, the centrally planned economy belonged to history.

Discussion

The ideas and theories that served as guidelines in organizing the Yugoslav economy immediately after the war are to be sought in prewar discussions among Yugoslav Marxists. They followed the well-known orthodox viewpoint which held that socialism meant state ownership cum central planning. Immediately after the war, there was so much to do that little time was left for leisurely reflections. Besides, everything seemed pretty clear, both theoretically and practically. One could rely on Marxist literature and on the experience of the Soviet Union, the first socialist country. What mattered most in those days was fast economic growth. And the Soviet Union showed how to achieve it.

But copying the Soviet blueprint did not produce quite the results expected. Besides, the savage attack of the Cominform countries forced people to reconsider their ideological positions quite thoroughly. And so preconditions were created for the emergence of a Yugoslav version of socialism.

Economic discussion before 1952 was dominated by two themes: planning for fast growth and the search for an authentic socialism. Since the former theme will be dealt with in the chapter on planning, we shall focus attention here on the latter.

The older theory maintained that under socialism there would be no market and prices. After the Revolution, Yugoslavia passed through a period of transition between capitalism and socialism. In this period, commodity relationships were still necessary because private ownership still existed and because labor was still heterogeneous [5]. Boris Kidrič, a statesman who dominated the economic thinking of the country until his premature death in 1952,[1]

---

1. Kidrič became President of the Economic Council of the government and Chairman of the Federal Planning Commission. He was also among the top Party leadership.

maintained that only state ownership was truly socialist [6, p. 8], that "the state sector was the highest form of our social owner-ship..." [6, p. 95]. The same opinion is still held by most econo-mists in the Soviet sphere of influence. In Yugoslavia, this idea did not survive beyond 1950. Consistent with the above reasoning was the extolling of the importance of state planning. R. Uvalić [51, p. 20], B. Kidrič [5, p. 42], S. Kraigher [52, p. 12], and others repeated the familiar thesis of Soviet economists that planning is a fundamental law of socialist economics. A few years later, this theory was described as a voluntarist fallacy.

A rereading of Marx and Engels demonstrated the possibility for great confusion in interpretation. Marx and Engels wrote seldom and very little about socialism. What they wrote amounted to two groups of statements: one dealing with the organizational form of a socialist economy, the other with the essential social character-istics of a socialist system. Marx and Engels maintained that com-modity relations and the market would disappear along with private ownership; there would be comprehensive planning; production and distribution would be organized without the mediating role of money. For many decades, it seemed obvious that comprehensive planning meant central planning exercised by the government and that the absence of private ownership meant state ownership. In 1950, it was discovered that Marx had never drawn the last con-clusion. In fact — and here they argued about the essential char-acteristics of socialism — Marx and Engels denounced the state, declared that it would wither away in a classless society, talked about the self-government of producers, and asserted that "a worker is free only when he becomes the owner of his means of production." Marx's insistence on the freedom of the individual was discovered in a statement that was later entered into the Party Program and that reads: "The old bourgeois society with its classes and class antagonism is being replaced by an association in which development of every individual is a precondition for the free development of all" [7, pp. 105-17].

Far from being truly socialist, state ownership turned out to be a remnant of capitalism, characteristic of backward countries that are building socialism and likely to generate dangerous bureau-cratic deviations [4, pp. 16-18]. In 1950 Kidrič wrote: "State so-cialism represents ... only the first and the shortest step of so-cialist revolution.... Persisting in state (bureaucratic) social-ism ... unavoidably leads to an increase and strengthening of priv-ileged bureaucracy as a social parasite, to a suppression ... of socialist democracy and to a general degeneration of the system into . . . state capitalism. . . . The building of socialism categorically requires the development of socialist democracy and a bold transformation of state socialism into a free association of direct producers" [8, pp. 5-6].

Very soon a similar position was accepted by practically all Yugoslav social scientists. M. Novak wrote that to keep state ownership would mean "not the abolition of the proletariat but the transformation of all people into proletarians, not the abolition of capital but its general rule in which a specific exploitation can be and necessarily will be developed" [9, p. 92]. Approaching the problem from a different point of view, N. Pašić came to the following conclusion: "In the past state intervention in the economy was erroneously identified with socialism. If this criterion were applied to the last several decades, it would bring into socialist ranks all eminent capitalist politicians of recent times, from Baldwin and Roosevelt to Hitler and de Gaulle" [10, p. 11]. A. Dragičević wrote: "Nationalization of means of production and planning are preconditions of socialism, but only preconditions and nothing more. In order to achieve 'fully developed' socialism, many more additional factors are required, in the first instance a socialist development of political relations and of economic structure of the society" [11, p. 218]. Similarly, P. Kovač and D. Miljević observed that "state ownership and state management by themselves lead to small or no change in the position of the producer in the production process and in his right to participate in the management of the economy. . . . In the countries in which socialist revolution was victorious, the state, instead of becoming an organ of the working people, may and does become an organ of the state and Party apparatus, which rules on behalf of the working people" [12, p. 13]. Milić observes that "state socialism in the USSR through bureaucratic socialism develops into state capitalism . . . [3, p. 21]. These statements are not quite so novel as they might appear. As early as half a century ago, Z. Fabria, in connection with a book by Lenin, wrote: "If the state becomes an owner, we shall have state capitalism and not socialism. . . . Under state ownership all proletarians would become workers hired by the state instead of by private capitalists. The state would be an exploiter and that means that an entire crowd of higher and lower managers and an entire bureaucracy with all its hierarchical strata would create a new ruling and exploiting class. It looks as if something similar has already been happening in Russia . . ." [13, p. 164].

Lately there has been a tendency to replace "state capitalism" by an emotionally more neutral term, "etatism" [14, pp. 328-36; 15]. The most radical in this respect is S. Stojanović, a philosopher by profession: "The term etatism denotes a system based on state ownership of means of production and state management of production and other social activities. The state apparatus represents a new ruling class. As a collective owner of means of production, it employs and exploits labor. The personal share of the members of the ruling class in the distribution of the surplus value is proportional to their position in the state hierarchy..." [16, p. 35].

If the state is an institution alien to socialism, who is to organize the economic process? Clearly, the only available alternative is that this job be undertaken by producers themselves. Centralization as the principle of organization is to be replaced by decentralization, a centrally managed economy by a self-governing economy. In mid-1950, a law was passed creating workers' councils. The draft of the law was introduced to the Federal Assembly in a speech by President Tito, who declared: "The slogan, the factories to the workers, the land to the peasants, is not any abstract propaganda slogan, but one which has deep meaning. It contains in itself the whole program of socialist relations in production and also in regard to social property and the rights and obligations of the workers, and therefore it can be and must be realized in practice, if we really desire to build socialism" (quoted in [33, p. 69]). By 1952 the new economic system was already in operation.

2. DECENTRALIZATION

Institutional Development

Preparation for the New Economic System, as it was called, started with the Law on Management of Government Business Enterprises and Economic Associations by Workers' Collectives enacted in July 1950, and ended with the Constitutional Law on Principles of the Social and Political System of Yugoslavia, passed by the Federal Assembly in 1953. The New Economic System (NES) became operational in 1952. It was transitional in character and lasted until 1960. During these eight years, the country achieved the highest rate of growth in the world: per capita gross national product expanded at the rate of 8.5 percent per annum, agricultural output at the rate of 8.9 percent, and industrial output at the rate of 13.4 percent [17; 18, pp. 363-64].

The law provided that workers' collectives should conduct all the activities of their respective enterprises through their managing organs, workers' councils and managing boards. The workers' council was to be elected by all the employees of an enterprise in a secret ballot. J. A. Schumpeter once remarked: "Wild socializations — a term that has acquired official standing — are attempts by workmen of each plant to supersede the management and to take matters into their own hands. These are the nightmare of every responsible socialist" [19, p. 226]. Such a nightmare was now made legal and obligatory by an act of the Belgrade National Assembly. "The principle of producers' self-management," explains E. Kardelj, a social scientist and one of the most active political leaders, "is the starting point of all socialist politics. ... Revolution that fails to open the door to such a development inevitably must ... stagnate in state capitalist forms and in a bureaucratic despotism" [30, p. 17].

In 1951 the government was busy dismantling the central planning apparatus, with its ministries, directorates, and administratively fixed prices. The last directorates disappeared in 1952. On December 30, 1951, a Law on Planned Management of the National Economy was passed. It replaced detailed central planning of production by planning of so-called basic proportions, such as the rate of accumulation and the distribution of investment. Enterprises acquired a large measure of autonomy. In 1951 there existed numerous categories of market and planned prices. This was all replaced by a single price structure which, with certain exceptions, was to be regulated by the market. The rate of exchange was made more realistic by devaluing the dinar six times. And so, in January 1952, the economy was ready to embark upon a new road of decentralization.

Once it was recognized that the essential features of socialism consisted in individual freedom and the autonomy of self-governing collectives, two important consequences followed. First, the political monopoly of the state and Party apparatus became incompatible with a social system conceived in this way. Second, in order to be really autonomous, work collectives had to have full command over the economic factors determining their position. The former consideration led to a gradual transformation of the Communist Party from a classical political party into what I have called

an association of political activists [7, p. 261]. The process was
initiated in 1952 when the Sixth Congress of the Party changed its
name to the League of Communists of Yugoslavia (LCY). The latter consideration led to a market economy with, hopefully, a minimum of government intervention.

In 1952 and 1953, several laws were passed regulating the formation, operation, and termination of business enterprises. The enterprises could be set up even by a group of citizens. The director
was to be appointed on a competitive basis by a joint commission
of the workers' council and the local government. Unsuccessful
enterprises could go bankrupt.

In agriculture, the collectivization drive increased the number
of peasants' work cooperatives, but with its compulsory deliveries,
administrative controls, and the rest, it depressed output [20,
pp. 99, 111].

	Index of output	Number of cooperatives
1930-1939	100	—
1948	103	1217
1949	103	6238
1950	75	6913
1951	106	6804
1952	75	4225
1953	106	1165
1954	94	896
1955	116	688
1956	97	561
1957	140	507
1964	170	16

Once the idea of all-embracing administrative state control was
abandoned, it was useless to insist on collectivization in agriculture, even less so because of the poor economic results. Ž. Vidaković gives the following explanation: "the massive participation
of peasants in the armed phase of the Revolution and in the setting
up of revolutionary political power contributed to the failure of
etatist-bureaucratic socialization of agriculture, since the socially
and politically active peasantry did not submissively accept the administrative methods of collectivization" [21, p. 42]. In 1953, the
Law on Reorganization of the Peasants' Work Cooperatives made
it easy for peasants to leave cooperatives, and most of them took
advantage of this opportunity. Those who remained were often
poor peasants, which meant that the remaining cooperatives would

not be viable. In order to prevent this from happening and also to curb income polarization in the villages, two months later the government carried out a new agrarian reform that reduced the land maximum to 25 acres.[2] Since before the war nearly nine-tenths of all peasant farms were smaller than 25 acres anyway, the new reform did not meet with much opposition. But the harmful effects of former policy were not wiped out. In Yugoslavia there was a long tradition of agricultural cooperatives. Forced collectivization did a great deal to discredit cooperatives. Later the general agricultural cooperatives, which were administratively established and given a monopoly in village trade, also helped to discourage a genuine cooperative movement.

After all these changes, the six-year-old etatist Constitution became grossly inappropriate, but the time was not yet ripe for a new constitution. The problem was solved by a constitutional law passed in 1953. In Article 4 it states: "Social ownership of the means of production, the self-government of producers in the economy, and the self-government of working people in the commune, city, and district represent the basis of the social and political system of the country. ..."

As a consequence of the self-government principle, another very important innovation found its place in the constitutional law. It became known as the principle of the fusion of political and economic sovereignty of the working people. The principle was implemented by creating the Council of Producers as a new house in the Assembly. The Council was composed of representatives of collectives of business enterprises.

In the following years, the government was engaged primarily in perfecting the monetary and fiscal systems. Interest rates were applied and there was some experimentation with investment auctions. Commercial banks were added to the hitherto all-embracing National Bank. Reserve requirements were introduced. Local governments acquired financial autonomy.

The First Five-Year Plan (1947-51) was extended for a year, but never really completed. The period from 1952 to 1956 was left with only annual plans. After the NES was well established, the Second Five-Year Plan, covering the period 1957-61, was launched.

---

2. As a result, Yugoslavia achieved the most egalitarian land distribution in the world. A survey of fifty countries shows a Gini index of inequality of 0.44 for Yugoslavia as compared with 0.45 for Poland, 0.46 for Denmark, 0.50 for Switzerland, 0.58 for Sweden, 0.60 for Ireland, 0.67 for West Germany, 0.71 for the United States, 0.82 for Uruguay, 0.86 for Argentina, and 0.91 for Venezuela [63, pp. 239-40].

It was carried out in less than four years.

Discussion

While the preceding period was characterized mostly by discussion of what was not socialism, the theoretical approach became more positive now. The discussion started with an exchange of opinions on the so-called transition period and ended with an analysis of what was to be known as self-governing or associationist socialism.

Marx wrote that the revolutionary transformation of a capitalist into a communist society could not be carried out at once. Between the two socioeconomic systems there must be a short transitional period. During this period, the state would be organized as a dictatorship of the proletariat. Marx's analysis seemed plausible and in fact proved to be a good anticipation of what happened in Yugoslavia in the first two decades after the war [7, ch. 2]. Around 1952, and intermittently thereafter, the main issue of the debate was whether socialism (considered to be the first of the two stages of a communist society) is to be included in or excluded from the transition period [23; 9; 24; 47; 49; 50]. The debate was highly scholastic, and yet the issue was of enormous practical importance. If the dictatorship of the proletariat is interpreted as a form of political regime and not as the class content of the government (which is what Marx had in mind), the identification of socialism with the transition period will produce a command society. If the political regime is democratic, but the transition period is extended to include socialism, the development of a classless society may be endlessly delayed. The issue was resolved in an indirect way after the essential characteristics of self-governing socialism had been elaborated.

Contrasting the old (administrative) and the new (self-governing) economic systems, R. Bićanić summarizes the actual developments by enumerating differences in goals, agents, and means [2, pp. 44-47].[3] The goals of the old system were to achieve socialism by means of state power, to equalize the position of workers in relation to the state-owned means of production, and to achieve the new social order for its own sake. Individual interests of producers

---

3. Bićanić completed his study early in 1961. Essentially the same comparative analysis had already been presented by M. Popović in 1952 [29]. Evidently, the system was being developed in a consistent way.

and consumers were subordinate to impersonal and superhuman goals of the economic system, and the state apparatus, entrusted with the achievement of this goal, was in a position to exploit the population. The new system presupposes the withering away of the state and the management of socialized property by workers, and makes the personal happiness of every individual a supreme goal.

As far as the agents are concerned, in the old system there was centralized state management by means of a hierarchically organized state apparatus. The directives were passed down the line in an authoritarian way, and enterprises had little or no independence. In the new system, the state apparatus cannot interfere with the business of individual enterprises, which are autonomous. Decentralization was applied not only to economic but also to social and political life. Authoritarianism was replaced by self-government as a basic principle of economic and social organization.

The means of the two systems are contrasted by Bićanić in the following way: state ownership versus social ownership; central planning versus social planning; administrative allocation of goods versus market; administrative rules versus financial instruments; administratively fixed wages versus free disposition of the income of the working collectives; all-embracing state budget versus the budget of the state administration, decentralized and separated from the economic operations; consumption as a residual versus consumption as an independent factor of development; collectivization versus business cooperation of peasants and large agricultural estates.

In the period under consideration, economists began to study intensively writings in the economics of socialism, particularly those of Western authors. This literature had hitherto been virtually unknown. I. Maksimović [54], F. Černe [55], and B. Horvat [25] produced extensive critical accounts of earlier economic literature. Černe attempted to provide an acceptable definition of socialism. In his view, socialism is characterized by the following three elements: (1) equal rights of members of the community as producers. This implies social ownership. Element (1) is a precondition for: (2) equal rights in terms of income distribution. This in turn implies distribution according to work. Both (1) and (2) are indispensable for the realization of: (3) equal rights in political life. As citizens, members of the community must enjoy political — Černe talks of socialist — democracy [55, p. 281]. It appears that socialism is essentially a philosophy of egalitarianism.

Černe's definition, although never explicitly quoted — references are not popular in this country — may be considered as commanding wide agreement among economists and other social scientists.

On a less abstract level, in an important article in 1953, R. Uvalić described the main intentions of the New Economic System [53]. In the administrative period, output was expanded regardless of cost. Now fast growth was to be maintained but cost considerations had to play an important role in the determination of the structure of output. The law of value, that is, the market, was to take care of that. But the operation of the law of value must be restricted in two important respects: income distribution and capital formation must be controlled. Otherwise, Uvalić warns, exploitation and market anarchy will reappear. These ideas were to dominate economic policy in the next decade. But clumsy bureaucratic and often incompetent controls of income distribution and capital formation were to become more and more irksome.

The relation between market and planning has become a recurrent theme in economic discussion. Usually market and planning are visualized as two different mechanisms. In the opinion of Černe, the planning mechanism is to be used for long-run and general decisions, while short-run and partial decisions may be left to the market mechanism [55, p. 11]. A similar position was taken by I. Lavrač [48]. B. Jelić explores in more detail the institutional arrangements necessary to harmonize the market and planning. He argues that unbalanced growth sometimes requires interventions even outside the general framework provided by the plan [56].

By the end of the period under consideration, the New Economic System had been given its first theoretical rationalization in a book by the present author [25].

Since the socioeconomic system is conceived as an association of (business, political, etc.) associations, I suggested that it be called associationist socialism. I pointed out that the old incompatibility of market and planning was nothing more than an ideological fallacy. The market is just one device of social planning — and a very efficient one at that. The integration of market and planning, of social ownership and business autonomy of enterprises, produces a system with interesting new practical as well as theoretical features. First reactions to this book were negative [26]. To insist on consumer sovereignty was considered to represent the (negative) influence of Western welfare economics. To insist on rigorous technical analysis was considered devoid of social content and thus anti-Marxian. To insist on market economy was considered to reflect the influence of the Western theory of free competition. The analysis of price formation, in which interest and rent played a certain well-defined role, was said to be a bourgeois theory.

A similar critique was given by some socialist economists abroad. E. Mandel maintained that "there is a definite incompatibility between socialism — or, put otherwise, a classless society and a high degree of social equality and economic efficiency — and commodity production" [27]. This is so because commodity production inevitably generates social inequality and produces waste of economic resources. The reader was not told why this should be inevitable.

In this debate, B. Ward came perhaps nearest to the truth. As to the method of analysis, he says: "In value theory Horvat manages to produce more or less Marxian results from more or less neoclassical assumptions" [28, p. 519]. As to the substance of the theory, he concludes: "Naturally enough this regime is essentially socialist; not surprisingly, it bears a more than casual resemblance to Yugoslavia. What is surprising is that it carries a more than expected measure of plausibility..." [28, p. 509]. Most of the ideas developed in this 1958 book have by now been absorbed and seem self-evident. The latest reform takes the market mechanism and the welfare of individuals as its main guiding principles.

3. SELF-GOVERNING SOCIALISM

Institutional Development

The last phase in Yugoslav postwar socioeconomic development was prepared by a series of political, economic, and constitutional reforms between 1958 and 1963. This turbulent period was inaugurated by the new Program of the League of Communists in 1958. In it, socialism is defined as "the social system based on socialized means of production in which social production is managed by associated direct producers, in which income is distributed according to the principle to each according to his work and in which, under the rule of the working class, itself being changed as a class, all social relations are gradually liberated from class antagonisms and all elements of exploitation of man by man" [31, p. 133]. Thus the Yugoslav variant of socialism appears to imply social ownership, self-management in the economy, and the absence of nonlabor income and exploitation. The term "working class," as explained a few years later by Kardelj, was to mean "all working people who are participating in the social process of labor and in socialist economic relations" [32, p. 1531].

By 1960, the Second Five-Year Plan was successfully completed. The economy was booming. Self-management in enterprises was already well established. The Program paved the way to an accelerated pace of change. The new five-year plan was prepared. The society felt ready for a new and important step forward. In 1961, three radical reforms were carried out. To increase the efficiency of the market organization and improve the quality of goods produced, the hitherto virtually closed economy was to be made more open to the influences of the world market. To achieve this, the system of multiple exchange rates was replaced by a customs tariff, the dinar was devalued, foreign trade was liberalized to a certain extent, and the country became an associate member of the General Agreement on Tariffs and Trade (GATT). Since developments in the field of money and banking were lagging behind the general institutional changes, an overhaul of the entire financial organization was undertaken. Finally, it seemed inappropriate for trade unions to continue to supervise wage levels and wage differentials in self-managed enterprises, and this control was discontinued. Since then, market competition in this field has gone further than in any other modern economy. These three reforms inaugurated in 1961 the beginning of the third distinct phase of economic development.

By that time, the country was institutionally ready for the new constitution. It was promulgated in 1963. Explaining the aims of the Constitution, Kardelj, one of its chief architects, stated that it was "not only the constitution of the state but also a specific social charter which will provide the material basis, political framework and encouragement for the faster internal development of the system of social self-government and direct democracy" [32, p. 1533]. Self-management was extended to cover not only business but also nonprofit organizations. It was generalized as a principle of self-government to be applied in all spheres of economic, social, and political life. In order to achieve this, the Constitution invented a new institution: the work organization [radna organizacija]. Whenever people associate in order to work for a living, they create a work organization and represent a work union [radna zajednica] which enjoys basic, constitutionally guaranteed rights of self-government. Work organizations include enterprises and other business establishments, as well as educational, cultural, medical, social insurance, and other public service establishments. As a consequence, the "fusion principle" of the 1953 constitutional law was extended to cover all work unions, and the Assembly was given three houses of work unions: one for the economy, one for education and culture, and one for health and social welfare.

The three reforms of 1961 were poorly prepared, partly inconsistent, and badly implemented. As one might have expected, the sensitive market economy reacted violently. Everything went wrong: in one year, the rate of growth of industrial output was reduced to one-half of its 1960 level, imports soared, exports stagnated, wages surged far ahead of productivity. The reformers, accustomed to a tardy half-administrative economy, were taken by surprise. Planners increased targets for 1962 in order to catch up with the five-year plan goals — and were, of course, deeply disappointed. The recession was deepened. It became clear that the plan would have to be abandoned. Administrators and political bodies were deeply disturbed. Conservative politicians and economists were busy explaining the failure of the market system and demanded that central planning be reintroduced.

Heavy pumping of money into the economy helped to generate recovery in the second half of 1962. In the next year, the economy was back to its normal path of fast growth. The upswing continued into 1964, ending in a boom with heavy inflation and a great balance of payments deficit. The new recession brought a new reform. Throughout 1964, assemblies were busy discussing the principles of this new reform [34]. In the beginning of 1965, the government administration was set to work. By May, technical preparations were completed. In July, the Federal Assembly enacted the package of laws inaugurating the reform [35]. Significantly enough, the solution to economic troubles was sought in further decentralization, perfection of self-government autonomy, development of a more competitive market, and integration into the world economy. What followed appeared to be a second, more radical and more consistent edition of the 1961 reform. The reform started as an economic one, but very soon yielded important social and political consequences. Multicentric planning could not help but produce a pluralistic society. Reform was in essence a new stage of the Revolution, asserted V. Bakarić, President of the Croation League of Communists [62, p. 231]. Self-governing autonomy became firmly rooted in the socialist establishment.

21

The Yugoslav Economic System

Discussion

The reform of 1961 — called also the New Economic System (II) — marked the beginning of real academic discussion of economic matters. Up to that time, institutional changes had been too fast, and economists too few, so rigorous analysis and discussion had been replaced by descriptions.

The discussion started with an exchange between R. Uvalić and R. Bićanić (both of them are dead now). Uvalić reiterated his views that income distribution and capital formation could not be left to regulation by the market. So far, distribution according to work had encountered serious difficulties. A capital market was unacceptable as a device for capital formation and allocation because it would lead to group ownership. Social profitability and individual profitability were two different things. The individual interest of a collective was inferior and had to defer to the social interest [57]. Bićanić objected that Uvalić failed to distinguish clearly between what is commonly called the economic system and the plan. The economic system (general conditions for business conduct) used to be an instrument of the Plan; now the relation had been reversed. (In fact, two years later a Party congress requested explicitly that the plan become an instrument of the system instead of the system's being accommodated to the plan [59, p. 29].) Uvalić offered no guidance as to how to replace labor and capital markets. He really implied central planning, with operational freedom left to planners and politicians and discipline reserved for the rest. Bićanić felt that this was unacceptable. A modern economy is essentially polycentric and not monocentric [58].

In December 1962, the Association of Yugoslav Economists organized a debate in Belgrade on the draft of the new constitution [60]. A number of participants — R. Davidović, M. Macura, N. Čobeljić, K. Mihajlović — argued that the role of planning was underestimated in the draft constitution. Macura explained that this was so because economic problems were approached from the point of view of an enterprise, even an individual, instead of from the standpoint of the economy as a whole [60, p. 462]. Čobeljić thought that planned market economy would in the future be replaced by market-planned economy [60, pp. 45-53]. Mihajlović argued that, while consumer and intermediate goods markets worked well, investment goods and capital markets were notoriously imperfect and needed strict control [60, p. 500]. The debate reached its climax at another meeting a month later in Zagreb.

Further discussion was prompted by the failure of the reform. The economy sank deeply into depression (relative to the standard Yugoslav state of affairs). From the beginning of 1961 to the middle of 1962, the annual rate of growth of industrial output dropped from 12 to 4 percent. The government was alarmed and asked a group of academic economists in a research institute to find out what had happened. This move set a precedent in the governmental attitude toward managing economic affairs. In a few months the group produced a report, popularly called the Yellow Book[36]. A second, even more important, precedent was established: the government accepted the report.

The findings of the Yellow Book may be summarized as follows: Inefficient planning resulted in economic instability. The structure of supply failed to match the structure of demand; there was a downward shift in long-run export trends; and a serious lack of skilled labor force was seen. The inherently unstable economy was exposed to the simultaneous shocks of the three poorly prepared and badly implemented partial reforms cited above. The insistence on financial discipline created a serious shortage of money with strong deflationary effects. The abolition of income control led to wild increases of wages unrelated to productivity increases. The liberalization of foreign trade increased the balance of payments deficit. The report emphasized the fundamental importance of economic research as a basis for economic policy and stability of the legal and policy framework as a precondition for the efficient operation of enterprises in a market setting.

In the meantime, another research institution produced an analysis of the defects of the economic system. This report, which became known as the White Book, criticized deficient planning, an imperfect market, arbitrariness in income distribution, and inconsistencies in investment decisions [37]. Both documents were discussed in a meeting jointly organized by the Association of Economists and the Federal Planning Bureau in Zagreb in January 1963 [38]. The former planning officials and a certain number of economists with a more centralist orientation criticized the two documents. They questioned the possibility of efficient investment and a high rate of growth in a decentralized setting. They thought that the market necessarily led to a destruction of the socialist principle of income distribution. Some of them pointed out that the classical conflict between the essentially social character of production and atomized decision making lay at the bottom of all economic difficulties [38, p. 192]. The majority of economists, however, agreed on the necessity of further decentralization and the perfection of self-governing autonomy. Since the Zagreb debate, the basic principles of the development of the economic system have never been seriously questioned among Yugoslav economists.

The well-known quip about doctors — "The operation was successful but the patient died" — might have been applied to discussions among Yugoslav economists: the causes of economic troubles were well explained, but the reform was dead. It soon became clear that the entire experiment had to be repeated. And so it was, in 1965. The situation was rather complicated. "The casual observer is often puzzled," commented Bićanić. "Only a few years ago Yugoslavia was presented as an example of a country with one of the highest growth rates in the world; now the foremost aim of economic policy is to reduce investment. For more than a decade the socialist economy struggled against bureaucratic command; now an administrative price freeze has had to be introduced. It was the first country in the world to initiate workers' management in business enterprises and to abolish the wage system; now there is discussion about whether this means too much or too little democracy.... National problems were said to have been solved; and now the country is pregnant with increased tensions among the constituent nations, tensions newly created and socialist in origin. Efforts to find solutions to all these problems are now concentrated into two words: 'The Reform'" [39, pp. 633-34].

Bićanić and Džeba [40] saw the aims of the reform to be the following. Its immediate purpose was to combat the increasing pace of inflation, to remove the chronic deficit in the balance of payments, to reduce drastically all sorts of subsidies (for exports, unprofitable production, etc.) in order to avoid the necessity of central administrative interventions, and to correct price disparities in order to establish more efficient market relations and to eliminate administrative controls. These were preconditions for some longer-term structural changes in the economy, such as revision of growth and investment policies, raising of the productivity of the economy to an internationally competitive level, liberalization of foreign trade and elimination of the balance of payments deficit, and convertibility of the currency in order to open the economy and expose it to the stimulating influences of the world market. In its broader social aspects, the reform was expected to impart a depoliticization of economic decisions, to double the share of enterprises in the control of national income, thereby

reducing the economic power of the state, to link the level of living
to the level of productivity, and to increase the rationality of economic decision making. Bićanić concluded that the fundamental
aim was in fact "to build a model of a socialist system for a developed country, one which will be able to stand the competition of
other developed countries without the constant tutelage of government machinery" [39, p. 643]. He and Horvat [47] pointed out that
this model is very different from the mixed economy of the welfare
state.

The goal was to be achieved by a process which Bićanić called
the four D's: decentralization, de-etatization, depoliticization, and
democratization.

As often happens, the ideas were good but the implementation was
poor. The reform was much better prepared politically than the
one in 1961, but not economically. Economically it was based on a
rather naive idea of the viability of the laissez-faire principle.
Monetary policy appeared to be practically the only available device of economic policy. In order to stabilize prices, the government applied a credit squeeze. It worked, but it also produced de-
flation with unemployment and stagnation. From the beginning of
1965 to the middle of 1967, the annual rate of growth of industrial
output dropped from 12 percent to −1 percent. Negative growth
rates had not been known since 1952. The government held that
this was unavoidable and that the reform "in its strategic aspects"
was proceeding as planned. Some economists and many businessmen were alarmed. For them, developments were catastrophic
and certain to produce another failure. Soon economists were to
discover the existence of business cycles. Since cycles had not
been known to the government — it was held as self-evident that
cycles could not exist in a socialist economy — the government
proceeded to frame economic policy as if they did not exist. The
results of such an economic policy could not be encouraging.

The discovery of business cycles proceeded in stages. The suc-
cessive retardations of growth described earlier in the Yellow
Book indicated that the Yugoslav economy might have been subject
to cyclical fluctuations. The research undertaken at the Institute
of Economic Sciences confirmed the hypothesis.[4] In the spring of
1967 in Ljubljana, the Association of Economists held a meeting
devoted to problems of stabilization [42]. Four papers dealt explicitly with business cycles. The Institute of Economic Sciences

---

4. See section 5 for a more detailed discussion.

ventured to make a forecast of the lower turning point (1967), boom (1969), and recession (1970) of the current cycle, which proved to be basically correct (see Chart 1 on p. 53).

A couple of months after the Ljubljana meeting, a public debate took place. It was focused on the theme "Economic Science and the Economy" [43]. Seven economists participated. A. Bajt raised the question of the responsibility for the reform and criticized the naive view that investment generated inflation. Z. Baletić evaluated the contention that there was a conflict between politicians and economists. Ž. Mrkušić analyzed the foreign trade equilibrium. B. Horvat pointed out a number of mistakes contained in currently popular economic reasoning (and, consequently, in economic policy) and in a separate article, which caused a newspaper explosion of discontent, calculated the losses due to cyclical instability. The output lost appeared to amount to about 40 percent of the social product. The three remaining economists supported the official view that everything was more or less all right.

In February 1968, the Institute of Economic Sciences organized an all-Yugoslav conference on the current economic situation. The study prepared for this occasion [44] described the cyclical mechanism operating in the Yugoslav economy and made a coherent proposal for an anticyclical policy. This was an important step forward. The proposal insisted on a combination of monetary and fiscal policies (the latter was virtually nonexistent at that time), a combination of price and income controls, and interrelations between aggregate demand and investment.

By the end of the same year, another feature of the unsuccessful 1961 reform was repeated: two research institutes were officially asked to assess the implementation of the reform. There was, however, an interesting difference in this demand: it came not from the government but from the Central Committee of the League of Communists. Two reports were prepared; the findings were more or less the same. I quote from the report that was published [45]. The report found that, in spite of a strong deflationary policy, prices were no more stable than they were before the reform; that the five-year plan was not likely to be fulfilled; that the administrative control of prices was extended over a greater percentage of output than before the reform; that the liberalization trends in foreign trade had been checked and reversed; that the balance of payments deficit was expanding; that the rate of saving was decreasing; that the losses and indebtedness of firms were increasing; that the rise in labor productivity was slightly retarded; and that unemployment was increasing beyond anything known in the country in the past two decades. Elaborating its early prognosis in more detail, the Institute predicted an acceleration of growth in the first half of 1969 (to a rate some 60 percent higher than the one forecast by the Federal Planning Bureau), an inflationary pressure in the second half, and the downturn of the cycle and the beginning of a new recession by the end of 1969 or the first half of 1970. The forecast proved to be correct, though the recession was not deep and was not followed by vigorous acceleration of growth (see Chart 1). A few months later, V. Rajković undertook to analyze the unpublished papers prepared by the administration as a basis for the reform. Rajković came to the conclusion that none of the important goals had been satisfactorily achieved [61, p. 47].

Once again the ominous question was posed: what had happened? A careful analysis of developments seems to suggest the following answer. Economic growth and institutional changes were too rapid for the government apparatus and other organs of economic policy to be able to cope with them efficiently. Almost overnight a backward Balkan country reached a European standard of economic development, and an administrative economy was transformed into a market economy. At the same time, responsible authorities often lacked the necessary understanding of how a modern market economy operated. If to all that we add the pioneering in the system of self-government — which did not exist anywhere else in the world — it becomes clear that the complexities of the socioeconomic environment had increased enormously and that it would take some time before the organizational framework was adapted, the necessary knowledge accumulated, and the new social system began to operate smoothly [43; 45; 46].

Economic Functions of the Federation

The laissez-faire-inspired reform of 1965 predictably fared rather badly. The rate of growth fell to almost half of what it was during the previous period. As a result, unemployment appeared. In a few years, several hundred thousand workers went abroad to find employment. After 1967, there was some acceleration of growth, but by 1970 the first serious signs of inflation became visible.

For a couple of years, the warnings of the leading economists were not taken seriously. Their suggestions of alternative economic policies were brushed aside with remarks that the authors were politically naive or simply not realistic. It was only in 1973 that, in an important political document, the following cautious admission was made: "There were some who laboured under the delusion that the market by itself could systematically solve all problems and assure optimum material development, remove structural disproportions, assign accumulation appropriately and guarantee dynamic and stable economic growth. Owing to the fact that the market had not been developed sufficiently in line with self-management socio-economic foundations, its negative qualities came increasingly to the fore..." [64, p. 14].

Since the federal government bears an obvious responsibility for the economic policy — and its failures — one of the key questions discussed was the economic functions of the Federation. It might have been assumed that economists would be in favor of centralized controls. But that was not the case. An unregulated market generated an environment of bellum omnium contra omnes in which the actors agreed on just one point: that centralized control, for which no satisfactory checks were established, ought to be reduced to a minimum and possibly abolished. After the Ohrid meeting of economists in October 1970, France Černe surveyed the opinions of his colleagues. It turned out that two-thirds of the 140 economists interviewed objected to federal interventions in general, and 43 percent were against any federal intervention whatsoever [65, p. 12].

In December 1970, the federal government asked the present author to prepare a report on the economic functions of the Federation. I invited leading economists from all federal states to participate, and the group produced a report that came to be known as the White Book [66]. The report insisted that the economy ought to be treated as a system and went on to discuss five current dilemmas.

1. Centralization or decentralization. In a self-managed economy, this dilemma is resolved in favor of decentralization. This means that all economic functions are in principle left to the economic base, and this principle is modified only when it is essential for the efficient functioning of the entire system. Accordingly, work organizations should carry out the maximum number of economic functions possible, and the Federation, only the essential minimum. The economic functions of the states are predetermined by this polarization, as well as by the fact that Yugoslavia is a federal community of several nations and nationalities.

Here the economic functions of the federal states ought to be mentioned as well. From the self-management rights of citizens and producers follows also their right to national and territorial organization (to be sure, only to the extent that the same self-management rights of other citizens and producers are not infringed). In that context, it would be mistaken to judge the state economies only from the standpoint of possible negative effects and deformations, possible autarchy and separatistic elements, although it is certain that these dangers really exist. Viewed from a positive standpoint, regional economies represent the necessary intermediate term to a decentralized and polycentric vision of the economy and society. It is a question of attaining regional balancing of economic development. This task is particularly urgent in the countryside, where the historically inherited differences in economic development, traditions, culture, language, and so on, are very pronounced. Under these conditions, overcoming the gap in economic development becomes the precondition of true equality of the nations and nationalities of Yugoslavia, and state or provincial autonomy the precondition for the harmonious functioning of the economy and society as a whole. In that sense, distinct state and provincial economies are not incompatible with the rapid, balanced, and efficient development of the entire Yugoslav economy. Provided that economic laws are respected, the harmonization of regional development with the particular national and economic characteristics of the states and provinces can give a powerful stimulus to general economic development.

2. The state apparatus as authority or as social service. The conception — and, consistent with it, the behavior — was inherited that the state apparatus is above all an apparatus of power. In that sense, the state apparatus was oriented almost exclusively toward granting permits and setting prohibitions (issuing direct orders is no longer possible, on the whole, because of the first decision, noted above). The consequences of this concept are borne by economic decision-making units, which can influence the state of affairs little if at all. Because of this, the efficiency of the entire system falls and the society suffers serious losses.

The state apparatus as authority is not the only possible solution. A certain number of developed nations — the Scandinavian countries are probably the best example — have organized their state apparatus as a public service. The task of a so-called state apparatus is to carry out coordinative and informative functions, to perform services for the population and work organizations, and to use force only exceptionally.

In a self-managing society, the second dilemma should be resolved by building a modern, highly expert state apparatus conceived as a public service. Among other things, this assumes the introduction of rigorous qualifying examinations for acceptance into the state service. So that people in the state apparatus can behave as responsible civil servants, they should be assured of a certain personal security and protection from various pressures.

3. <u>The Federation as the state or as the Yugoslav community</u>. The former conception of the state as authority prevails almost exclusively, and thus the weakening of the Federation necessarily leads to weakening of the Yugoslav community. However, there are very important economic problems, such as anticyclical economic policy, that should be solved on the Yugoslav level, although not necessarily within the framework of the state apparatus and in a bureaucratic way. The view can be taken that, even in the case of reform of the state apparatus in the sense of the second point, it still remains desirable for this apparatus to be left with only a minimum of essential functions, and for decisions on the Yugoslav level to be made in bodies that also include other social elements.

In the report, the Federation is conceived as the Yugoslav social community, and economic decisions at the level of the Federation represent decisions for the Yugoslav economy as a whole. Viewed in this context, the Federation should have four main types of organs. The first is the top political body which forms the institutional system and determines developmental and general economic policy on the basis of the broadest democratic agreement of the nations and national minorities of Yugoslavia, or of producers and citizens. This is the parliament. The government, or Federal Executive Council, should be that organ of the parliament which (a) undertakes expert technical work and (b) executes current economic policy within the framework determined by the parliament. In addition to these two government organs, a certain number of special (mixed or more directly social) organs can exist on the level of the Federation, of which the report authors mention several (a Council of Economic Advisers, Arbitration Commission for Incomes and Prices, Scientific Council, Monetary Council, and an agency for the administration of federal funds). These special social organs probably will increase in number over time. Their role is often of an arbitrational, consultative, or expert advisory character, but they sometimes also have operative functions, as, for example, that for the administration of federal funds. An increase in the number of special social organs on the federal level can be expected to hasten the transformation of administration by government clerks into more direct social regulation, and of bureaucratic state authority into a civil service. Finally, the fourth type of federal organ in the economic sphere includes interest associations, such as the trade union and chamber of commerce.

4. Authority to the Federation or agreement of the states. This is, in fact, a pseudodilemma, for both should be used, depending on the nature of the problem. What is basic is the distinction between determining policy and carrying out the policy decided upon. The former is a matter for political forums, in which agreement of the states plays a basic role. The latter is the task of executive organs, hence the federal apparatus. The execution of a determined policy can take various forms, however, and for the most important decisions it is desirable to obtain the agreement of the states. From the nature of the situation, it follows that ad hoc agreement has no place: (1) when operational measures that do not tolerate delay (for example, interventions on the market) are involved; (2) when complete discretion is required to ensure the economic interests of the country (for example, a decision on devaluation); and (3) when decisions of secondary importance are at issue. Category 3 includes so many matters, and agreement on them would absorb so much of the time and capacity of the administration, that discussion of truly serious tasks and key decisions would be neglected. Such a situation was to a large extent characteristic of then current practice, when infinite energy was lost in bargaining over peripheral matters and important decisions with far-reaching consequences were made in an improvised way. Eventual abuses, irresponsibility, or insufficient expertness of federal organs cannot be prevented by the continual interference of the organs of the six states in operational decisions. When this occurs, in fact, responsibility is removed from the federal apparatus, and the efficiency of administration is reduced to a minimum. The federal government should be given all the necessary authorization, and control should be exercised through analysis of the results of the government's work. When a proclaimed program is not carried out, the degree of confidence in the government should be discussed. When deviations from proclaimed goals, adopted plans, and published forecasts are significant, the government should resign. If one wishes to replace the mystical aura of authority that surrounds the state administration with the attributes of a public service, then the government should be treated in large measure as the business board of the society. And just as the

business board of an enterprise is not a coalition of representatives of sectors and work units but an organ of the enterprise as a whole, so also the government cannot be primarily a coalition government but ought to be primarily a federal government.

5. Sociopolitical communities or economic organizations. Unless one considers creating some parallel economic "government" — which probably would not be advisable, and the group authoring the report did not examine this assumption further — this dilemma is also artificially created. There is a clear social division of labor between economic organizations and organs of sociopolitical communities. Economic organizations acquire income in a competitive struggle on the market. Organs of sociopolitical communities harmonize interests of the economic decision-making units in a particular territory. If one sought harmonization from the former, one would obtain monopoly. If one sought entry into the market from the latter, one would obtain etatism. In fact, precisely because of these insufficiently controlled tendencies, very marked symptoms of both of these appear.

Next, the group established three basic functions of economic policy at the federal level: (1) equalizing conditions of economic activity, without which there is no distribution according to work and monopolistic exploitation appears; (2) viewed from the short run, ensuring market equilibrium, without which the first function is impossible to achieve or the autonomy of work organization is liquidated; (3) viewed from the long run, ensuring economic growth, without which functions 1 and 2 and the building of socialism are impossible.

A very widespread misconception was found — namely, that the organs of the community were responsible only for those tasks that they could carry out by administrative directives. Because of this, if mistaken investments occur, the enterprises that undertook them and the banks that financed them are blamed with no consideration for the fact that the production-investment behavior of economic organizations is a function of the economic system and economic policy. If prices rise, enterprises are blamed for driving prices up. If personal incomes rise faster than productivity of labor, work collectives are blamed for insufficient social consciousness. If the economy becomes illiquid, exports too little, or imports too much, the economy is blamed for failing to adapt to the intentions of the reform and to adhere to recommendations and political resolutions. This reasoning runs through the daily press, parliamentary debates, and the pronouncements of some state functionaries. It is deeply mistaken, however. The organs of the community, and the executive state organs, in particular, are responsible for economic occurrences even when they cannot intervene administratively. This responsibility follows from the fact that, in addition to administrative methods, there are also other means of economic coordination that the organs of the community can and must use.

The autonomy of work organizations is not only the basic organizational principle of the Yugoslav economic system, but also the motor of economic growth. Work collectives operate under certain conditions that are given to them as parameters for decision making. Taking into account these parameters, they are led in their decision making by their material interests. Precisely because the motivation for economic activity comes from material interests, bureaucratic subordination becomes unnecessary and real autonomy possible. But the satisfaction of some partial interests must not harm other partial interests; otherwise, exploitation, which is incompatible with socialism, will occur. Whether exploitation will occur or not, and whether the decisions of self-managed work organizations will lead to economic equilibrium and growth depend on the parameters of the system. But, by the nature of things, work organizations cannot bear the responsibility for these parameters — for the conditions of economic activity. The organs of the community bear this responsibility.

Let us amplify what is meant by each of the three basic functions of federal economic policy listed above.

Equalizing the conditions of economic activity means organizing the economy so that all economic decision-making units acquire income under the same conditions. Whatever differences in income then appear will be the result of differences in work and entrepreneurship, and not of external conditions beyond the control of work collectives. To achieve the equalization of conditions, it is necessary: (a) to ensure the stability of the economy; (b) to eliminate administrative interventions, and particularly the constant changing of regulations and other parameters of economic activity; and (c) to prevent the creation of monopolies and to eliminate imperfections of the market. The last condition requires free movement of labor, material, and financial resources throughout all of Yugoslavia, which should be guaranteed by the Constitution and carried out by means of federal inspectorates.

The degree of equality of conditions of economic activity is objectively rather simple to determine. Although personal incomes

can vary substantially from individual to individual or from enterprise to enterprise (and this is desirable), because of statistical
laws the income for a certain skill should be the same for all industries if calculated as average income within each particular
industry (provided that statistically the industries are sufficiently
large). To the extent that industry averages differ among themselves, the principle of distribution according to work is negated.
The report pointed out that it was notorious that these differences
were very large, which meant that there were privileged and deprived work collectives and that the former, by means of the imperfect market, exploited the labor of the latter.

Equalization of the conditions of economic activity cannot mean
state subsidization of work organizations that operate with losses,
which has often enough been the case. But it ought to mean com-
pensating for damages to industries that are discriminated against
in earning income by decisions of economic-political organs (fixed
prices and such). Equalizing the conditions of economic activity
also has its regional aspect and represents the economic justification for the existence of the fund supplying credit for the development
of the less-developed regions. To avoid misunderstanding, it
should be added that the requirement for equalizing conditions
does not contradict favoring or disfavoring certain production
when this is an accepted goal of economic policy directed at stimulating or checking such production.

Ensuring market equilibrium means: (a) achieving full employment of the labor force and of other factors of production; (b) stabilizing prices; and (c) achieving balance of payments equilibrium,
along with convertibility of the domestic currency. To attain these
goals, constructing an adequate economic system is not enough;
appropriate anticyclical economic policy must be undertaken against
stagnation and unemployment, on the one hand, and against inflation, on the other. As basic forms of anticyclical policy, both
monetary-credit and fiscal policy are essential. During periods
of cost inflation, an anti-inflationary incomes policy is also necessary to limit the overall change in personal incomes by the change
in productivity of labor. A well-formulated incomes policy, on its
part, should also contribute to solving the problem of distribution
according to labor and to increasing the reproductive capability
of economic organizations. For special types of structural and
regional unemployment, a corresponding labor force policy is also
necessary (information, retraining, transfer of labor, etc.).

Ensuring economic growth is the ultimate test of the progressiveness of a socioeconomic system. One need not cite Marx to understand that social systems which lag in economic development necessarily decline. And, contrariwise, the world economy models itself according to those systems that expand the fastest. An essential component of economic growth is also the regional balancing of development. Research has shown that, the faster the overall economic growth, the more rapidly the gap between the undeveloped and developed regions is overcome.

A clear determination of the relationship between the federal government and the labor-managed firm merits special attention. In a mutually dependent system such as an economy, very little can be done independently at individual points. The business success of each individual enterprise is in good part predetermined by the functioning of the economic system as a whole. If that system functions poorly, then the efforts of the collective and the expertise or skill of the enterprise's management cannot ensure exceptional business results. This naturally does not mean that the efficiency of enterprise organization is irrelevant to the success of the economy as a whole. On the contrary, it has a significant bearing and, viewed from the long run, constitutes a key factor.

In an economy subject to strong cyclical fluctuations, however, one cannot expect high incomes or high labor productivity in a recession, no matter what individual collectives have done; likewise, one cannot expect that good organization of individual enterprises will prevent recession or ensure high growth rates. An enterprise can plan inventory changes by the most modern statistical methods, but this is not worth much if deliveries of production materials can be unexpectedly interrupted because somewhere in the chain of production someone has failed to carry out essential import transactions or, for example, railroad freight cars are lacking. Enterprise experts can faultlessly program the optimal production plan, and then, for instance, there may be a reduction in the supply of electrical energy, or transportation channels may become clogged somewhere. The workers' council can formulate a long-run investment and business policy very conscientiously, only to have prices, interest rates, taxes, and other conditions of economic activity changed administratively, so that what appeared profitable becomes unprofitable, and vice versa. The work collective, like a good householder, can allocate substantial amounts to the investment fund at the expense of personal incomes, only to see the state, the commune, or someone else block those funds or forcibly convert them into long-term deposits. The enterprise management, in estimating market demand and programming production, relies on the parliament's social plan, and that plan may not be carried out or may be abandoned. When everything is this way, work collectives are not interested in modern statistical methods, nor in thoroughly prepared investment programs, nor in a well-founded longterm business policy, nor do they pay much heed to social plans; rather, they respond in kind to administrative measures.

It is therefore mistaken to give collectives and enterprise managements recommendations on how the good businessman should behave and expect that matters will then essentially change. It is much more realistic to assume that, under the given conditions, Yugoslav economic decision makers on the whole act in an economically rational way. If their behavior is not the most desirable, and if it should be changed, then the conditions of economic activity should be altered accordingly. Economic decision makers will then adjust to these changed conditions. Obviously, the organs of the community are responsible for creating conditions for more efficient business activity, and thus also for increasing the rate of production.

From what has just been stated follows the principle of economic policy that runs: the typical work organization — that is, the average enterprise — cannot err. If it behaves mistakenly, makes the wrong decisions, this is because it is correctly reacting to mistaken stimuli of the wider system. This is one of the axioms of economic policy which, it seems, is not sufficiently understood.

After administrative planning was abandoned, the state organs increasingly withdrew from the economy (and nonmarket sector). This process was particularly intensified after 1960. Such a course of events naturally should be welcomed. But during this process, a rather dangerous theory and practice developed. That is, it began to be believed that the state apparatus and other organs of the community are responsible only for those actions in which they can intervene administratively by commands. This trend in economic policy has already been described above in some detail.

The destiny of the White Book was very different from that of the Yellow Book prepared eight years earlier. It was not discussed either publicly or in the government. It was quietly shelved. The climate in the country was not favorable to economic reasoning. The dismantling of the economic policy apparatus of the Federation was continued vigorously. The solution of the problems of planning and coordination was sought in the sphere of politics and was attempted by political rather than by economic means. In the meantime, economic difficulties were mounting.

The New Constitution of 1974

The reform of 1965 intensified the process of political democratization. But at the same time the laissez-faire market generated various nonsocialist and antisocialist tendencies. There were monopolistic abuses of the market. Economic power tended to become concentrated, particularly in the financial sector (banks, exporting and insurance firms). Income differences increased. Due to misconceptions about the proper role of government described in the preceding section and the resulting passivity of an poor control by governmental agencies, there was a massive abuse of taxation and other regulations. As usual, governmental inefficiency began to generate corruption. A certain number of clever and ruthless individuals exploited the deficiencies of social organization and quickly accumulated personal fortunes by legal and illegal means. Discontents and protests became more and more numerous. The 1968 student revolt was just one incident, though the best known. And on top of all this, latent nationalist antagonisms suddenly erupted. Political instability increased substantially.

Thus, applying the familiar rule post hoc ergo propter hoc, to a superficial observer it might have looked as if political democratization generated antisocialist tendencies, nationalist conflicts, and political instability. One moves closer to the truth if one observes that good wishes do not suffice for an efficient economic and social organization of a society. A full sociopolitical analysis of this highly significant development is beyond the scope of the present book. To the few hints that have been scattered throughout the text, let me add only a word or two about nationalism.

Nationalist conflicts were quite serious and, for almost everybody, completely unexpected. Yet, with the wisdom of hindsight, they could have been easily predicted.[5] In a separate study on the

---

5. As a matter of fact, to a certain extent they were. In March 1969, the Central Committee of the League of Communists asked a selected group of economists to give their views on the current economic situation in a closed session. Two studies were prepared, one of them by the Institute of Economic Sciences, which I directed at that time. In the oral presentation, which was later published in a newspaper without my permission, but which I may now quote, I gave the following warning: "Accordingly, this is not a permanent upswing; on the contrary, there will be a new recession...which necessarily must bring about an increase in unemployment, centrifugal tendencies, fragmentation of the economy, administrative interventions and political complications such as strikes, nationalistic excesses and similar that will contribute to a certain discrediting of our self-governing system." The minister of the economy called this evaluation a "half-truth" [74].

subject [67, pp. 19-31], I identified four main reasons for the revival of nationalism: (1) Insecurity. Rapid economic development
caused a transfer of population from agricultural to urban occupations at a rate of 1.5 percent annually. Decentralization, democratization, and individualization of the society, occurring in a haphazard fashion, left these migrant individuals increasingly to themselves. In such a situation, the search for support and identity is
naturally expressed in identification with the social group within
which the individual has experienced fateful changes in his life.
Thus nationalistic feelings become hypertrophied. (2) Frustrations
generated by a divergence between the proclaimed ideals of the
Revolution and their realization. Frustrations lead to apathy,
apathy to introverted individualization, and from there the road
naturally continues to nationalism. (3) Authoritarianism of the
political system. Self-management in the work organization was
not accompanied by the development of self-management on higher
levels and in the political sphere. Gradually, a dualistic system
developed in which the authoritarianism of the political superstructure increasingly came into conflict with the self-managed
nature of the rest of the system. (4) National-political quid pro
quo. In a nationally heterogeneous environment, political authoritarianism is interpreted as the hegemony of the other, larger or
economically more developed nation.

These were the four hidden roots of nationalism. Once the rate
of economic growth had been drastically reduced and serious unemployment began to appear, fertile soil was provided for the wild
plant of nationalism to blossom.

In the environment just described, an enormous amount of discontent about decisions in the center accumulated. And there were
good reasons for distrust, since many of these decisions had been
arbitrary. State parliaments and ordinary citizens became nationally hypersensitive, carefully calculating the costs and benefits of every central decision. Thus the only solution that appeared
politically feasible — that is, acceptable to all concerned — was a
radical dismantling of the central apparatus. Economic policy was
to be replaced by direct political bargaining, subject to unanimity
on all important, even professional or routine, economic issues.
These feelings were fully reflected in institutional changes.

On the other hand, there was a strong desire and pressure to
continue with the development of self-management at the level of
the firm. That implied further economic decentralization. Economic decentralization without appropriate instruments of economic

policy, however, requires strong central political power in order to make the system work at all. And this is what happened in fact. Thus the formula applied was economic and administrative decentralization and political recentralization, all in quite extreme forms. The solution, probably unavoidable under the circumstances, can hardly be considered inherently consistent. The economic and social price paid was substantial.

When in 1963 the country got its third constitution in twenty years, the general feeling was that it would provide a lasting legal basis for many years to come. But the eventful decade that followed proved this belief ill-founded. Only five years after its passage, the Federal Assembly promulgated the first nineteen constitutional amendments. By 1971, the number of amendments had increased to forty-two, and it became clear that it would make more sense to prepare a new constitution than to continue to amend the old one. The new Constitution was adopted in 1974. In the present context, the most important innovations were as follows.

The basic market decision-making unit is the firm. Below the level of the firm, the market ceases to operate and is replaced by a very different type of decision-making and coordinating mechanism. Above the level of the firm, the market is modified. The 1963 Constitution specified the autonomy of the firm or, more generally, of the work organization. But very soon it became apparent that the solution was too rigid because the firm was both too small and too large to satisfy all the requirements. Modern economy — and society — requires permanent forms of cooperation above the level of the work organization. Thus, the new Constitution determined the conditions for self-managing business associations. Even more important was the introduction of subfirm units known as basic organizations of associated labor [osnovna organizacija udruženog rada]. If self-management is to be really meaningful, it must result in direct decision making. For that, a firm — a work organization — has to be broken into constituent units characterized by technological and economic unity of the work process, by autonomous organization of work, by direct management, and by direct distribution of income [68, p. 51]. The firm appears as a federation of basic organizations of associated labor. Since in a socialist system no one owns anything, each of these basic organizations may break away from the mother firm provided it compensates for possible damage [69, p. 22]. A merger of two firms, on the other hand, must be agreed upon by all basic organizations of the two firms, and changes neither the position nor the structure of each basic organization.

If state intervention in the economy and society is to be mini-
mized, laws and administrative orders must be replaced by direct
agreements among the interested parties. The Constitution provides for two types of such agreements. Self-management agreements [samoupravni sporazum] are made between buyers and
sellers, or, in the nonmarket sector (education, medical services,
etc.) between users and suppliers of services, and are intended to
reconcile the divergent interests. If any level of government is
included, the agreement signed is called a social compact [društ-
veni dogovor]. For instance, the distribution of income is regulated by social compacts among the local or state governments,
trade unions, and chambers of commerce.

In the political sphere, the main innovation was the replacement
of traditional elections and parliaments by a system of delegations.
The idea is a very old one in the socialist movement and has now
been implemented for the first time nationwide. The "substance
of the delegation system," according to Edvard Kardelj, one of its
architects, "lies in the fact that the interests of the working people in the assemblies should be directly expressed and defended
by their delegates, who retain their regular jobs and so cannot
turn into one or another kind of professional political representative.... The basic organizations of associated labor as well as
each local community would have a delegation — just as they have
various committees and commissions — which would be a standing
organ of the workers' collective and the workers' council, on the
one hand, and the local community, on the other" [69, p. 33]. Members of a delegation are elected by direct secret ballot. Delegates
representing their respective delegations in the assemblies are
elected from among the members of the delegation as a kind of
collective deputy. They make up chambers of self-managed communities in the Assembly. A self-managed work organization or
community gives instructions to its delegation, and the latter in-
structs its representative delegate in the Assembly how to act,
but does not specify how he is to vote on each individual issue. As
the system has been in operation for only a short time, it is
too early to comment on its efficiency.

Federal and state investment funds (except the fund for less developed regions) and banks have been liquidated and resources
transferred to business firms. Customs duties are almost the
only independent source of federal revenue. The federal government cannot pass any important economic decision at all without
the unanimous consent of the appropriate interstate committee

composed of the representatives of the state governments. There is also a system of compensations designed to deal with the adverse effects of federal regulation on particular state economies [75, pp. 104-10].

It is still too early to judge how all these provisions will work in everyday practice. In the discussions that preceded the adoption of the Constitution a certain scepticism occasionally was shown. Lj. Madžar expressed the widely shared opinion that the development and deepening of self-management has been accompanied by institutional changes that have affected economic efficiency and the pace of development very unfavorably [70, p. 16]. Nikola Čobeljić, on the other hand, expressed doubts about the meaningfulness of the statement that there was both a progressive development of self-management and increasing unemployment, emigration of workers, increased social differentiation, consumerism and commercialization of social services, and so on [71, p. 63]. Research workers at the Institute of Social Studies in Belgrade reached the following conclusion: "The political system is not in line with the evolution in the economic base, and this is reflected in the paradox that, while our society is the bearer of an exceptionally progressive idea of self-management, it has also manifested a repugnance toward innovations with respect to the modernization of the political system" [72, 276]. Similarly, Veljko Cvjetičanin, a sociologist, observed that the development of self-management has been retarded because of an inadequate political system: "The political system is a limiting factor of self-management. All segments of social labor are directed toward the political system, which arbitrates, instead of becoming integrated directly through association" [76, p. 487]. Another sociologist, Stipe Šuvar, who at the time of this writing is Secretary of Education in Croatia, also pointed to a stagnation of self-management and added that it is almost nonexistent above the firm level: "Social-political power ... is still possessed and exercised by narrow ruling groups. ... For instance, all essential functions in the Federation and the states are performed by at most a hundred-odd people" [77, pp. 17, 19, 20].

In the final analysis, politics, not economics, determines the pace of development of socialism. Further discussion of this problem, however, is beyond the scope of the present work.[6]

---

6. The author deals with this subject in his book on the sociopolitical development of Yugoslavia [73].

PLANNING AND GROWTH ‖

4. FIVE FIVE-YEAR PLANS

The rationale for central planning was explained in the preceding chapter. By 1947 the machinery for central planning was completed. Hierarchically organized planning commissions on various
levels — federal, state, district, and city — were entrusted with
comprehensive planning in their respective territories. Operational planning and implementation was carried out by ministries
and then, down the line, by general and chief directorates and
planning sections in the enterprises. Annual plans were broken
down into quarterly, monthly, and ten-day plans. In 1949 about
13,000 groups of commodities were planned [1, p. 15]. In the same
year, the state budget comprised two-thirds of the national income
[2, p. 453]. Every enterprise had to supply the higher authorities
with 600-800 different reports per year. The annual economic
plan weighed some 3,300 pounds [42, p. 65]. Suppliers and cus-
tomers were assigned to every enterprise in advance. The administrative allocations were not quite perfect, however, and the
enterprises were asked "to probe the ground themselves." The
planning authorities would provide them with money — more than
they wanted — and would ask them to spend it. Since prices were
fixed, spending money meant finding raw materials and investment
goods necessary for the fulfillment of the plan. In a market economy, one endeavors to save money; in the centrally planned economy, one is at great pains to spend it. In the former, selling is
the most difficult task; in the latter, buying is the greatest worry
of businessmen.

The economy was run as a single mammoth enterprise. That
required establishing a system of continuous control of operations
of all enterprises. In 1948 B. Kidrič voiced complaints against

those who felt there was no need for daily reporting and were satisfied with ten-day reporting [2, p. 468]. A number of years later,
J. Stanovnik, now Secretary of the UN Economic Commission for
Europe, was asked at a lecture delivered to Swedish economists
in Stockholm what sort of devices were used to implement plans
in Yugoslavia. He answered, "Telephones!"

The First Five-Year Plan covered the period from 1947 through
1951. It proclaimed four main goals:

1) to overcome economic and technological backwardness;
2) to strengthen the economic and military power of the country;
3) to strengthen and develop the socialist sector of the economy;
4) to increase the general welfare of the population.

Consumption was taken care of, but it was last in the order of
priorities. The goals enumerated were to be achieved by an explosive increase of output; compared with the prewar level, national income was to increase 1.9 times, agricultural output 1.5
times, industrial output 4.9 times. Due to poor statistical records,
however, the prewar level seems to have been greatly underestimated, and the three targets were achieved only by 1954, 1959,
and 1961, respectively.

At first, the implementation of the plan proceeded satisfactorily,
though not as well as it was believed.[1] In 1959 the economic block-
ade of the Cominform countries forced Yugoslavia to search for
trading outlets for about one-half of its exports and to secure the
same proportion of imports from other sources. Substantial foreign aid was obtained, but in spite of this, two years later the sudden reorientation of foreign trade had stifling effects on growth.
The next blow came from nature in 1950: a severe drought reduced agricultural output by one-third. Collectivization helped to
aggravate agricultural problems. The radical economic reorganization in 1951 could only complicate matters. Industrial output
fell by 4 percent in 1951, and by one more percent in 1952. The

---

1. Thus V. Begović reported the overfulfillment of the first half of the five-
year plan [3]. But later statistical estimates showed that the data produced by
the Federal Planning Commission [4, pp. 251, 484] were inflated. For the output of manufacturing, mining, and power plants, the differences are as follows:

	Indexes		
	1948	1949	1950
	1946	1948	1949
Federal Planning Commission	267	116.6	106.3
Federal Statistical Office (later estimates)	190	111	103

plan was extended for a year, but that was already pointless, and the report on the fulfillment of the First Five-Year Plan was never published.

And yet, if not a full success, the plan was far from being a failure. It generated output substantially above the prewar level, raised the share of gross investment in fixed assets to 33 percent of gross national product (material product definition — close to 30 percent on the standard national accounts [SNA] definition), and created entire new industries.

In 1952 rigid central planning was replaced by "planning by global proportions." These proportions were: minimum use of output capacity and the corresponding wage fund, profits as a percentage of the wage bill (a device for wage planning), basic capital formation, and taxes and allocation of budgetary resources [5, p. 31]. In this way the central plan was expected to regulate general economic activity without administrative orders by influencing the rate of growth and the proportion between investment and consumption, and by effecting structural changes in the economy [6]. The old Planning Commission, which had acted as a superministry controlling the activities of all economic ministries and was in charge of the overall implementation of the plan [19], was replaced by the Federal Planning Bureau, an expert institution with no administrative powers. State planning became social planning, which meant wide consultations among all interested parties, inclusion of nonprofit institutions, and independence of the plans of the enterprises.

The next three years were used to complete the key investment projects of the five-year plan in annual installments. In the discussion of the 1955 plan, the new mood was already apparent: agriculture seemed neglected, investment too large and one-sided [7, pp. 147, 150]. By the end of that year, M. Popović could say in the Federal Assembly that one period of economic development was completed [7, p. 160]. The year 1956 was used to prepare the Second Five-Year Plan for the period 1957-61. In this plan, increase of consumption already ranks third among the five main goals [8, p. 220]. Growth of investment was somewhat retarded and its structure changed radically. The share of industrial investment was substantially reduced in order to double the share of agriculture and increase the shares of transport and trade [7, p. 211]. Within manufacturing, consumer goods industries were to expand faster. So-called nonproductive investment was also accelerated. All these changes proved beneficial, and the plan was carried out in four years. The planning system seemed to be well adapted to the needs of the economy and worked satisfactorily. This system was described by J. Sirotković [9], S. Dabčević-Kučar [10], and B. Jelić [11].

The first plan distorted the structure of the economy by forcing investment into heavy industries. The second undertook to make corrections but went to the other extreme by overexpanding consumer goods industries. Thus, the third plan was left with the task of redressing the balance again by accelerating investment in power generation, metallurgy, and intermediate goods industries. These fluctuations in investment induced N. Čobeljić and R. Stojanović to invent a theory of investment cycles inherent in a socialist economy with an uneven pace of technological progress [12]. Z. Baletić, A. Bajt [15], and others criticized this theory as unacceptable on the grounds that mistakes in planning are due to ignorance rather than necessarily intrinsic to socialism, and technological progress is rather innocent in this respect.

The Third Five-Year Plan for the period 1961-65 endeavored to accelerate the growth of output even further. Personal consumption ranked second among the goals [8, p. 221]. But the plan was hardly launched when the country found itself in the middle of a recession, the reasons for which were explained in the previous chapter. The plan was doomed to fail. To avoid unpleasant discussions, the Federal Assembly decided to replace the five-year plan with a seven-year one covering the period 1964-70. For that purpose, the Assembly passed a Resolution in which the basic political and economic goals of the new plan were defined as follows [13]:

1) to raise steadily the level of living, first of all of personal consumption, and realize a higher share of personal incomes in national income;

2) to catch up with international standards of productive efficiency and labor productivity;

3) to expand external trade through more intensive participation of Yugoslavia in the international division of labor;

4) to accelerate the development of underdeveloped areas;

5) to develop further socialist society by strengthening the role of the direct producers and work organization in management.

A comparison of these goals with those of the First Five-Year Plan shows very clearly the distance that separates social planning from state planning. The welfare of individuals is moved from the bottom to the top of the list of priorities.[2] This change is both fostered and pervaded by the philosophy that economic welfare is the purpose and the most powerful incentive for production. Autarchical orientation is replaced by openness toward the world market and international influences. The measure of perfection of a socialist economy is no more to be found in the share of the state in national capital but in the development of self-government. Yet, the first plan and the Resolution had one thing in common: neither of them was implemented.

The Resolution, in fact, foreshadowed the reform of 1965. The changes in the economic institution were so radical that it became necessary to prepare a new five-year plan for the period 1966-70. This plan incorporated the goals of the Resolution. It envisaged a somewhat lower rate of growth of GNP (7.5 to 8.5 percent a year) and a relatively modest expansion of manufacturing (9 to 10 percent), but a high rate of productivity increase (6 to 7 percent a year). These targets were not achieved either.

Thus, in the 1960s, one after another of the plans remained unfulfilled. The result was serious structural discrepancies, unemployment, and so on. The task of the Fifth Plan 1971-75, was to repair the damage. It envisaged an acceleration of investment and rate of growth, structural changes in favor of industries that were lagging behind, faster increase of productivity, and a substantial slowing of price increases. Analyzing the fulfillment of targets for the first three years, Nikola Čobeljić [14] comes to the conclusion that not only were the targets unfulfilled, but the observed trends have been exactly contrary to the trends envisaged by the plan. A comparison between the targets and the achievements of the last four plans is given in Table 2.

Only the first of the four social plans was very successfully carried out. In fact, it was fulfilled in four years, and so the next plan was designed to start with 1961 to catch up with calendar decades. The following three plans were disappointing, particularly with respect to the most important indicator — the rate of growth of social product.

The period after 1960 may be described as a crisis in Yugoslav planning. Elsewhere I explained this crisis in the following way [29, pp. 203-5]. In the last half-century, Yugoslav economic

---

2. Personal consumption was reduced at a rate of 2 percent annually during the period 1948-52; it began to expand at 4.6 percent per annum in 1953-56; it grew at approximately the same rate as national income, 9.3 percent, in 1957-63; and its rate of growth surpassed that of national income afterward [18, pp. 207-9].

Table 2

Planned and Achieved Rates of Growth

	1957-61		1961-65		1966-70		1971-75	
	P	A	P	A	P	A	P	A[a]
Social product	9.5	10.3	11.4	7.0	7.5-8.5	6.3	7.5	6.3
Industrial output	11.0	12.6	13.0	10.7	9-10	6.1	8.0	8.0
Agricultural output	7.1	6.5	8.3	2.8	4.6	2.6	3.5	3.9
Gross fixed investment	9.1	15.9	12.0	5.4	7.0	7.1	7.0	2.4
Personal consumption	6.7	9.3	8.8	7.3	8.5	5.9	7.0	6.0
Exports	11.9	11.9	13.6	13.9	13-15	12.2	12.0	11.4
Imports	8.0	14.0	9.6	9.9	10-12	18.0	10.0	7.4
Employment	4.4	6.1	6.0	4.3	2.5-3.0	1.1	3.0	3.9
Labor productivity	7.5	4.6	6.8	4.7	6-7	5.8	5.0	2.7

P = plan; A = achievement.

Sources: Vukčević [50, p. 45]; Čobeljić [14, p. 67]; Službeni list, 35, 1972; SGJ-1974.

a. 1971-73.

development has been extremely uneven. One world economic depression, one world war, and a period of administrative planning cum collectivization left per capita output stagnant for almost a quarter of a century. The initiation of self-government in 1950 liberated latent growth potentials and generated an economic explosion in the next decade and a half. Between 1952 and 1966, the development lag of Yugoslavia in comparison with France was reduced from 130 years to 53 years; in comparison with Belgium, from 100 years to 40 years; in comparison with Sweden, from 90 years to 44 years; and in comparison with Italy, from half a century to a decade. In other words, the development period comparable to the last 14 years for Yugoslavia lasted 80 years in France, 60 years in Belgium, 46 years in Sweden, and somewhat more than 40 years in Italy.

Rapid economic development produced difficulties of adjustment. Almost overnight a peasant economy with an illiterate population was transformed into an industrialized modern economy with highly complex social institutions. That was too much of a rush for the state apparatus to cope with. Since the problem was not realized in time, things got out of hand. The pace of economic growth was not the only factor of strain. After all, several other countries grew at comparable rates. But superimposed on economic development were quite radical political and social changes. Yugoslavia was not only to be economically developed but also socially transformed. In this latter respect, it has turned out (so far) to be the single member of its class — and pioneering is a very exhausting activity.

State machinery, institutions, and individuals in responsible positions began to lag behind the general pace of economic and social development. Many of the old leaders retired, and masses of young people were brought to positions of responsibility, even to top political positions. Rotation of cadres — another sociopolitical invention — was put to work quite vigorously. But there was a general lack of social experience to aid in coping with continual eruptions of new problems. Two improvised reforms after 1960 only made things worse. The country found itself in the middle of a very turbulent adjustment process. This is what constitutes the crisis of planning in Yugoslavia.

5. GROWTH AND CYCLES

In postrevolutionary economic development, three distinct phases can be observed: the central planning phase immediately after the war; the transformation phase, or decentralization; and, finally, the self-governing phase, in which economic organization assumed more permanent forms. The exact dating of the three phases is somewhat arbitrary. In this connection, it should be noted that the impact of legal-institutional changes is not immediately reflected in economic behavior; the lag amounts to about two to five years. Thus, the basic law on workers' management was passed in 1950, and about two years of organizational work were necessary before the new economic system began to function in 1952. However, as will be mentioned in a moment, a production function analysis shows that for three more years the economy continued to behave as it had in the central planning phase. Thus both 1952 and 1955 could be taken as cutoff years. In the first edition of this book, I opted for 1952 in order to bring legal-institutional and economic periodization closer together. Later analysis [49] convinced me that 1955 was more preferable, among other reasons because it gives a more realistic picture of the general efficiency of both central planning and transition organizations. Since the economy matched the prewar level of output in 1947, this year was taken as the beginning year.

Similar considerations apply to the second cutoff year. The new phase was politically foreshadowed by the Program of the League of Communists in 1968 and legally-institutionally established by the Constitution of 1963. The first reform, carried out in 1962, proved abortive, and so the transition period was prolonged until 1964. The radical change in economic behavior occurred after the inauguration of the reform of 1965. In the first edition of this book, I could not take 1964 as a cutoff point because that would have left the third phase with only four rather disappointing years. Now the periodization can be corrected.

Five basic groups of indicators for twenty-six years of post-revolutionary economic development are given in Table 3.

In the central planning period, collectivization caused stagnation of agriculture until 1953, when collectivization was discontinued and reversed. Consequently, a low rate of growth was seen for the entire period. The economic boycott of the Cominform countries depressed foreign trade, and exports, in particular. As a result of both factors, investment could expand only slowly, and the overall pace of development was not impressive. The rapid expansion of employment was an indication of the inefficiency of economic organization.

In the second period, the unfettered economy was in full swing in all spheres. Foreign trade expanded faster than output, and exports faster than imports. Prices were stable except in agriculture, where the disparity from the first period had to be corrected. Personal consumption and real wages were rising as fast as one could wish. The overall performance of the economy set a standard against which alternative economic policies could be evaluated.

In the third period, trends were reversed and performance dropped to the standards of the central planning phase. The dismantling of federal investment funds (with no adequate institutional change to replace them) reduced the growth rate of investment to less than half of what it had been before. This, together with poor coordination of activities and poor economic policy, reduced the rates of growth of output. As a result, employment possibilities were drastically reduced, and the rate of employment growth dropped to almost one-third of what it was previously. Slow growth of output implied unimpressive increases in real wages and personal consumption. On the other hand, trends in people's aspirations that were formed in the preceding period generated much faster increases in nominal wages than a sluggish economy could absorb. Inflation occurred and soon began to feed on itself and on international inflation. Administrative interventions multiplied and efficiency dropped.

49

Table 3

Yugoslav Economy, 1947-73: Percentage Rates of Growth per Annum

	Central planning, 1947-55	Decentral- ization, 1955-64	Self- government, 1964-73
1. Output and investment			
Social product (1966 prices)	5.4	8.2	5.7
Manufacturing and mining	9.1	12.4	7.0
Agriculture	1.6[a]	4.3	1.5
Gross fixed investment (1966 prices)	4.2	11.8	4.8[b]
2. Foreign trade			
Export of commodities	0.3[c]	12.8	7.8
Import of commodities	4.9[c]	11.6	8.8
3. Prices			
Industrial producer prices	—	1.6	8.8
Agricultural producer prices	—	8.2	16.0
Cost of living	—	6.9	15.3
4. Level of living			
Real wages	—	7.1	4.5
Personal consumption (1966 prices)	—	7.8	5.4
Employment in collective sector	8.4	5.7	2.0
5. Efficiency			
Labor productivity in collective sector	—	5.1	4.6[b]
Investment efficiency[d] in collective sector	—	0.9	−3.6[b]

Sources: Jugoslavija 1945-1964; Statistical Yearbook 1974; Horvat [49, p. 52].

a. 1947/48-1954/55.

b. 1964-1972.

c. 1948-1955.

d. Efficiency of investment is defined as the ratio of the increment of so-cial product and the increment of fixed capital a year earlier corrected for cyclical fluctuations.

Because I denoted the third phase as "self-government," one might infer that self-government is economically inefficient. That would be a false conclusion. Since basic inefficiences were correctly forecast by economists, their causes may be considered as known and understood. The reasons that alternative policies were not accepted must be sought in the political sphere. One almost trivial reason is that all personnel at the senior levels of the

governmental apparatus were trained and mentally formed in an
environment of administrative controls, and these people have
both a poor knowledge of the functioning of the market and few
sympathies for its complexities. In general, it may be said that
not self-government but the inconsistencies and poor development
of integral self-governments are the real causes of the deterioration
of economic performance. Since lessons are usually learned after
some time and the political superstructure usually adapts to the
economic base, one may expect an improvement in efficiency beyond even 1955-64 standards. The following question may be
asked: Suppose economic policy and planning are efficient enough
so that they do not pose barriers — continuous changes of regulations, poor forecasts, wrong incentives, administrative interventions, and the like — to expansionary efforts of working collectives; what would the rate of growth be? After a brief analysis,
I came to the conclusion that the rate of growth of nonagricultural
output would be on the order of 13 percent per annum [17, pp. 134-
35]. If agricultural growth at the rate of 3 percent is assumed,
and account is taken of the agricultural share in social product
(20 percent), the potential growth of material social product in a
self-governing setting amounts to about 11 percent.

In its quarter-century of postrevolutionary development (1947-
74), the Yugoslav economy expanded its total output five and a
half times. Agricultural output increased more than two times,
industrial output eleven and a half times, and employment in the
collective sector (i.e., outside peasant agriculture and private
handicraft) four times. The material base for socialist development has been created.

Since Yugoslavia has so far been the only country to have lived
through three different economic systems — capitalist, etatist,
and self-governing — in a relatively short period of time, it may
be possible to evaluate the comparative efficiency of the three
systems. Something of the kind was attempted by T. Marschak.
He reduced the dimensions of the problem by studying comparative efficiency in a centralized and decentralized setting. Marschak's results were not conclusive. He felt that the lessons to
be drawn by the current de riguer of new economic systems from
the Yugoslav experience were "staggeringly obscure" [21, p. 586].
Later research was undertaken at the Institute of Economic Sciences [16]. In this study, efficiency was measured in terms of the
rates of growth of output attributable to technical progress, defined as the residual after the contributions of labor and capital

Table 4

The Use of Labor and Capital and Technical Progress in Yugoslavia

		Rates of growth per annum (%)		Rates of growth of GNP due to increased efficiency
		GNP	Employ-ment	Fixed assets	
Capitalism:	1911–32	3.28	1.87	3.52	0.71
	1932–40	4.67	0.72	2.59	3.16
Etatism:	1940–54	5.91	4.76	9.99	−1.04
Self-government:	1954–67	10.31	4.44	7.84	4.44

Note: The war years 1914-18 and 1941-45 are excluded. The data refer to manufacturing, mining, power generation, construction, and crafts.
Source: Horvat [16].

have been accounted for. The results are summarized in Table 4.

The periodization in the table is not ideal and is determined by data availability. Yet the results of the analysis are extremely suggestive. In the foregoing section, it was stated that the investment program of the First Five-Year Plan was completed by 1955. Statistical testing in the IES study showed that the Yugoslav economy operated on the basis of two completely different production functions, one applying to the period 1947-55 and the other to the years after that. The former had a negative residual, the latter a positive and very large one. Data in the table seem to suggest that, under central planning, output and employment expanded rapidly, and capital formation even more rapidly, as compared with the private capitalist prewar economy. But overall efficiency was also reduced. Under self-government, the growth of output and technical progress accelerated beyond anything known before, while rapid employment expansion was preserved.

As might have been noticed, growth was rapid but not at all smooth. At first, the possibility of regular cyclical development was rejected by some economists. Yet in another IES study, business cycles with periods of about four years were identified [17]. The periods tend to lengthen. These cycles, which manifest themselves as fluctuations in the rates of growth (see Chart 1), have interesting features not found elsewhere. Inventories are accumulated during the downswings and decumulated during the upswings; the accelerator is not operative; prices tend to vary inversely to the cycle; and so on. The upper turning points seem to be generated by divergent changes in import and export elasticities that

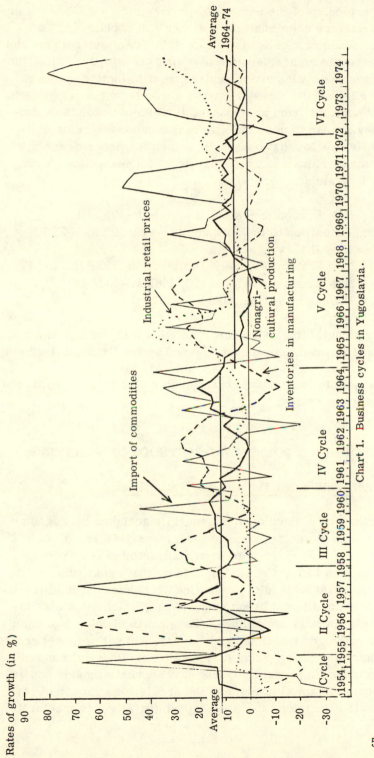

Chart 1. Business cycles in Yugoslavia.

53

end in an explosion of the balance of payments deficit. The lower turning points are somewhat more difficult to explain. A. Bajt feels that consumer demand is to a certain extent autonomous and helps to generate an acceleration of output growth [48; 52]. If the beginnings of the cycles are measured from inflection points in the downswings of the rates of growth (these points correspond to peaks of deviations from an exponential trend of absolute magnitudes), they appear to coincide with major economic reforms. Thus, the five cycles that have occurred so far describe in an interesting manner the history of postwar economic policy (Roman numerals indicate quarters):

Cycle 1: New Economic System (I), 1949 III-1955 III
Cycle 2: Transition to the Second Five-Year Plan, 1955 III-1958 II
Cycle 3: New System of Income Distribution, 1958 II-1960 IV
Cycle 4: New Economic System (II), 1960 IV-1964 IV
Cycle 5: Economic Reform, 1964 IV-1972 II

The beginning of the sixth cycle coincides with the implementation of constitutional amendments passed by the National Assembly in 1971.

Cyclical institutional development seems also to be a novel feature of business cycles.

6. DEVELOPMENT POLICY AND METHODS OF PLANNING

Development Policy and Functions of Social Plans

The philosophy of development generally accepted by Yugoslav economists and by the government until about 1956 is well described by N. Čobeljić, former Deputy Director of the Federal Planning Bureau [20]. Čobeljić maintains that rapid industrialization is the chief method of generating development. Industrialization creates additional urban employment, which alleviates latent unemployment in agriculture. The growth of the urban labor force generates additional demand for agricultural products and so stimulates the development of agriculture. Physical control of foreign trade (to prevent imports of nonessential goods and secure imports of capital goods) and the accelerated growth of consumer goods industries (so-called department I) help to accelerate industrial growth, which in turn generates development impulses throughout the economy. Imports are paid for by exports of raw materials and agricultural products. Necessary saving is secured by a proper price policy. Prices are kept low in predominantly private agriculture and are inflated in consumer goods industries by means of large turnover taxes.

The policy described was not only advocated but also consistently implemented. In the period 1950-56, investment in industry (manufacturing, mining, and power generation) absorbed 51 percent of all investment. The share of industry in national income rose from 21 percent in 1939 to 40 percent in 1956. Four-fifths of industrial investment was channeled into heavy industry and power generation. The share of saving in national income increased four times compared with the prewar level [20, pp. 178, 366].

The planning system in 1947-52 was consistent with such a development policy. The main characteristics of this system, as described by B. Jelić, another Deputy Director of the Federal Planning Bureau, were as follows: (a) decisions regarding priorities, timing, and structural changes are strictly centralized; (b) physical allocation of resources is a basic method of planning; (c) financial elements play a secondary role and serve to achieve balancing in value terms; (d) targets represent directives; (e) production is planned in terms of commodities and capital formation is planned in terms of individual investment projects; (f) prices are administratively fixed; (g) the elements of which a plan is composed are also the means for its implementation [11, pp. 102-5].

After the engine of growth has been set into motion in the manner described and the economy organized along socialist lines, a different approach is both possible and necessary. Čobeljić expects a more balanced growth to occur now. Jelić refers to Rostow's takeoff theory and to Bicanić's threshold of growth theory [22] and insists on decentralized initiative as a further vehicle of growth. Self-government implies separation of the function of planning from the function of operational management. Jelić points out that social plans, if they are to be efficient devices for implementation of social preferences, should determine at least three global proportions — the basic division of national income, the structure of investment, and the relations with foreign countries [11, p. 144].

The same three global proportions were accepted as basic by D. Bjelogrlić, Director of the Planning Bureau of Serbia. He adds a fourth one, however: the relatively greater growth of the less developed states and regions [23, p. 118]. Bjelogrlić presented his paper to a conference on social planning held in Belgrade in 1965. There, Čobeljić and K. Mihajlović spoke in favor of introducing more directives into planning, while M. Samardžija and M. Korać maintained that the planning of even the share of accumulation and the structure of investment, meant a violation of self-government. This discussion — which covered a wide spectrum of opinions, from those favoring semicentral planning to those advocating an almost complete laissez-faire approach — has been characteristic for Yugoslav economic professionals since the enactment of the new Constitution in 1963. The trend has been toward the laissez-faire extreme. In 1960, the federal government controlled 48 percent of business investment directly through its General Investment Fund, as well as 14 percent indirectly through tied loans [21, p. 158]. In 1969, the Party Congress decided to liquidate so-called state capital and in the future the federal government was not supposed to retain any direct control over investment resources.

The advocates of the new approach to planning — J. Sirotković [25], former Director of the Planning Bureau of Croatia, and R. Štajner [24], Director General of the Federal Planning Bureau — as well as M. Mesarić [26], and others argue that the professional function of planning should be supplemented by an emphasized social function; that annual plans should be abandoned and replaced by parliamentary resolutions (which has been done since 1966); and that medium-term plans should be continually revised and extended every two to three years. These ideas have been more or less accepted, but in parliamentary debates criticisms were voiced that it was not at all clear how the plans were to be implemented [24, p. 91]. In practice, the implementation of plans has left much to be desired, and a satisfactory law on social planning has still to be produced.

The functions of social planning in the present Yugoslav setting have been described by the Institute of Economic Sciences [27, p. 20] and by M. Mesarić [28] as follows: (1) A plan is, first of all, a forecasting device. (2) As such, it provides economic subjects with necessary information for their autonomous decision making. This, together with institutionalized consultations, makes the plan an instrument for coordinating economic decisions. (3) After relevant social preferences have been determined by an essentially political process, the application of modern tools of economic policy make the plan an instrument for programming economic development. (4) Once the social plan has been accepted by the parliament, it becomes a directive for the government. This is the only administrative or compulsory aspect of social planning.

Institutional Framework

The precondition for efficient social planning is an adequate analysis of the functioning of an institutional framework. R. Bića-nić speaks of a polycentric planning model [51, pp. 41-62]. A general idea of how the system works or is supposed to work can be obtained from a description by Horvat [29].

The Yugoslav economic system consists of autonomous, self-governing, work organizations[3] and individual producers in market and nonmarket sectors, and government machinery. The task of the latter is to use nonadministrative means to coordinate the activities of market and nonmarket agents and to organize public administration in certain fields of common interest (judiciary, defense, foreign affairs, etc.).

The functioning of this economic system is based on the assumption that the self-governing collectives are materially interested in maximizing their incomes and that the government and the parliament are able to create an economic environment in which autonomous decision makers behave in accordance with general social interests. Both assumptions seem to have been proved by modern theory of economic policy and by experience in decentralized market economy. Between the center (parliament) and the periphery (work organizations), four types of gravitational forces are active in keeping the system in equilibrium and the economic agents on the predictive trajectories of social interest. These forces are information-consultation ties, market ties, economic policy ties (instruments of economic policy and legislation), and administrative ties. The last mentioned are exceptional as far as economic agents are concerned and apply to various organs of the center such as ministries, the National Bank, certain bureaus, and the like.

I should add that there is also a fifth type of tie — political ties — which closes the whole structure connecting the work organizations

---

3. "Work organization" is a constitutional term meant to underline a fundamental equality in rights and status of every group of citizens organized with an intention to earn a living, regardless of the activity they perform. An enterprise, a theater, a government office — all are work organizations.

with the parliament and with flows of commands from the periphery toward the center. To keep this section short, I shall not analyze these ties.

Let us now take a look at the market half of our economic cosmos. The market coordinates the activities of enterprises and individual producers. It is a very rough and unreliable mechanism, however, requiring constant adjustments. These adjustments are achieved through general regulative measures and economic policy instruments of the government. The financial flows, intended to achieve desirable allocation of resources, are regulated by the National Bank within the framework of the social plan. There are two additional types of specific financial interventions: in the area of foreign trade (credits and exchange insurances) and in the area of investment (insuring of the proper structure and regional allocation of capital formation). These three purposes are served by three federal funds: the funds for export credits, for underdeveloped regions, and for investment.

Market equilibrium is influenced by three institutions. Two of them — the Directorate for Food and the Directorate for Industrial Reserves — intervene whenever supply and demand do not match. The former directorate also administers agricultural support prices. The third institution — the Price Control Bureau — is now a somewhat alien element in the system. I expect that in the future this governmental bureau will evolve into a Price and Wage Arbitration, an institution in which all relevant interests would be represented and all decisions made jointly. At the moment, more than 40 percent of industrial prices are controlled.

Statistical and planning bureaus have only informative-consultative functions in this system.

A rather peculiar arrangement of the Yugoslav system is to be found in what I term a quasi market. The market cannot coordinate the activities of schools, hospitals, museums, and other nonmarket work organizations as directly as it does those of the enterprises. In a socialist society, sick persons should be healed, talented youths educated, regardless of whether and how much they can afford to pay. On the other hand, the traditional budgetary financing of nonmarket activities has led to bureaucratic practices incompatible with a self-governing system. The solution of this dilemma was sought in an interpolation of a special self-government mechanism between the government and nonmarket work organizations. This mechanism is the "interest communities" [interesne zajednice]. The communities obtain their financial resources through parliamentary decisions and then buy services of nonmarket producers on behalf of the society. The nonmarket producers compete for available resources by offering their services on differential conditions. In this way, there emerges a special type of market — a quasi market — which makes it possible for the relations between the nonmarket sector and society to be economically conditioned and for the collectives in the nonmarket sector to preserve their self-governing autonomy, and, at the same time, for relations within the fields of education, culture, and social welfare to be based on the principle of "distribution according to needs," which is one of the preconditions of a socialist society. It is clear that the enterprises can also intervene in the nonmarket sector — either by buying services directly or by creating special foundations.

Apart from economic relations between federal bodies and economic agents, there are relations between federal and state and local authorities, between the latter two and the work organizations, and among all of them. I must, however, skip the description of all these relations, although they are extremely important for the functioning of the system as a whole.

Other Issues

One of the recurring issues of the planning controversies is the problem of optimum investment and saving. Impressed by the unpleasant contraction of personal consumption during the First Five-Year Plan, Čobeljić maintains that a certain minimum rate of growth of consumption represents the upper limit for the share of accumulation and the growth of output [20, p. 188; 43]. Similarly, Stojanović argues that reduction of consumption growth below a certain limit reduces the growth of labor productivity and that this functional relationship determines the optimum rate of investment [44]. Bajt also agrees that the optimum rate of investment is determined by the rate of consumption which maximizes labor productivity [45], but this is not necessarily the socially desirable rate of investment. The purpose of production is to increase economic welfare, and the maximization of welfare over time can be discovered only by a discounting procedure [46]. Horvat argues that pure time discounting is inconsistent because an individual will regret his present impatience at some later date, and utility discounting is impractical since it cannot be ascertained empirically. The other theoretical solution often suggested — social determination of the terminal stock of capital — is irrelevant, since no sensible planner ever insisted in carrying out a long-term plan. One constructs, say, twenty-year plans in order to take into account all relevant consequences of the decisions that are taken now; in time, with every new piece of information, the plan is revised and the planning horizon pushed forward. Since every economy has a definite and very strictly limited capacity to absorb investment (in Yugoslavia, the limit is around 35 percent GNP, SNA definition), maximum growth is achieved when marginal efficiency of investment is reduced to zero. If a lag of several months in achieving a certain level of consumption is an acceptable price to pay for maximizing consumption within one's lifetime, then the maximum rate of productive investment is identical to the optimum rate of saving. Thus maximization of the rate of growth appears to be a proper target for socialist planning. The trouble with the First Five-Year Plan was not a low level of consumption but an inappropriately high level of investment. Pushed into the region of negative marginal efficiency, investment depressed output. A large part of such a stagnating output (up to 20 percent of national income) was used for defense. On both counts, potential consumption was seriously reduced [34; 35].

Economic analysis and planning methods have become considerably more sophisticated since the telephone age described by J. Stanovnik. Yet, they are still far from impressive. Interindustry analysis has been adapted for planning purposes [36; 37]. It was used in calculating the new exchange rate and the price levels in the last reform. Simple econometric models are now regularly used in the early stages of the preparation of a plan [39; 40]. An integrated system of social accounts, specially adapted for planning needs, has been produced recently [40; 41]. For the rest, planners rely on abundant statistics, old-fashioned balancing, and hunches. A satisfactory methodology of planning is yet to be developed.

7. REGIONAL DEVELOPMENT

Institutional Development

Postwar Yugoslavia inherited an underdeveloped economy with a highly heterogeneous regional structure. The northern and northwestern parts of the country were considerably more developed

than those in the south and east. Due to varying historical conditions in the past, among which we can list the different directions
of the spread of industrialization in Europe and different socioeconomic systems of the empires ruling over the territories forming present-day Yugoslavia, and due to the strong polarization of
development between the two wars, two types of areas arose: those
that were partly industrialized and those with a traditional economic structure [53, pp. 14-16]. While the more developed areas
had the basic prerequisites for industrialization, conditions for
the development of a modern economy were sadly lacking in the
underdeveloped areas. As a result, regional development policy
was faced with a highly unfavorable dual structure of the economy,
in which there were two substantially different types of areas
whose development was to be synchronized.

The per capita national income figures given in Table 5 (column
1) also indicate the marked regional differences. In Slovenia, the
most developed region, the per capita income was three times
higher than in Kosovo, the least developed region. The differences
between Slovenia and other underdeveloped regions were also very
high. Substantial discrepancies were seen in all measurable growth
indicators [88, p. 283]. In addition, one should take into account
the considerable qualitative differences between the two types of
regions, as well as the fact that they have approximately the same
order of land area and population. Such a serious problem had to
be solved at the level of the community as a whole, despite the
fact that in many other areas the states represent independent
policymaking units.

Society's active involvement in the problems of development of
the underdeveloped regions, as seen in the policies favoring an
accelerated development of those areas, was one of the basic characteristics of economic policy throughout. In line with its basic
aim — rapid development and overcoming of economic backwardness — accelerated development of the underdeveloped regions
became an important element of development policy. As pointed
out by Bićanić [51, pp. 182-84], there were four important reasons behind this policy. To begin with, the purely humanitarian
aspects of the disparity among regions strongly militated against
impermissible differences in the living conditions of the population. Furthermore, the underdeveloped regions made a very large
contribution to the country's liberation during World War II. Later
the 1963 Constitution obliged the more developed regions to help
in their development. As Yugoslavia is a multinational community,

61

Table 5

Per Capita National Income[a]
(at 1966 prices, in thousands of new dinars)

	Per capita national income in absolute and relative terms								Index of growth of per capita national income			
	1947		1955		1964		1973		1947-55	1955-64	1964-73	1947-73
1. Yugoslavia	1682	100	2306	100	4276	100	6456	100	137	185	151	384
2. Developed regions	1874	111	2643	115	5087	119	7874	122	141	192	155	420
Slovenia	2571	153	3958	171	7575	177	12337	191	154	191	163	480
Croatia	1758	105	2776	120	5048	118	7769	120	158	182	154	442
Vojvodina	2045	122	2641	115	5189	121	7784	121	129	196	150	381
Serbia proper	1668	99	2090	91	4258	100	6525	101	125	204	153	391
3. Less developed regions	1241	74	1592	69	2704	63	3887	60	128	170	144	313
Bosnia and Herzegovina	1380	82	1770	77	2786	65	4120	64	128	157	148	299
Montenegro	1332	79	1620	71	2895	68	4383	68	122	178	151	329
Macedonia	1157	69	1598	69	3284	77	4696	73	138	206	143	406
Kosovo	839	50	936	41	1528	36	1966	31	112	163	129	234
Difference, 2-3	633		1051		2383		3987					
Ratio, 3:2	66%		60%		53%		49%					
Ratio, 3:1	74%		69%		63%		60%					

Source: SZS, Jugoslavija 1945-64, SGJ 1967, 1974, Studija br. 45.

a. In calculating per capita national income, the effect of exceptionally good or bad years in agricultural production was offset by taking the averages of the preceding and following years. The figures for 1947 had to be estimated, since data on national income at 1966 prices are available from 1952 only.

the principle of solidarity acquired an additional dimension: assistance to the nations living in the underdeveloped areas became an element of national cohesion. From a general social point of view, assistance to the underdeveloped areas served the precept of equal conditions for the development of all parts of the country. The accepted principle of transferring resources from the developed to the underdeveloped areas therefore does not run counter to the principle of remuneration according to performance, because it was designed to permit faster development of the underdeveloped areas — in other words, to equalize conditions for the development of socialism. Helping the underdeveloped areas is justified from an economic point of view because, in the long run, it has a positive effect on the growth of the more developed areas and because an economic policy is more easily carried out in a homogeneous and unified economy.

As regards the basic principles of financing the development of the underdeveloped regions, the following should be pointed out [54, p. 116].

First, the adopted policy of assisting the development of the underdeveloped areas has led to a situation in which permanent aid has become one of the basic features of this policy.

Second, a relatively large territory has been defined as underdeveloped, in which regions are represented by sociopolitical units. These units are defined on the basis of the federal structure of the country. As will be seen later, there have been many changes not only in the selection of regions but also in terminology: the officially accepted term "underdeveloped" was replaced by "insufficiently developed."

Third, industrialization was thought to be the quickest possible method for developing these areas; in accordance with this policy, direct investments and some other types of material intervention have been the main means of financing development, with the result that other sectors have been considerably neglected.

Fourth, indirect methods have also been used to reduce inequalities in the sphere of public services through interventions in the secondary distribution of national income. Budgetary and other subsidies at all levels of the sociopolitical communities were designed to raise social consumption to a level higher than the level of economic development of these regions. In view of the continuousness of these subsidies, this method of financing could also be regarded as direct [54, p. 116].

In line with the essential changes in the socioeconomic system, the developmental policies for underdeveloped regions have passed through different stages; of these, special consideration will be given to the period of centrally planned economy, the period of decentralization, and, finally, that of self-managing socialism.[4] Financing of the development of underdeveloped regions was made principally in accordance with the current system of financing social reproduction; in addition, the federal government also used some special measures to ensure that part of the accumulation flowed into underdeveloped regions [55, p. 117].

During the period of administrative control, allocations from centralized accumulation to different industries or different areas were made according to priorities defined under the First Five-Year Plan. Although the entire economy was regarded as underdeveloped, special attention was devoted to the less developed states. In accordance with this, during the period 1947-51 the underdeveloped states of Bosnia and Herzegovina, Montenegro, and Macedonia were expected to have a higher rate of investment and faster rate of development mainly in the basic industries and power generation. This was because, due to insufficient accumulation at a time when it was necessary to build up that structure of the economy which would allow for rapid development of the entire country, the underdeveloped regions could develop only insofar as they fit into the general framework of overall development.

The period of decentralization was characterized by the removal of investment from among the budget items, by the tendency of the states to rely upon their own resources in financing the underdeveloped areas, and by a more precise definition of the underdeveloped areas. As regards development policies for underdeveloped regions, the period can be divided into two subperiods.

In the subperiod 1953-56, the policy of bringing the underdeveloped regions into pace with general economic growth was similar to that in the administrative period. Since economic development was regulated by annual plans, measures providing for the development of the underdeveloped regions were not part of a comprehensive system. The system of financing retained certain characteristics of centralized decision making (credits for some precisely determined projects). As financing from investment funds was separated from budgetary investment, a distinction was introduced between credits and grants; new forms of financing included interest-free loans matching the amounts of deposited accumulation,

---

4. See section 5.

investment credits at privileged interest rates, special global subsidies to investment funds, and so on.

The system of investment was closely connected with the plans
of the Federation and the states. As pointed out by B. Srebić [54,
p. 116], federal investments were characterized as follows: (a) their
amount was not fixed; (b) territorial allocation was made administratively; and (c) distribution among different regions under-
went several changes. Besides the Federation, the states did some
financing of investment in underdeveloped areas, but it was not of
a permanent nature. The states were included in the financing of
the development of the underdeveloped regions as part of the policy
of increasing the participation of the recipients, in accordance with
the system of self-management. One way of achieving this was to
waive repayments on loans. The new system also demanded a
more accurate definition of underdeveloped regions; as a result,
priorities were granted to Bosnia and Herzegovina at the beginning, to Montenegro and Macedonia throughout the period, and occasionally to certain regions of Serbia and Croatia.

The partial approach to the problems of underdeveloped regions
as well as the differences in the treatment of individual regions
brought about marked disparities in development level. A much
more efficient way of financing development had to be found. So in
the second subperiod of the decentralization period, some important changes took place: a long-term and more stable policy of development was created, the underdeveloped regions were firmly
defined, participation of the resources of those regions was secured, and a new relationship was established between the developed and underdeveloped areas. The Second Five-Year Plan made
provision for faster development of the underdeveloped regions
and of those regions that lagged behind. It observed the following
principles: (a) in financing investment, the amount of resources
supplied by the underdeveloped regions was to be increased; (b) not
only federal but also state, district, and communal authorities were
obliged to help develop the underdeveloped regions; (c) assistance
to underdeveloped regions was not to jeopardize the development
of the already developed regions [51, p. 187]. The following regions were to be regarded as underdeveloped: Montenegro, Macedonia, Kosovo, the southern districts of Croatia, most of the districts of Bosnia and Herzegovina, and some districts of south-
eastern Serbia. As regards the definition of underdeveloped regions, there were discussions concerning the adequate determining
criteria, but these were not applied in practice. All this resulted

in the intervention of political elements in the distribution of resources for investment.

An important innovation in the financing of development was the so-called guaranteed investment. Under this program, investments in the economies of Montenegro, Macedonia, and Kosovo were considerably larger than in the previous period. In addition to guaranteed investment, some other measures were applied, such as waiving repayments on loans, waiving down payments for investment, financing overdraft, and giving priority in granting credits from the General Investment Fund provided all the criteria of profitability were met. Because of a limited capacity of absorption, however, the underdeveloped regions were not able to avail themselves of all the advantages of this system.

The system of guaranteed investment was a much more efficient method of assisting the development of underdeveloped regions, since (1) a certain volume of investment was indisputable and (2) it provided a comprehensive program of development. And although centralized decision making with a well-defined purpose, structure, and size of investment slowed to some extent the rate of realization of this program, the important investment activity secured an initial acceleration of development (the construction of facilities in power generation and basic industry, the development of communications, manufacturing industries, agriculture, and extraction of natural resources). Owing to their permanent and comprehensive character, these investments constituted a turning point in the policy of development for underdeveloped regions [55, p. 121].

With the Second Five-Year Plan having been fulfilled within less than four years, the period of self-managing socialism was entered with high hopes and ambitions. Since the capabilities of the economy were increased, the social plan for 1961-65 could foresee greater activity in accelerating the development of underdeveloped regions, whose resources were still insufficient (because of the price system, differential investment capacities of individual industries, and unfinished projects). Policies were laid down to accelerate their development in relation to the previous period as well as in relation to the developed areas. Industrialization continued to represent the main method of development; in addition, special attention was paid to the development of the economic and social infrastructure. The plan provided for the establishment of a special federal fund for the development of underdeveloped regions, which was mainly to give loans for the development of the manufacturing industry. The most important change in financing was the increased role of the states, not only in participating in the fund loans but also in directly distributing resources (the fund's resources were distributed to the states, and they were to carry out the direct allocation according to projects; the states were also responsible for the efficient utilization of resources). The following additional measures were envisaged: (1) termination of guaranteed and other current investments; (2) priority in granting resources out of the General Investment Fund. The fund's resources were distributed to the underdeveloped regions of Montenegro, Macedonia, Kosovo, and some parts of Serbia, Croatia, and Bosnia and Herzegovina. Although the plan was subsequently abandoned, these measures remained in force until 1965 [55, p. 125].

Under the new Constitution of 1963, an obligation was undertaken to assist the underdeveloped states and regions, and in this connection provision was made for the establishment of the fund for development of the underdeveloped regions in order to ensure a continuous source of finance in the form of loans. Accordingly, a law was passed in 1965 establishing the fund as an independent finance institution to engage in crediting development, give technical aid, and study the possibilities for and conditions of development in underdeveloped regions. Since loans from the fund, together with all other types of financing, were designed to ensure faster development of the underdeveloped regions, during 1966-70, as well as in the next midterm period, the financing covered only those states and regions that were not capable of independently ensuring faster development. Under a special law, Bosnia and Herzegovina, Montenegro, Macedonia, and Kosovo were defined as insufficiently developed areas (as noted earlier, this replaced the label "underdeveloped"). The underdeveloped regions elsewhere were to be aided by their respective states.

The earlier practice of establishing a fixed amount in financing development was replaced by a relative measure. The fund was supplemented by fiscal methods; the appropriate taxes were imposed on developed states. During the period 1966-70, 1.85 percent of the social product of the developed states was to be earmarked for aid to insufficiently developed regions. The main source of finance was the tax on fixed assets. In the next five-year period, 1971-75, this percentage was to be increased to 1.94, of which 0.09 percent was to be allocated to Kosovo as the least developed region. Kosovo enjoys preferential treatment with respect to the repayment of loans. While the average repayment period is fifteen years with 4 percent interest, the respective figures for Kosovo are nineteen years and 3 percent. In addition, there is a three-year grace period which, combined with the high rate of inflation in Yugoslavia, creates further benefits for the less developed regions.

On the basis of national income analysis, presented in Table 5, several conclusions could be drawn about the efficiency of regional policy in the three subperiods under consideration. First, postwar development led to an increase in the absolute difference between the developed and less developed regions. This difference in per capita national income grew from 633,000 new dinars at the beginning of the period to 3,987,000 new dinars at the end. Nor did the relative growth indicator show any narrowing of differences. If the Yugoslav development level is taken as 100, the relative index of the developed areas changed from 111 to 122, and that of the less developed ones from 74 to 60.

The above-described tendencies were not equally strong in the different subperiods. The tendency toward relative improvement of the developed areas was less evident in the period of self-managed socialism. Such changes indicate an increase in the efficiency of regional policy.

Discussion

During the administrative period, the problems of regional development failed to receive sufficient attention (partly because of theoretical inadequacies). Yet, some basic principles for subsequent elimination of regional differences were laid down. Boris Kidrič's 1946 statement on uneven development contained essential arguments against the continuation of regional differences and for the design of efforts to reduce them. "The unevenness of development is one of the difficulties of the present economic development of our country. It can be eliminated in two ways: (a) by a general leveling on the basis of the existing economic situation; or (b) through industrialization. Although aid to the underdeveloped and war-devastated states has been the duty of the economically developed and less distressed states, the principle of general leveling on the basis of existing conditions would be wrong. The proper way to do away with unevenness in the economic development of our states is to industrialize. Industrialization will secure the intermittent progress of the economically developed states and (under the plan) enable the other states to catch up, in revolutionary

jumps, and if necessary to surpass the more developed states"
[56, p. 172]. Even development, as defined above, implies balanced economic growth and social equality [57, p. 38]. Kidrič's
statement was to become the official policy on development and
was quoted in various resolutions by Party congresses, in constitutions, and in Program documents.

Although the practical aspects of regional planning received only
partial and inadequate treatment, several papers and monographs
elaborating regional problems appeared during the period of decentralization. One of the essential practical questions — the definition of underdevelopment — was studied in 1954 by B. Kubović
[58]. After analyzing the underdeveloped districts of Croatia, he
ranked regions according to their level of development, using per
capita national income and some other criteria. In another paper,
the same author pleaded in favor of correcting the per capita national income; he proposed both a narrow and a broad list of indexes for correction [59]. In 1956, at a meeting at the Federal
Planning Office, it was agreed that national income would be the
basic criterion, while some other indexes were listed as subsidi-
ary criteria. That was the first time use was to be made of the
I-distance method based on discrimination analysis, designed by
B. Ivanović [60]. Districts were listed on the basis of seven indexes. In considering the approach to a long-run development
plan, R. Lang and D. Gorupić stressed the need to analyze the degree of development and the possibilities of area development.
After pointing out the inadequacy of national income as the exclusive criterion, they considered a number of indexes and attempted
to make a selection and categorization of areas [61].

Another problem that attracted the attention of economists was
the selection of suitable locations for industries when funds were
insufficient. I. Krešić analyzed the importance of transport costs
[62]. Gorupić pointed out the necessity of considering not only
individual but also social effects in selecting a suitable location
[63]. In his analysis of the role of individual factors in the location of industries, B. Srebrić called for finding optimal locations
from the standpoint of the national economy [64].

As decentralization and development of self-management entered
all fields of social life, the significance of the development of backward areas was considerably enhanced. In 1962 the scientific section of the Association of Economists of Yugoslavia organized a
conference on the problems of regional economic development. On
this occasion, K. Mihailović stated that regional development

received its full scope in a socialist society, but that it must not be given a one-sided treatment that deals only with the problem of backwardness [65]. He also stressed the need for faster development of the backward areas, as did R. Stojanović, who stated that, in the long run, there could never be economic aid because "aid implies something that is a loss for the one who offers it in favor of someone else" [66, p. 62]. Pointing out that the regional aspects of development must not be limited to the development of the underdeveloped areas, Kubović analyzed the relationship between regional development and self-management and proposed a method for guiding regional development [67]. Considering the industrialization of backward areas, B. Čolanović expressed the belief that without a comprehensive, long-term policy it would be impossible to eliminate regional differences, and in this context stressed the role of the formation of areas for development, the role of gravitational centers, and the role of methods for development financing [68]. N. Mladenović defended the idea of creating long-term programs of development and the need for defining economic regions on the basis of natural, economic, geographic, and historical factors [69]. The assessments of national wealth by states made by I. Vinski revealed vast differences between the developed and the underdeveloped regions, notable in particular in some of the indexes of wealth [70]. By using a simplified inter-regional input-output analysis, Horvat concluded that increased final consumption in an underdeveloped area results in bigger production increases in the developed than in the underdeveloped area [71].

At this conference a general consensus already appeared to have been achieved on the need for a faster development of underdeveloped regions in order to reduce regional disparities. Much stress was placed on the economic justification for accelerated development of the underdeveloped regions. In this connection, the following arguments were advanced: reduction of general social costs, better utilization of natural resources and other available factors of production, creation of increased demand for products from developed regions, transition from a nonmonetary to a market economy, greater indirect effects of investment in underdeveloped regions, contribution toward the creation of a uniform national economy, more efficient implementation of economic and political measures, and so on [65; 66; 67; 72; 73]. Yet, as pointed out by Horvat, the thesis that the backward areas should be developed more rapidly for economic reasons has never been rigorously proved [74].

Although general agreement was achieved on the need for faster development of backward regions, parity as a policy principle has not been sufficiently elaborated from a theoretical standpoint, and that created problems in application, allowing even development to be treated arbitrarily. Furthermore, such a policy takes no account of the stages of development and the general level of development, has no respect for the individual possibilities of the regions, and essentially constitutes a static approach because it ignores the significance of migratory movements, polarization, and a selective regional policy [72, pp. 69-71]. As regards the time range in which an equalization or reduction of regional differences could be achieved, Mihailović believes that, at Yugoslavia's present level of development, the time is ripe for this process to begin. The Federal Bureau of Statistics has devised a method, based on the criterion of per capita national income, for gauging the number of years necessary for backward regions to reach the national average or the level of the developed regions. This method has relatively little practical value, however, because it is based on per capita national income only.

In connection with regional differences and regional levels of development, mention should be made of the works that accentuate the theoretical and practical significance of the problems of measurement. An analysis of the levels of development of the states, provinces, and districts has been made at the Institute of Economic Sciences [75]. To classify the states and provinces for 1952, 1957, and 1964, the method of I-distance was used. Measurements based on per capita national income and ten other indexes grouped under four headings have shown that the differences were significant during all the periods. An analysis for districts was made for 1964. Another of the Institute projects makes measurements for 1966 through I-distance, using eleven indexes [76]. On the basis of per capita national income analysis, it was shown that the gap between the developed and underdeveloped areas had widened between 1952 and 1966.

In addition to the analysis based on administrative-territorial units, efforts have been made to examine economic development at the level of economic regions. Thus Kubović accentuated the need for defining the region before attempting to make measurements. According to his conception, the principles of homogeneity and gravitation cannot be used as criteria for forming economic regions under Yugoslav conditions, because a region should constitute an entity from the standpoint of economic development.

With this aim in mind, he defined four categories of common perspectives of territorial development, through which ninety-two districts in the country were classified into twenty-five regions. By combining two criteria — the corrected values of production funds per active inhabitant and the share of the collective sector of the economy in the total corrected value of production fixed funds — a combined index of development was obtained which was used for classification. The analyses made for 1957 and 1965 have shown that, notwithstanding considerable progress, the differences in the levels of development are still considerable and are greater in the sphere of the means of production than in other fields. An important conclusion to be drawn from this is that no state as a whole constitutes an underdeveloped area, because the regions at the bottom of the list have made notable progress [77].

Results achieved in regional development have also been analyzed. In one of his papers, Srebrić concludes that, whereas the rates of growth of national income are fairly even, the movement of per capita national income indicates an increase in both relative and absolute differences among states in the period between 1947 and 1966 [54]. On the other hand, some positive changes have been registered in the structure of underdeveloped economies with regard to decreased participation of agriculture and increased shares of other sectors. According to Mihailović, though all the regions have recorded important progress, differences have not been reduced; the underdeveloped areas have lagged less with regard to increase in fixed assets than to increase in income, and have fallen behind most in increase in employment. Accordingly, the influence of an increase in income and employment is less in underdeveloped areas than in developed ones [53, p. 97]. Analyzing regional differences within states and provinces, P. Sicherl [76] concludes that, of eleven indexes under consideration, the largest differences are seen in per capita national income, and that this criterion overestimates the development of the developed regions and underestimates the level of development of the backward regions. Consequently, social intervention has helped achieve greater results than has been indicated by income analyses. Since differences in availability of fixed assets are smaller, differences in incomes can be explained by some other factors. Of these, Mihailović [71] points out the inadequacy of the investment structure in the backward regions. Despite major investments in underdeveloped regions, there was unequal treatment among these as well as among developed areas. Montenegro and Macedonia had much larger per capita investment, whereas Bosnia and Herzegovina, and Kosovo in particular, lagged behind. Although much was invested, because investments were made mainly in raw materials production, the underdeveloped areas did not achieve substantial development (terms of trade were unfavorable). Furthermore, the processing industry in these regions has a traditional character [53, p. 48]. Consequently, lower effectiveness of investment in the underdeveloped regions is explained largely by their unfavorable structure, as well as by the lack of adequate infrastructure, production tradition, terms of trade, and so on.

Because of the transition to market production and the existence of price disparities, the correction of unfavorable terms of trade, that is, compensation to underdeveloped areas for unfavorable market conditions — has become a question to which considerable thought has been given. The subject was discussed in the Resolution of the Ninth Congress of the Yugoslav League of Communists: "The nations and the working people in the socialist republics must be entitled to control the results of their labor. Within a unified Yugoslav market, all the instruments of the economic system should be so elaborated as to ensure the realization of this principle. Should measures of economic policy infringe upon this principle, a system of compensation has to be provided to palliate the negative consequences of the effects of the unified instruments and measures of economic policy passed by the Federation." Compensation has become a topical question of the economic system and economic policy. Provision has been made for the fund for development of underdeveloped regions to use part of its resources to correct the unfavorable terms of trade.

As Mihailović and Berković [53, p. 131] pointed out, however, because of the vagueness of the concept and the scope of compensation, different regions have been giving it different interpretations to suit their own interests. There are different opinions on this subject [81]. At a discussion [82], N. Uzunov pointed out that compensation should be made according to the principle of industries. H. Hadžiomerović wanted it to become a permanent institution, whereas Mihailović considered it an instrument of a provisional nature because the remedy was elimination of the causes of inequitable trade. Since compensation has appeared as a new instrument in the sphere of interventions in underdeveloped areas, there have been frequent disputes as to whether the underdeveloped areas have been gaining because of additional financing or losing because of worsened terms of trade. Attempts were made to examine different measures of economic policy from the viewpoint of their influence on regional differences [83]. In this connection, D. Bjelogrlić [82] stated that, although it was impossible to make an accurate calculation of transfer of resources, the present contributions by the developed areas have not been so great as to threaten their own development.

As we have already pointed out, the different economic structures of the states have been inherited from both the recent and the not so recent past. As decentralization proceeded, the influence of the states and provinces in interregional relations became stronger [57, p. 153]. Ideas on separate state economies and on the existence of separate regional interests appeared. These were frequently in contradiction, particularly with regard to the allocation of investments, and in discussions on the adoption of institutional solutions. At a conference on the integration of the Yugoslav economy held in 1969, Hadžiomerović [84] noted that, owing to differences in the levels and structures of the economies of the states, their interests and possibilities were different. V. Rakić [85] also differentiated the national economy and the economy of the states because the latter are not indifferent to their development possibilities within the framework of the Yugoslav community. In this sense, the separate nature of national economic interests is a fact. Despite all this, on the basis of an analysis of regional cycles, Horvat [86] concluded that the Yugoslav economy was unified but that the economies of the underdeveloped areas were less stable.

In practice, there has been an increased tendency to achieve a comprehensive economic structure within the states. It was felt not only in the underdeveloped states that wanted to extend their economic structures, but also in the developed regions that wished to retain and complement theirs [82]. Consequently, these tendencies cannot be termed simply autarkic. There were actually two versions of national economies: a positive one in the sense of increased diversification of development, and an autarkic one, which prefers integration within the states to the integration of industries. The intensive assertion of regional interests in practice has resulted in a reorganization that, while strengthening the status of the states, calls for an interregional coordination of sectors at the level of the entire economy through regional agreements [57].

Finally, a few words should be said about the assessment of the economic policy by economists [53; 54; 55; 72; 78; 79; 82].

(a) Great efforts have been made to reduce regional disparities.
(b) Investment activity was important, so that throughout the period the share of investment in the national income was greater in underdeveloped areas. For example, Montenegro had a share of nearly 100 percent, and sometimes even higher [54, p. 125]; in Kosovo and in Macedonia, the share frequently exceeded 50 percent, while Bosnia and Herzegovina had a favorable situation in this regard only in the early postwar years. (c) Investments had started the process of economic development, but the lower growth of per capita investments and their unfavorable structure contributed to still greater regional disparities. (d) An inadequate treatment of the problem of investments and lack of funds did not permit the creation of the necessary conditions for achieving all the positive effects. (e) Hence, investments were less effective and were also influenced by an unfavorable economic structure, lack of tradition, and inadequate organization of the economy.
(f) The institutional setup has favored more the growth of the developed regions, primarily because of the price disparities that were protecting manufacturing industries and because of the system of import restrictions. (g) Lack of long-term territorial division of labor and reduction of the policy of regional development to simply development of underdeveloped regions have also impeded the development of the underdeveloped regions and consequently of the economy as a whole.

III

8. AGRICULTURAL POPULATION, LANDOWNERSHIP PATTERNS, AND PRODUCTION

Agricultural Population

Over the course of economic development, the share of agriculture both in the labor force and in total output is reduced. At first, the agricultural population increases absolutely, but falls relatively. After a certain stage of development, absolute decline begins and relative decline accelerates. The share of agriculture in total national product declines still faster. Rudolf Bićanić studied this phenomenon, finding that the absolute turning point in the agricultural population occurred in Great Britain as early as 1820, in Sweden in 1880, in France in 1900, in the United States in 1910, in Italy in 1920, in Germany and Denmark in 1925, in Finland in 1930, and in the Soviet Union in 1956. Individual countries reached this turning point at different levels of per capita national income and when the proportion of agricultural population was between 31 and 60 percent [9, p. 740]. In Yugoslavia, the turning point occurred immediately after the Liberation when the proportion of agricultural population was 75 percent. This is a unique record and indicates the development potential created by the Revolution. The data in Table 6 show the development over the last eighty years.

Prewar Yugoslavia was a peasant country like the present-day less developed nations of Asia and Africa. After the Revolution, an explosive development took place that was three to five times faster than in other countries. Using Kuznets's data, Stipetić notes that Sweden needed sixty years to reduce the share of agricultural population from 71 to 50 percent (from 1840 to 1900); the United States also required sixty years (72 percent in 1820, 50 percent in

Table 6

Agricultural Population and Income, 1890-1971

	Million persons	Agricultural population as % of total	Agricultural income as % of total
1890	8.9	83.8	—
1910	10.5	81.0	—
1921	9.9	78.8	43.2[a]
1931	11.1	76.6	46.9[b]
1939	12.1	75.1	47.3[c]
1945	11.3	75.0	—
1948	10.6	67.2	35.9[d]
1953	10.3	60.9	30.3
1961	9.2	50.5	25.4
1971	7.4	36.4	23.7[e]

Sources: S. Livada, "Osnovne strukture i pokretljivost seoskog i poljoprivrednog stanovništva u Jugoslaviji," Sociologija sela, 29-30, 1970, p. 83; V. Stipetić, "Ekonomika poljoprivrede i ribarstva," in J. Sirotković and V. Stipetić, Ekonomika Jugoslavije (Zagreb: Informator, 1971), p. 10; V. Stipetić, Stočarstvo (Belgrade: Jugoslavija, 1969), p. 3; SZS, Statistički bilten 700, Jugoslavija 1945-1964; SGJ-1971.

a. 1926-29.
b. 1930-35.
c. 1936-39.
d. 1947-52.
e. 1969.

1880); to reduce the agricultural population by the same percent took France eighty years (43 percent in 1866, 21 percent in 1946); Japan needed forty-three years (78 percent in 1887, 52 percent in 1930) [2, p. 11].

During the postwar period as a whole, 3 percent of the population left agriculture annually. This indicates the large hidden unemployment in agriculture and the huge pressure on employment in other sectors. During the etatist period, the transfer from agriculture was absorbed through excessive employment in nonagricultural activities. After 1952, this transfer was taken up by the exceptionally high rate of economic growth. In the 1960s, when economic expansion slowed, unemployment appeared, and soon after mass emigration of the labor force occurred. The indicator cited also shows the falsity of the notion that the peasant holds firmly onto his land, that he has an ownership mentality, that he is conservative and unenterprising. When the opportunity is offered him, the peasant either improves his farm or accepts a more rewarding occupation. In Yugoslavia, as elsewhere, two modes of leaving agriculture were established: (a) definitive abandonment of the farm and agriculture; and (b) steady employment off the farm in the collective economy and public services while remaining on the farm [10]. The latter creates the special problem of the worker-peasant; there have been polemics about just how desirable it is to have such a group [2, p. 98; 24; 25; 26].

The accelerated abandonment of agriculture while agricultural output nevertheless continues to rise indicates the existence of great agrarian overpopulation. This problem was already being discussed before the war, and the concern continued in the postwar years. The definition of the phenomenon itself [30] and the methodology of measuring it were discussed, and various measures were made. Bićanić [29], Čobeljić and Mihailović [33], and Tomašević [17, p. 26] take agrarian density (the number of peasants per 100 hectares) as the criterion for measuring overpopulation. Since there is no standard for density, this is a rather arbitrary criterion, and estimates differ greatly. V. Figenwald [34] calculated the surplus labor force by contrasting the necessary labor for given production with the available labor; he established that in 22 percent of Croatian communes there are surpluses of over 25 percent, but that in 20 percent of communes deficits are found. Z. Ružić used the same method, but arrived at a substantially higher percentage of surpluses in 1960: 34-40 percent, on the average, for Croatian agriculture as against 12 percent according to Figenwald [32]. In a study by the Community of Research Institutes for Agricultural Economics, it is asserted that in 1960 the amount of potential work time in agriculture that was actually used ranged from a low of 48 percent in Kosovo to a high of 80 percent in Slovenia [37]. J. Klauzer criticized this estimate, holding that an adequate definition of the labor force was not used [31]. According to his calculation, the excess labor force varies from 19 percent in Slovenia to 44 percent in Kosovo and for Yugoslavia on the average amounts to 30 percent.

Abandonment of agriculture will continue very rapidly in the future. Practically the entire younger generation in rural areas wishes to leave agriculture. This extreme attitude is obviously in large part the result of sociopolitical neglect and discrimination against the peasant after the Revolution. S. Šuvar analyzed a survey conducted among pupils in the final grades of 128 village primary schools in 1963-64; data from the study indicated that, in all, 0.8 percent of youth want to remain on their family's land, and another 0.5 percent want to be employed on collective farms [11, p. 835].

Šuvar considers present-day village youth in Yugoslavia to be largely unadjusted to their current social position and striving to change it. As causes of youth's attitude, Šuvar cites: (1) the low level of living (housing comfort, health protection, etc.) of those who live on peasant farms; (2) the economic and social dependence of youth in peasant families; (3) the unavailability or lesser availability of cultural and social goods and means of entertainment in the village environment; (4) the low social prestige of agricultural occupations; (5) the lack of leisure; (6) the lack of some social benefits; (7) the lack of prospects for the peasant agricultural holding; and (8) the lack of mobility (professional, social, and geographical) in the village environment [11, pp. 846-47].

The rapid exodus from the village seriously disturbs the social equilibrium in rural (as well as in urban) surroundings. "The craftsmen and other social segments have left the village, and youth are leaving; there is a reduction of economic functions as well as of social life, for which both a range of age groups and other variety are the basic precondition. Once the young created the social climate in the village, the adults carried economic life and production, and the oldest transmitted the cultural heritage. Now the young are leaving, economic life is being transferred outside the village, and the cultural heritage is not respected. The fulcrums of the social system are destroyed. Because of the penetration of industry and tertiary activities, in the more developed villages differentiation occurs as the economic functions of the impoverished social structure of the village population are reduced. Worker-peasants, pensioners, and new craftsmen are social groups that are offshoots of overall structures representing the village's links with the total society; on the other hand, however, they weaken the internal mechanism of the village system, its completeness. The village disintegrates and is included in general social currents, but still has not found a new social and economic equilibrium" [35, p. 24].

Agrarian Reform and the Landowning Structure

The gradual abolition of feudal relations in the South Slav lands in the course of almost a century — from 1833 in Serbia to 1928 in Bosnia and Herzegovina — is described in the monumental work of Jozo Tomašević on the Yugoslav peasants [17]. Feudalism was in fact definitively abolished only by the agrarian reform after the country's unification. This reform, gradually watered down and subject to various forms of corruption, was drawn out until 1931, and its liquidation extended over the entire prewar period. According to the preliminary regulations for the preparation of the agrarian reform in 1919, holdings larger than 57 to 288 hectares of arable land, depending on local conditions, were sequestered and the land rented out to the peasants. The law on the liquidation of the agrarian reform in 1931 increased the agrarian maximum to 100 to 500 hectares. In addition, a supermaximum of 1500 acres was allowed for so-called model agricultural holdings. The agrarian reform affected 369 large landowners, of whom 310 were foreigners. On the average they were left about 1300 acres, and about 42 percent of their former land was taken away [40, pp. 177-78]. About 700,000 peasants received ownership of 3 hectares of land each [23, p. 78]. However, these measures could not prevent a new polarization in the village. In 1931, 2098 large landowners (holdings of over 100 hectares) possessed more land than 710,473 small peasants (with less than 2 hectares) [22, p. 22].

A new and radical agrarian reform was begun immediately after the Liberation in August 1945. It was largely completed by the fall of 1946 and entirely accomplished by 1948. The law proclaimed the principle: The land belongs to those that cultivate it. In accordance with this principle, the arable land held by peasants was limited to 25 to 35 hectares. The reform was accelerated and eased by the fact that almost half of the stock of land represented confiscated — and often abandoned — holdings of enemies and collaborationists. The stock of land included 1.2 million hectares, or 8.5 percent, of the arable land. A total of 745,000 hectares were given to 330,000 families. About 67,000 families were resettled from the mountainous to the plains areas. State agricultural estates [poljoprivredna dobra] obtained 304,000 hectares and peasant work cooperatives 47,000 hectares [19, pp. 441, 451]. Two years later the leading agrarian economist, Mijo Mirković, concluded: "Land is ceasing to be the source and cause of social differences, and land ownership is taking on its true meaning of a collective productive function. In the division of the fruits of agricultural production, land fertility and human labor, inherited ownership, and force no longer will be decisive, but rather the socialist principle. This is the realization of that social justice for which the peasants of all countries and all times have struggled. ... The agrarian reform of 1945 expelled from the land the foreign and domestic usurpers of land ownership, broke the private and church land monopoly ... eliminated the capitalist relations that arose from land ownership and the use of others' labor in the cultivation of land, and also reduced large peasant holdings to the limit, where they could be cultivated by the labor of the members of the peasant families alone without using hired labor. These were the first and direct results of the agrarian reform, from which it went immediately on to the construction of a cooperative system of agricultural production" [20, p. 48].

The reform helped to reduce differences in the village. Other measures — prohibition of sale and mortgaging of land and buildings, and compulsory sale of agricultural produce at fixed prices [21] — aimed at preserving this situation or inducing peasants to form cooperatives. After the collectivization campaign was halted and a reorganization of the cooperatives carried out in 1953, a second agrarian reform was introduced. Some 276,000 hectares of arable land representing the excess above 10 hectares per holding were purchased from 66,000 peasants and distributed to agricultural estates and work and farming cooperatives [zemljoradničke za- druge]. Ten hectares of arable land was considered the upper limit of the holding that the average family could cultivate without hired labor [22, p. 90]. After the agrarian maximum was reduced, the ban on sale of land was eliminated as no longer necessary.

The agrarian reforms changed the landowning structure, as shown in Table 7. Around 1960, Yugoslavia had the most egalitarian distribution of land in the world, as has already been noted.

A polarization of holdings is seen before the war, and averaging — that is, an increase in holdings of 2 to 8 hectares at the expense of those in the extreme categories — is observed in the postwar period. The average size of all farms declined before the war and stagnated afterward, as follows [2, p. 41]:

1900	8.0 hectares	1949	4.7 hectares
1931	5.8 hectares	1955	4.8 hectares
1941	4.6 hectares	1969	4.6 hectares

The number of individual landholdings increased slightly in the country as a whole; in the more developed areas and Montenegro, the number fell, but this reduction was more than compensated for by increases in the underdeveloped regions.

The ownership structure is corrected by renting. In this, the trends are precisely the opposite of those before the war, and small owners rent out land to larger owners. The reason is that peasants with small farms find employment outside agriculture, but retain their property [22, pp. 30-31]. In that way, the economic

Table 7

Ownership Structure of Individual Farms, 1931-69 (in percent)

Size of farms	1931		1941	1949		1955		1969	
	Number	Area	Number	Number	Area	Number	Area	Number	Area
Up to 2 hectares	34.3	6.5	47	37.2	10.4	35.3	9.6	39.0	9.7
2-5 hectares	33.6	21.5	24	34.7	26.2	36.9	29.8	35.6	30.8
5-10 hectares	20.4	26.6	20	14.8[a]	21.0[a]	15.3[a]	22.5[a]	19.8/14.8[a]	35.8/24.2[a]
Over 10 hectares	11.7	45.4	9	13.3[b]	42.5[b]	12.5[b]	38.1[b]	5.6/10.6[b]	23.7/35.3[b]
Total	100.0	100.0	100	100.0	100.0	100.0	100.0	100.0	100.0

Sources: P. Marković, Strukturne promene na selu kao rezultat ekonomskog razvitka (Belgrade: Zadružna knjiga, 1963), pp. 22, 26, 27; SGJ-1970, p. 147.

a. 5-8 hectares.
b. Over 8 hectares.

position of the peasants is further equalized: small farms have less income from agriculture but larger income from nonfarm work [22, p. 58]. In large part, land of relatives and aged households is rented, and by this means holdings of arable land are sometimes increased above 20 hectares [104, p. 29]. It is of interest to note another observation of Marković [22, p. 88]: household members from families with larger landholdings more often leave the farm, while those from families with small holdings more often are employed off the farm (while continuing to live there). Small farms are mixed, and from these, above all, the worker-peasants are recruited.

The increase in the number of worker-peasants is a phenomenon accompanying industrialization. The percentage of farm households with members employed outside of agriculture is constantly increasing [2, p. 98]:

1931	9%	1955	32%
1949	19%	1969	43%

Today, almost half of agricultural households, which hold over 30 percent of the arable land, include members employed outside of agriculture. These worker-peasants earn more than pure workers and pure peasants, and the farm solves their housing problem, supplements income, and serves as insurance until a definitive break with agriculture is made. In 1960, 44 percent of all employees in the collective sector of the economy were from individual farms [24, p. 99].

As noted earlier, discussion developed about the role and place of worker-peasants. S. Krašovec maintained that in other countries mixed households comprise one-fifth to one-half of all farms and have similar characteristics as in Yugoslavia [25]. S. Livada argues with conceptions of the worker-peasants as less productive workers who bring a peasant mentality into industry, are often absent from work, and cultivate their land primitively [26, pp. 39-40]. Levstik also maintains that the productivity and work discipline of worker-peasants and workers are the same on the whole. He emphasizes that the urban consumer spends half of his income on food, while the worker-peasant produces the larger part of food for his own needs, and therefore spends a larger part of income on industrial products [100]. Puljiz and Stipetić [2, p. 98] consider that mixed households lag in agricultural production, but lead in their standard of living [2, p. 98; 24, p. 102]. In addition, it is emphasized that worker-peasants are the pioneers of progress in the village and provide the basis for changing traditional and backward forms of peasant production and life [26, p. 41].

In his sociological monograph, C. Kostić traces the appearance of the worker-peasants from the very beginning of the country's industrialization in the last century until the middle of the 1950s [38].

Finally, two more characteristics of the current transformation processes should be observed. Because of the departure of men, there is a feminization of the work force on the mixed farms; and because of the departure of young people, the average age of the work force in agriculture as a whole is rising. The proportion of active men over 50 years old increased from 23 percent in 1948 to 34 percent in 1961. This causes the phenomenon of so-called aged households; before the war, there were 30,000 to 40,000 such households and in 1970 there were estimated to be over 600,000, or more than a fourth of all farms [16, p. 87]. Livada states that in the majority of industrially developed zones the senilization of the agricultural labor force has affected almost every village. According to some estimates, in a third of villages persons older than 50 have become the basic or sole agricultural labor force [27, p. 5]. Magdalenić studied the behavior of aged farm households and found that they achieve lower yields, do not carry out net investment, hire labor, rent out their land, and recently have begun to sell their land [28]. Leaving the land is made easier by arrangements with the local authorities by which, in exchange for their land, aged peasants receive pensions.

In connection with the ownership structure, we shall also consider the question of the categorization of the peasants into small, middle, and large, which is very important from the standpoint of formulating Marxist economic policy. The following categorization is most frequent in Yugoslavia: "The small peasant is one who has enough land for subsistence, or less; the middle peasant is one who does not have more land than can be cultivated without hired labor; the large peasant has so much land that he is forced to make use of hired labor ..." [51, p. 5].

In the first decade after Liberation, these categories were defined as peasants with holdings up to 5 hectares, from 5 to 10 hectares, and over 10 hectares. In practice, there were attempts to lower the limits — up to 2 hectares for the small peasant and below 8 hectares for the medium peasant — in order to fabricate as many "kulaks" and "capitalistic elements" as possible. M. Bogdanović follows N. Rapajić in determining the limits at 3 and 8 hectares;

small farms (up to 3 hectares) earn most of their income by work
off the farm; medium farms (3 to 8 hectares) earn 35 percent by
work off the farm; and large farms (over 8 hectares) earn 20 percent total income by work off the farm [23, p. 95]. Engels set the
limits higher: "By small peasant we understand here the owner . . .
of a piece of land no larger than that which he can as a rule cultivate along with the help of his own family and not less than that
which will feed his family" [53, p. 403]. Middle and large peasants
use hired labor — the former sometimes and the latter constantly
— and both represent capitalists in the village. Lenin's classification is similar, with the difference that he also emphasizes two
groups below the small peasant: the agricultural proletariat and
semiproletariat peasants [54, pp. 626-31]. However, Lenin later
changed his definition of the middle peasant, whom he freed of
using hired labor [50, p. 51]. This categorization later served
Stalin's well-known policy of alliance with the village poor, neu-
tralization of the middle, and liquidation of the kulak, which also
was repeated sporadically in Yugoslavia. Stojanović discussed
these categorizations, drawing a pessimistic conclusion with respect to their usefulness [50, p. 54].

Under contemporary Yugoslav conditions, such classifications
are truly rather dubious, for besides land several other factors
substantially determine the economic position of the peasant. From
Table 8 it can be seen that "large farms" achieve more than three
times greater agricultural income than the small. However, since
agricultural income represents only the lesser part of the total income of small owners, when total income is considered the differences are halved. Furthermore, both the number of active workers
and the number of household members increase with the size of
the holding. Hence, when calculated per household member, the
income span is further drastically reduced. Finally, investments
in farming and tax contributions increase with the size of the holding. As a result, personal consumption per household member is
almost ideally equalized. The size of holding — and, accordingly,
land ownership as well — no longer play any role in economic differentiation in the village. Differentiation, insofar as it exists,
must be traced to other causes. A certain difference does exist
between purely agricultural and mixed farms, and these differences
seem to be increasing.

If we take average income per household member in 1967 as 100,
then on agricultural farms income per household member amounts
to 91, and on mixed farms, 111 [102, p. 331]. The basic reason for

Table 8

Income on Peasant Farms in 1967

Category of farm	Agricultural income			Total income					Personal consumption per member		
	Dinars	Index	% of total income	Per household		No. of household members	Per member		As % of income	Dinars	Index
				Dinars	Index		Dinars	Index			
Up to 2 hectares	3,876	100	37	10,046	100	4.2	2,392	100	70.6	1,690	100
2–3 hectares	6,103	158	57	10,674	106	4.4	2,426	101	68.4	1,690	100
3–5 hectares	7,497	194	63	11,894	118	4.8	2,479	104	64.1	1,590	94
5–8 hectares	9,837	254	75	13,160	131	5.1	2,580	108	63.6	1,640	97
Over 8 hectares	12,232	318	74	16,454	164	5.8	2,837	119	57.8	1,690	100
Average	6,879	178	59	11,731	117	4.7	2,496	104	65.8	1,640	97

Sources: J. Simić, "Vidovi i faktori promena u strukturi dohotka domaćinstava na individualnim poljoprivrednim gazdinstvima," Ekonomika poljoprivrede, 5, 1970, pp. 328–29; M. Petrović, "Raspodela dohotka seoskih domaćinstava Jugoslavije," Ekonomika poljoprivrede, 7–8, 1970, p. 554.

this difference is the greater income outside of agriculture. However, even this difference is insignificant compared with the differences that exist in nonagricultural activities.

Agricultural Production

For the sake of a full understanding of the discussion on agricultural problems as well as easier judgments of the effects of individual turning points in agrarian policy, it would be useful to cite basic statistical data and to establish periods of agricultural development or policy.

The overall results of the development of agriculture can be judged on the basis of comparison with the results of other countries or with prewar development. As can be seen from Table 9, in the period 1948-1963, Yugoslavia was sixth in the world in the rate of expansion of crop production, while it held the record in the percent contribution of increased yields to increasing output.

Table 9

Countries with Fastest Growth of Crop Output, 1948-63

	Period	Annual rate of growth	Contribution of increased yields to growth, in %
Israel	1948-63	9.7	76.8
Sudan	1948-62	8.0	47.0
Mexico	1948-60	6.3	46.7
Philippines	1948-62	5.2	18.6
Tanganyika (Tanzania)	1948-63	5.2	26.6
Yugoslavia	1948-63	5.1	79.2

Source: V. Stipetić, Poljoprivreda i privredni razvoj (Zagreb: Informator, 1969), p. 301.

In relation to the prewar period, the tempo of agricultural development increased by over 50 percent, and on a per capita basis grew by two and a half times.

The picture is filled out by data on yields, which stagnated before the war and doubled in the postwar period (see Table 11).

Production and yields did not increase evenly in the postwar period. Three very different periods are observed, which we shall call the periods of collectivization, cooperation, and search for a new way.

Table 10

Rate of Growth of Yugoslav Agriculture, 1920-70

	1920-40	1946-70
Farming	2.7	3.4
Livestock raising	3.0	3.8
Total agriculture	2.3	3.6
Population increase	1.4	1.2
Per capita increase in production	0.9	2.4

Source: J. Sirotković and V. Stipetić, Ekonomika Jugoslavije (Zagreb: Informator, 1971), p. 56.

Table 11

Average Yields of Wheat, Corn, and Sugar Beets, 1909-69
(in 100 kilograms per hectare)

	1909-13	1926-30	1936-40	1947-51	1967-69
Wheat	10.4	11.4	11.9	12.0	23.7
Corn	14.8	13.6	17.5	16.2	29.7
Sugar beets	223	160	199	150	370

Source: Same as for Table 10.

9. THREE STAGES IN AGRARIAN POLICY

Etatist Collectivization (1945-53)

In the first postwar period, agriculture was treated as a source of capital accumulation and the peasants as a social group of small property and (potentially) capitalist elements that should be re-educated by administrative measures and included in the socialized, that is, state, sector of the economy. As a result of revolutionary élan, prewar production was matched again in 1948, after only three years (see Table 12), while after World War I the recovery of production took twice as long, until 1924 [2, p. 60]. But then etatist pressure led to stagnation, and even to a fall in production. Unsuitable programs of production were often imposed by compulsory deliveries, and all surpluses were absorbed by fixed low prices of agricultural products and high prices of industrial products. The tax on individual production was sharply progressive and apportioned very subjectively with the aim of "curbing capitalist elements."

Table 12

Agricultural Production, Number of Tractors,
and Use of Artificial Fertilizer

		Agricultural production		Share of agriculture in total investment (%)	Number of tractors	Use of artificial fertilizers (thousand tons)	Standard head of livestock (millions)
		Index	Rate of growth				
Prewar 1930-39		100	—	—	2,500[a]	31[a]	—
Collectivization	1948	103	0.6	11.7	—	74	4.2[c]
	1953	106		5.0	6,266[b]	75	4.2
Cooperation 1964		170	4.5	9.1	43,264	1,904	5.5
Search for a			1.9				
new way 1971		194		6.5	66,861	1,679[d]	5.2[d]

Sources: SGJ-1971; SZS, Jugoslavija 1945-1964; Vasić [36, p. 42].
a. 1939.
b. 1951.
c. 1949.
d. 1970.

In his report at the Fifth Congress of the Communist Party of Yugoslavia, held in the middle of 1948, Edvard Kardelj presented the generally accepted thesis that the basic form of organization of the peasantry on the road to socialist transformation of agriculture is the farming cooperative and cited three reasons: (1) the cooperative is an organization familiar to the peasant; (2) it is a flexible form of organization that can comprise all activities in the sphere of agriculture; and (3) it is built on the principles of internal democracy and hence represents for the peasant a guarantee that the progress of agriculture will not proceed in ways that are unacceptable to him. Kardelj stated that the work cooperatives, "which by their form and content approach the type of the Soviet kolkhozes," already were playing an important role. But, because of the backwardness of the village, they could not represent a general movement of the peasants. Consequently, concluded Kardelj, citing Lenin and Stalin, the lower forms of the farming cooperative remained the principal ones [14, p. 385].

Under the pressure of the Cominform criticisms, half a year later the conceptions were changed. At the January plenum of the Central Committee in 1949, forced collectivization according to the Soviet model was initiated. In the Resolution of the plenum,

the socialist sector is defined as state and cooperative [13].
Faster development of the state sector and devotion of greater attention to agricultural machine stations were sought. In Kardelj's
report, which served as the explanation of the Resolution, it is
stated: "While in 1947 almost all the peasant work cooperatives
had yields below those of individual peasants, in 1948 the overwhelming majority of peasant work cooperatives exceeded the
yields of individuals" [14, p. 62]; nevertheless, the Resolution
categorically concludes: "Peasant work cooperatives have shown
themselves to be the most successful means for the socialist transformation of the village and the progress of agriculture" [p. 5].
As a political principle, it is emphasized that "the creation of
peasant work cooperatives must continue to be carried out exclusively on the basis of the free will and conscious decision of
the working peasantry itself..." [p. 5]. In practice, however,
rather severe administrative and political pressures were applied
which were interpreted as limiting and repressing capitalist elements, as embodying a struggle for limiting the monopoly of individual farming, and as linking the peasant with the socialist sector [14, pp. 45-46]. In spite of this, there were objections that
the rich peasant got along best and that he was not sufficiently
constrained [14, pp. 46-47]. In the next two years, the number
of peasant work cooperatives and their landholdings increased by
six times, so that they accounted for practically a fifth of agricultural land in 1950. Since neither the organizational nor the material preparation had been made for such a radical transformation, the consequences soon had to be felt. In 1951, an otherwise
fruitful year, cooperation stagnated. During the following year,
there was a drought and agricultural production fell to a fourth
below the prewar average. Compulsory sale was abolished and
the system of controlled prices practically abandoned (except for
the purchase prices of wheat). In 1953 the idea of collectivization
according to the Soviet model was finally abandoned. Yugoslav
agriculture was ready for a new start, but eight precious years
were lost.

Cooperation and the Duality of Agriculture, 1953-64

During the next three years, new ways of organizing agriculture
were sought. The peasant work cooperatives were gradually dissolved. The prices of agricultural products continued to be relatively low. In order to stimulate the producers, as early as 1952,

federal subsidies for agricultural machines, artificial fertilizers, fuel, and other materials were introduced. In 1954 the tax system was changed: a tax according to cadastral revenue [1] was introduced with rates determined annually by the federal government. In that way, the earlier arbitrariness in taxation was eliminated and stimuli for greater production were built in. However, agricultural production continued to lag behind the country's needs. Food prices rose in spite of large imports. In 1956, 80 percent of the deficit in the balance of trade was accounted for by food imports. Energetic measures had to be undertaken to correct the situation and compensate for failures.

During 1956 and 1957, the state organs analyzed domestic and foreign experiences in the development of agriculture; in 1957, on the basis of this study, the federal parliament adopted a Resolution on the Prospective Development of Agriculture and Cooperation [3]. The Resolution, which became the basis for a new conception of agrarian policy, was later supplemented by some other programmatic documents (the Program of the League of Communists of Yugoslavia, the Conclusions of the Seventh and Eighth Congresses of the League of Communists, the Ninth Plenum of the Socialist Alliance of the Working People of Yugoslavia, and the Resolution on the Development of Agriculture of the Federal People's Parliament of 1964) without essential changes. Stipetić summarizes the bases of the new agrarian policy as follows [2, pp. 86-88]:

1. It was intended to achieve the necessary faster development of agricultural production by greater investments (which in 1959 reached the maximum share of 15.9 percent of total investments), by a change in the conditions of economic activity, and by certain technical and systemic solutions (imports of machinery, fertilizers, pesticides, breeding livestock, and seeds; credits for working capital, guaranteed prices, rebates for basic inputs, etc.).

2. Because domestic and foreign experience was interpreted as showing the impossibility of faster expansion of production on the basis of the small peasant holding, it was insisted that the technological breakthrough be carried out on large collective farms (combines, estates, cooperatives), while including individual pro-

---

1. Cadastral revenue is the value of the average yield of a specific land category under average weather conditions and using a standard land cultivation technique.

Table 13

Collective and Individual Farms, 1956–70

	Production index, 1955=100		Share of sales (%)	Arable land (million ha.)		Tractors (thousands)		Standard head of livestock (millions)		Use of artificial fertilizer (million tons)
	C	I	C	C	I	C	I	C	I	C
1956	84	83	24a	0.8	9.4	11.4	3.3	0.2	4.0	0.2
1960	250	117	34	1.0	9.2	30.7	5.1	0.5	5.0	0.6
1962	308	114	40	1.2	9.1	35.3	–	0.5	5.0	0.8
1964	411	129	41	1.3	8.9	40.3	–	0.5	5.0	1.1
1965	411	115	44	1.4	8.8	40.3	–	0.5	5.0	1.2
1966	493	132	44	1.4	8.8	38.8	12.2	0.5	5.3	1.2
1967	504	130	48	1.5	8.8	34.8	–	0.5	5.3	1.2
1968	507	123	49	1.5	8.7	31.3	–	0.4	5.4	1.1
1969	544	135	48	1.5	8.7	29.2	39.0	0.4	4.6	1.0
1970	525	130	44	1.5	8.7	27.8	–	0.4	4.8	0.8

C = collective farms (agricultural combines, estates, general agricultural cooperative farms, agricultural cooperatives).
I = individual farms.
Sources: SGJ–1971; SZS, Jugoslavija 1945–1964.
a. 1957.

ducers in modern, highly productive agriculture by means of
cooperation.

The effects were felt immediately. High-yielding varieties of
Italian and Soviet wheat and American hybrid corn — which after
some time were replaced by still higher yielding varieties produced in domestic scientific institutions (see [117, pp. 126 ff.])
along with adequate cultivation of the soil brought about by investments in modern technology, made possible phenomenal increases
of yields on collective farms. The former estates — now self-
managed agricultural combines — instead of showing chronic
losses, began to earn profits. Cooperation was well received by
the peasants and individual farms also began to increase production. In the five-year period 1957-61, agricultural production
was 48 percent greater than in the previous five-year period.
Prices on the agricultural products market stabilized. For the
first time in many years, supply exceeded demand and food imports were decreased and exports increased. The agricultural
balance of trade became positive.

In this period, the Yugoslav economy took on a new, apparently
permanent characteristic. A very specific duality appeared: large
collective production and small individual production. These two
organizations of production differ in many respects. These differences created great confusion among insufficiently critical or
insufficiently Marxist-educated economists and politicians, and
socialized or socialist farming was often opposed to the private
nonsocialist peasant holding. The former should be helped and
developed, and the latter transformed and checked. We shall discuss this problem further below. Here it is sufficient to state
that it was necessary to regulate and institutionalize the relations
between these two sectors in some way. In the period under consideration, the solution was found in cooperation. It will be useful to cite some statistical data to make the text that follows more
understandable.

In 1970, the last year for which data is currently available, a
synthetic picture of the duality of Yugoslav agriculture is given
by the statistics in the table on page 94.

One can see that the duality means substantially greater productivity (per worker and per hectare) on the collective farms, but
there is also a certain complementarity: the collective sector
specializes in the production of some industrial cultures and
wheat, and the individual in the production of milk, meat, fruit,

Number of farms	
Collective	2,073
Individual	2,599,552
Labor force	
Collective sector	208,000
Individual sector	5,100,000
Share of the collective sector	
Number of farms	0.1%
Labor force	4
Livestock	9
Arable land	15
Social product	29
Marketable surpluses	40
Value of all deliveries	44
Deliveries of corn	55
Deliveries of wheat	70

Source: SGJ-1971; Stipetić, "Ekonomika poljoprivreda i ribarstva," p. 96.

and potatoes.[2] The collective sector provides almost half of wholesale deliveries and, because of the specific market, about two-fifths of marketable surpluses. This means that in the individual sector agricultural production is still of a peasant nature, diversified, and primarily for the needs of the peasant's own family. Increasing marketable surpluses in the individual sector presuppose the transformation of the peasant into a farmer, and for that it is essential, among other things, to open up the necessary number of new jobs in the nonagricultural sector to absorb the surplus of peasant manpower. How large this surplus is potentially is seen from a comparison of the labor force in both sectors relative to the achieved production. It should be kept in mind, however, that the collective sector is very capital intensive: it disposes of five to six times more capital per worker than the individual producer [2, p. 47]. The capital equipment of labor in collective agriculture corresponds to that in industry.

It is of interest to note the yields in both sectors, as shown in Table 14.

If it is kept in view that the collective farms are located on the best land (and in the developed regions) and that among many

---

2. In 1969-70, the share of the following products (as percentage of total production) produced by individual farms was: sunflower seeds, 35 percent; sugar beets, 30 percent; wheat, 63 percent; meat, 74 percent; eggs and grapes, 84 percent; corn, 85 percent; milk, 87 percent; fruit, 90 percent; and potatoes, 98 percent [105, p. 99].

Table 14

Yields on Socialized and Individual Farms, 1956-69

	Collective farms			Individual farms		
	1956-58	1963-65	1967-69	1956-58	1963-65	1967-69
Crop yields (q. per ha.)						
Wheat	20.8	29.7	35.8	12.2	18.4	20.1
Corn	34.2	46.2	54.5	16.1	23.0	27.0
Sugar beets	254.2	357.6	431.6	195.4	243.0	313.0
	1956	1965	1969	1956	1965	1969
Meat production (per head in kg.)						
Per cow	184	270	285	84	150	170
Per pig	553	1220	1650	493	639	642
Milk production (liters per cow)	1955	3018	3615	1038	1050	1070

Source: D. Drače, "Development of Agriculture, 1945-1970," Yugoslav Survey, 4 (1970), p. 21.

peasants production of meat and milk is still not market oriented, it can be estimated that, with respect to yields, individual farms lag behind collective farms by approximately a decade. Because of the nature of things — and given normal conditions — this gap will be reduced in the future: further increases of already high yields become increasingly difficult, so that the laggard may be able to catch up. This process will be accelerated by the raising of the general level of education. That it has already begun can be seen from the data of Tables 12 and 13: in relation to collectives, individual producers are increasing the number of tractors and the input of artificial fertilizers. A comparison of yields on individual farms of the developed regions with collective farms of the undeveloped regions casts an interesting light on these problems. As representative of the first category, we take Vojvodina and for the second, Kosovo; data are for 1968

	Individual farms in Vojvodina	Combines and estates in Kosovo
Yield of wheat (q. per ha.)	25	20.3
Yield of corn (q. per ha.)	36	37.9

Sources: SGJ-1970; SZS, Statistički bilten 720.

The data are not entirely comparable, for the factors of climate and soil fertility cannot be eliminated. Nevertheless, they are very suggestive. The Vojvodina peasant, who has begun to transform himself into a modern farmer, achieves on the average yields equal to those of collective producers in economically undeveloped Kosovo, with substantially less investment. These data at the same time indicate where the greatest unused potentials of Yugoslav agriculture lie today. As for collective farms, at present they achieve yields characteristic of the most developed agriculture in the world. For example, in wheat the highest yields in 1963 were attained in Holland (42.1 quintals), Great Britain (39 quintals), and West Germany (35.1 quintals); in corn, the Yugoslav yields are higher than the average in other countries [5, p. 1551]. Labor productivity is still substantially lower. For example, in comparison with American agriculture, Yugoslav collective farming expends up to 12 times more time for the production of 100 kilograms of corn, 4 times more time for wheat, and 2.5-3 times more time in milk production [5, p. 1558]. But labor productivity is rapidly increasing. For three representative crops, the necessary human labor in hours per quintal of output was as follows:

	Wheat	Corn	Sugar beets
1960	2.58	8.56	2.21
1968	1.14	2.99	0.93

In seven years, labor productivity increased 2-3 times, and now corresponds to American productivity in the period 1945-49 [106, pp. 668-69].

After we have considered the collective and individual sectors separately, we must also consider their mutual relations through cooperation. The basic carrier of cooperation, both in conception and in reality, was the agricultural cooperative. The relevant data are cited in Table 15.

Following a period of rapid expansion, the number of cooperants as well as the area included in cooperatives began to decline after 1964. The volume of work performed cooperatively also declined, except in sowing, where it increased further, and in harvesting, where it stagnated. It is obvious that the peasants began to equip their farms themselves and that they began to master modern technology, so that the general agricultural cooperatives were no longer so economically interesting to them.

In the collectivized sector, striking changes are also observed.

Table 15

Cooperation

	1956	1960	1962	1964	1965	1966	1968	1970	1973
Number of cooperants									
(thousands)	55[a]	801	877	1261	1231	1241	1082	929	—
Amount of work									
Plowing (thousand ha.)	245[b]	366	607	599	680	671	485	406	220
Sowing (thousand ha.)	56[b]	116	122	211	226	258	326	340	145
Harvesting (thousand ha.)	68[b]	194	150	303	230	294	316	331	136
Threshing (thousand									
wagons)	87[b]	142	86	130	154	163	138	102	43
Area in cooperation									
(thousand ha.)									
Wheat	9[a]	263	281	499	363	978	357	320	—
Corn	5[a]	119	279	528	586	590	495	436	—
Sugar beets	2[a]	39	30	33	27	46	34	36	—

Sources: SGJ-1963; SGJ-1971; SGJ-1974; SZS, Jugoslavija 1945-1964.
a. 1957.
b. 1958.

The intensity of cultivation declined. The number of tractors fell on combines, estates, and cooperatives, with the reduction less on the first two (from 20,574 in 1966 to 17,572 in 1970) and partially compensated for by the purchase of heavier tractors. On all of them, the use of artificial fertilizers per hectare fell (on combines and estates, from 978 kilograms in 1965 to 625 kilograms in 1970). The number of livestock also fell, which Stipetić explains by the low prices of livestock products, especially milk, and the high input of feed per unit of output [2, p. 94]. If we add that agricultural expansion began to slow after 1960, then it is obvious that in 1965 one of those discontinuities characteristic of Yugoslav economic policy occurred. That was the year of the economic reform.

Stipetić sees the main reason for the slower growth of the collective sector to lie in the lower efficiency of the resources invested in relation to the alternative investment opportunities, which demobilized sociopolitical organs in efforts to broaden the collective sector and reduced the capability of the agricultural organizations themselves to accumulate capital. The overcapitalization of the collective sector, in which organizations with losses are perceptibly more capital intensive than profitable organizations, is especially evident. Although the productivity of labor is increasing rapidly, the efficiency of capital — because of over-capitalization — is rapidly falling, and, as a result, according to the measurements of Marković, the aggregate productivity of agriculture is stagnating.[3]

Economic Reform and Attempts to Achieve a Laissez-Faire Market after 1964

The symptoms of stagnation in agriculture coincided with crisis phenomena in the rest of the economy, so that the 1965 reform embraced the entire economy. The basic idea of the reform was to increase the role of the market and reduce state interventions. In agriculture, this meant the elimination of rebates for all inputs except artificial fertilizers. The total amount of annual rebates fell from 454 million dinars in 1954 to about 280 million dinars in the next six years. The total premiums for livestock, grains, milk, and cotton were halved, and premiums were retained only for the last two products. Federal funds for financing investments were reduced from over 900 million dinars in 1964 and 1965 to about 500 million dinars in the following years [8, pp. 77, 78]. Thus inputs became more expensive and subsidies were reduced at the same time that the need for capital accumulation by the organization itself grew. The resulting problem could be solved only by a substantial increase in prices; this was done, with the expectation that the prices of agricultural producers would increase by 34.6 percent [8, p. 79]. In reality, in the first two years of the reform, producers' prices in agriculture increased by 66 percent compared to 28 percent in industry and 59 percent in retail trade. The movement of agricultural prices generally illustrates well the stages of economic policy. In Table 16 we present a short comparative survey.

---

3. In the period 1955-62, the index of net product per worker increased to 179, and the sum of depreciation and materials consumed in the course of the year per worker to 183. Marković obtains his index of overall productivity = 98 by taking the ratio of these two indexes. The index is methodologically erroneous: (a) overall productivity is measured by the product per unit of combined input of labor and resources, but the number of workers and the value of resources cannot be combined, for they have different dimensions; (b) the index arbitrarily gives the same weight to labor and resources; (c) it is calculated on the basis of net price. (For the calculation of overall productivity, see [55, ch. 17].) But even with these deficiencies Marković's index in a certain way illustrates Stipetić's proposition.

Table 16

Producers' Prices in Agriculture and Industry and Retail Prices, 1956-73

	1956	1960	1964	1966	1970	1973
1. Producers' prices for agricultural products	100	117	206	342	402	990
2. Producers' prices for industrial products	100	103	113	145	168	278
3. Retail prices	100	112	147	234	306	556
4. Price ratios						
1:2	100	114	182	238	240	356
1:3	100	105	140	147	131	178

Source: SGJ-1971; SGJ-1974.

Between 1956 and 1960, prices were rather stable. In the next four-year period, the increase accelerated, especially for agricultural prices. The 1964-66 price jump caused by the reform is described above. In the next four-year period, the increase in prices slowed down, but it is nevertheless greater than in the initial period. Price relations changed in favor of agriculture very quickly and substantially until 1966, reflecting the disparities inherited from the etatist period. After 1966, agricultural prices follow industrial prices and lag behind retail prices. In 1971, a new acceleration of the increase in agricultural prices appears to begin.

The first effects of the reform were positive. Record production was achieved in 1966. Furthermore, collective farms began to reorient themselves from maximizing production to maximizing efficiency, which led to a reduction of outlays for mechanization and fertilizers, as noted above. After 1968, however, new difficulties began. The reform was conceived as an extreme liberalization of the market without any important regulatory role of state organs; this was quickly shown to be unmaintainable in the concrete international and internal circumstances. It was not perceived that the alternative to etatist control consists not in a laissez-faire market and the abandonment of regulation, but in modern regulation by indirect methods with the full responsibility of the economic policy bodies. A complete opening up toward the world market that was insufficiently thought out led to the import of products at dumping prices, which seriously checked domestic production (in sugar, denatured alcohol, butter, fruit, and other products). The closing of the West European market, along with the simultaneous absence of systematic socially organized aid to exports, perceptibly hindered the marketing of Yugoslav agricultural products. The lack of a stabilizing policy increased the cyclical character of production, especially meat production. Phases of surplus and deficit alternated, accompanied by the negative effects of badly timed imports and large price variations. As a result, a substantial reduction in the number of livestock occurred after 1968 (see Table 17).

Table 17

Changes in Selected Input Prices and Retail Prices
for Agricultural Products, 1966-70 (1966 = 100)

	1967	1968	1969	1970
Producers' prices for agricultural products	97	93	102	117
Prices of agricultural tools and equipment	112	118	121	124
Prices of chemical inputs	103	104	99	99
Prices of fuel and lubricants	117	117	117	117
Prices of construction materials	123	129	133	149
Services	113	126	142	–
Retail prices	107	112	120	131

Source: SGJ-1971; M. Trkulja, et al., Politika dugoročnog razvoja poljoprivrede (Novi Sad: Zavod za ekonomiku poljoprivrede, 1970), p. 83.

As early as 1967 the relative price relations were disturbed: prices of inputs rose faster than product prices. The mechanism of guaranteed and minimal purchase prices did not function well because of the inefficiency of the federal administration (prices were not determined on time; the financial means for purchase were not provided on time; because it had to wait for political decisions, the Directorate for Reserves of Food Products could not intervene on time, etc.). Repayment of earlier excessive loans created chronic overindebtedness in the collective sector. The rate of investment in agriculture slowed down, and its share in total investment fell by a third (see Table 12).

Finally, after a three-year delay, the state administration took action. In May 1968, protection of domestic agricultural production was again introduced. In the middle of the same year, a fund for the stabilization of production and promotion of exports of livestock products was founded. Improvements in the credit system were carried out. It was understood that subsidization of agriculture could not be suddenly ended. Control over the prices of basic inputs was introduced (see Table 17) [8, p. 82].

In October 1970, the First Conference of the League of Communists of Yugoslavia concerned itself particularly with agriculture. In the Conference Resolution, the following judgment of the development of agriculture in recent years is given:

Parallel with major results in the development of agriculture and the village, there occurred the phenomena of instability on the market for agricultural products, the lagging of livestock raising and the slowing of the growth rate of aggregate agricultural production. This affected the overall development and stability of the economy, and caused certain difficulties throughout the country.... This occurred because in the conditions of increased production and more difficult marketing, above all of livestock products, there was not a sufficiently defined place and role of agriculture on the domestic and foreign market, nor adequate instruments for insuring the necessary stability in the development of production and the market, and partially also because at a higher level of production high rates of growth cannot be attained [12, p. 360].

As the basic orientation for solving the problems that had arisen, the Resolution cites the replacement of state regulation by self-management mechanisms such as contractual agreement, the formation of funds for the stabilization of the market, the advancement of production and marketing of food products, and the formation of common reserves. It is especially emphasized that "the responsibility for the stable development of production, markets and sale of agricultural products is primarily the affair ... of the working people in agroindustrial production, of their joint efforts," and only after that "also of the sociopolitical communities" [12, p. 361]. Here it can be observed that, while a self-government orientation is the only correct alternative in a socialist society, nevertheless the shifting of responsibility to farmers and their organizations is mistaken and based on misunderstanding of the functioning of the economic system. Agriculture is only one sector of production, and its efficiency and stability depend mainly on the functioning of the overall system. Stipetić has pointed to the empirical correlation between the development of agriculture and the development of the economy as a whole [2]. Hence, the economic policy bodies — that is, the government and its organs, political bodies, and chambers of commerce — bear primary responsibility for the development of agriculture. Their own material interest will automatically lead farmers to rational solutions — the enormous importance of the market as an organizational mechanism lies in this — while this need not be so with the organs of economic policy, whose behavior is determined rather differently.

The Resolution further insists on association, in which informed agricultural cooperatives are to play a special role. These cooperatives must "develop as self-managed work communities of agricultural producers (those who are permanently employed in them and those who cooperate with them, temporarily or permanently), in which business will be conducted on the principles of income and distribution according to the results of work. ... In this connection the management organs in cooperatives and units for cooperation should be so formed that their internal structure and management organs maintain the linking of the work of individual producers with the work of those employed in these organizations" [27, p. 363]. Related to this is the demand for greater inclusion of individual farmers in the LCY.[4] A clear position was adopted that "the equipping of individual farms with suitable mechanization" not only is not unsocialist nor the road to small property anarchy, as was often thought earlier, but is "a component part of the process of their linking with work organizations in the socialized sector and the socialization of their production. This presupposes ensuring their adequate treatment with respect to opportunities of obtaining loans for production, purchase of agricultural machines and such" [p. 363].

The First Conference of the LCY, as well as later constitutional amendments, removed some ideological prejudices in the approach to agriculture. However, the entire conception of the self-management organization of the economy is still not worked out. Some mistaken and, in their political-economic effects, very dangerous conceptions, such as that of who bears final responsibility, are still maintained. Expert solution of a whole series of technical organizational problems still lies ahead.

10. COLLECTIVIZATION: IDEAS AND IMPLEMENTATION

In the Soviet Union, there are sovkhozes, machine-tractor stations, and kolkhozes. In Yugoslavia after Liberation, state agricultural estates, agricultural machine stations, and peasant work

---

4. One peasant was elected to the federal parliament and a total of about forty peasants to all the state and provincial parliaments. After the Liberation, more than half the members of the Communist Party of Yugoslavia were peasants; by 1972 their participation had fallen to about 5 percent [116, p. 13].

cooperatives were organized. There were also other cooperatives, but they were considered to be transitional forms. There were, of course, many individual peasant farms, but this was considered a reflection of the initial stage of socialist transformation of the village. The parallelism, accordingly, was complete.

Nevertheless, it was not a matter of imitation. The Yugoslav authorities started from the belief — one not founded on statistical data, however, which is not uncharacteristic of this region — that Soviet institutional solutions had shown themselves to be efficient, and that they therefore could be usefully applied. Nevertheless, in application Yugoslavia's own experiences played the decisive role. Hence, it is not surprising that the system developed rather differently than in the Soviet Union.

V. Begović has succinctly reviewed the substance of the conception of socialist transformation of the village at that time [39]. He polemicizes about the postulate that transformation should begin with nationalization of the land, for the same effects can be achieved much more efficiently by limiting and forbidding sale of land and by similar measures [p. 11]. Begović points out essential differences between industry and agriculture, because of which "the inclusion of agriculture in socialism must go and does go by another way.... Here it is not a matter of a parasitic class, but of millions of small landowners who actively participate in social production and comprise the majority of our people" [p. 5]. However, agriculture, with its small-owner structure, could not keep up with the rapid development of industry, and therefore would become a brake on general development. That is, it is necessary (1) to produce new market surpluses to feed the new labor force in industrial centers; (2) to supply expanding industry with increasing quantities of raw materials; and (3) to free sufficient manpower from agriculture for increased industrial production. These effects can be achieved only by large-scale, that is to say, collectivized, agriculture [pp. 7-8].

State Agricultural Estates and Agricultural Machine Stations

The state agricultural estate (SAE) represents the first and, in some ways, the most socialist link in the socialist chain, for it involves social property. The task of the state sector, emphasized Kardelj in his report, is to show the peasantry in practice all the advantages of a large-scale socialist economy, to aid in improving their technical skills, and, by daily services, to help the farming cooperatives and peasants in improving their farms. In addition, the SAEs should contribute to supplying the large cities and industrial centers as cheaply as possible [15, p. 389]. M. Mirković had the same conception — in fact, it was generally accepted: "The state agricultural estate, applying the best techniques of production, appropriate crop sequence, good division of types of production, and appropriate division of work tasks, draws all production forward after it..." [20, p. 72]. Mirković adds that agricultural estates will have a lasting importance in socialism and that their role will increase with the development of socialism.

In relation to prewar conditions, the state sector substantially increased after the agrarian reform. Before the war the area of state agricultural estates amounted to 96,000 hectares, or 0.7 percent of the total agricultural area in 1931. In 1950, estates possessed 323,000 hectares, or 2.2 percent, and, with agricultural institutions, 438,000 hectares or 3.9 percent of the agricultural area [40, p. 328]. Data on the development of agricultural estates comparable with that for later years are incomplete; we cite them insofar as they are available in Table 18.

Table 18

State Agricultural Estates, 1949-53

	Number	Employed persons (thousands)	Area (thousand ha.)	Tractors (thousands)	Cattle (thousands)	Yields (q./ha.) Wheat	Corn
1949	1255	—	—	—	54	—	—
1950	858	52	413	1.4	52	14.0	12.0
1951	1422	—	—	2.1	65	—	—
1952	737	—	—	—	60	—	—
1953	666	—	—	—	56	—	—

Source: SZS, Jugoslavija 1945-1964, p. 110.

The SAEs were treated with particular attention and given special aid. The results, however, were not impressive. Almost all the estates operated at a loss [40, p. 333], which one can assume was partially the result of low prices. According to Vladimir Bakarić, in 1949, "among our enterprises the agricultural estates are distinguished by their carelessness, negligence, and lack of effort. With a few exceptions, the spirit of old Yugoslavia still prevails among them. Already in advance they cannot fulfill any task, they regularly work with large losses (which have a tendency to increase), they do not show any initiative whatsoever toward correcting this condition, and so on" [41, p. 99].

Agricultural machine stations (AMSs) appeared immediately after the Liberation, when collective farming was not organized on some of the confiscated large holdings and colonists on small holdings could not use the confiscated machines and equipment rationally. In the first two years, the AMSs worked as agricultural institutions (Law on the Organization of the State Agricultural Machine Service, July 1945), and from 1947 as state enterprises. At first the stations helped in cultivating the land of SAEs and peasant work cooperatives, and later predominantly of the latter and to a certain extent of individual farms. According to Mirković, the AMSs had the task of facilitating the systematic transition from peasant small production to cooperative, collective large-scale production [20, p. 76]. Mirković cites with approval the following conclusion of S. Sinanović of the same period (1949): "The state agricultural machine stations showed in practice the advantage of the large socialist farm over the small holding, both in increasing productivity of labor and in the timely performance and better quality of mechanized operations. On the other hand, the state agricultural machine stations exercise tremendous influence on the ripening among the working peasantry of consciousness of the necessity for transition to large-scale socialist farms and the further development of peasant work cooperatives" [42, p. 43]. This attitude is a good example of the substitution of subjective desires for empirically founded conclusions that was typical of this time.

At the end of 1948, there were 109 stations in the country with 3820 tractors [20, p. 76]. Two years later, after the introduction of workers' self-management, the centralistically conceived AMS came into conflict with the system (i.e., with the concept that agricultural producers should manage the fixed capital they use), and they were disbanded and replaced by funds for mechanization and the building up of cooperative agriculture. After mid-1950, there was no longer even one AMS, and the new funds were given the task of distributing the machinery taken over to the peasant work cooperatives as well as purchasing and distributing new machines. The funds for mechanization were liquidated after two years [40, pp. 318-24].

Concerning the shortcomings of the AMS, Lj. Božić notes that there were no skilled workers to repair and maintain the machines, no attachments for the tractors, and no spare parts [40, p. 321].

The Yugoslav Economic System

The sociopolitical criticism of M. Todorović, who was to become
Secretary of the LCY, at that time is much more serious [43,
pp. 79-81]. Todorović ironically quotes the position of the Soviet
academician P. Maslov that the machine-tractor station "represents the greatest discovery of the current century in the area of
production, since the creation of the MTS introduces a turnabout
in an economic branch in which a great majority of the population
of the globe is employed and hastens the transition from socialism
to communism. This greatest discovery of Stalin still has not been
judged properly." Todorović states that over 90 percent of the
sowing area of the kolkhozes is worked by machines of the MTS
and that, accordingly, the kolkhozes are not in a position to cultivate the land regardless of price, whose level is determined by
the government. In that way, "the bureaucratic caste holds the
kolkhozes in a directly dependent position through the MTS" [p. 79].
It follows that the transformation of the kolkhoz into a modern
large-scale agricultural enterprise is not desired, but the kolkhoz
is "necessary only and exclusively as a forced organization for
labor" and "Stalin's epochal discovery reduces to the forced investment of capital in agriculture." Todorović continues: "Since
the MTSs play such a role toward the kolkhoz peasantry, it is then
understandable that, together with tractors and agronomists, various political authorities also travel from them to the villages...."
The MTSs are transformed "into, so to speak, a unified center in
the village for the operations of the NKVD, the court executor, the
tax administrator, the landowner-capitalist creditor (manager)
and, of course, the Party political department. For the new capitalist monopolist is the 'soviet' state, that is, the bureaucratic
caste. It finds itself in that most ideal position sought after by all
capitalists in the wolves' fight of mutual extermination; in its hands
is all power and property. Wherever economic monopoly is insufficient, force, terror, and oppression appear. Alongside the
agronomist appears the NKVD agent; along with the tractor, the
rifle butt" [pp. 80-81].

After such an assessment, it is natural that agricultural machine stations never appeared again in Yugoslav agriculture.

The kolkhozes represent the third link in Stalinist collectivization. In Yugoslavia the peasant work cooperatives correspond to
the kolkhozes [68, p. 203]. However, general agricultural cooperatives existed alongside the peasant work cooperatives and
had a much greater role, so we shall concern ourselves with
them first.

General Agricultural Cooperatives

The general agricultural cooperatives (GACs) inherited the pre-war cooperative organizations. In a programmatic article in 1947, Kardelj sets out from this proposition, but simultaneously disassociates himself from the negative elements of prewar cooperatives, which should be avoided [44]. These negative aspects emerged from the fact that, in a capitalist environment, the cooperatives also behaved in a capitalist fashion. (M. Vučković adds as negative characteristics that the prewar cooperatives were to a large degree nondemocratic and were under the influence of political parties [46, p. 83].) Credit cooperatives transformed themselves into banks, nonpeasant elements dominated cooperative leagues, and cooperation was generally exploited for the enrichment of the village bourgeoisie. Kardelj cites Stalin, who said that peasant farming is not capitalistic, for it is predominantly small-scale farming. However, immediately afterward he quotes Lenin's well-known thesis "that small-scale commodity production generates capitalism and a bourgeoisie, every day, every hour, spontaneously and on a large scale...." This position was to be repeated as a refrain in the next two decades and served as a justification for discrimination against the peasants, who, as property owners, were considered predisposed to an antisocialist orientation. Kardelj did not fall into this error, however, but drew the correct conclusion that Lenin's statement holds in conditions of the spontaneous development of small peasant production, but that in the framework of socialist construction peasant farming develops in the direction of socialism. Now, in order to make this correct general conclusion operative, it was necessary to determine the conditions and framework of socialist construction very precisely; but it was exactly here in the following years that there was the greatest wandering.

If the process of socialist development should be controlled, then the cooperative is the most suitable organizational form of that process, for to the peasant it is the most understandable and most acceptable form of economic unification. However, cooperatives cannot develop automatically, for, as prewar experiences show, that would mean the development of cooperatives under the leadership of the village rich man, which would again lead to the strengthening of capitalist elements through the cooperatives [p. 47]. This correct conclusion was also given a mistaken interpretation and appreciation in practice: every expansion of an individual peasant farm was proclaimed as capitalist and suppressed, and the village was subjected to extreme income leveling.

Kardelj thought that the Soviet Union "gave a practical example of how a socialist country can rapidly carry out the industrialization of the country by reconstruction, advancement, and improvement of agriculture by the hands of the peasants themselves, at the same time improving the living conditions of the peasantry" [p. 58], and then cited Stalin's demand that agriculture be made large scale, capable of net investment [p. 62]. But to that end, he did not propose relying on machine tractor stations, which he considered as temporary, but rather mechanizing cooperatives [p. 69], and he did not propose exclusive reliance on kolkhozes, but on several types of agricultural cooperatives that already existed in the country. These were: (1) credit cooperatives, reformed so that they would no longer be an instrument of finance capital; (2) buying-selling cooperatives, which were most widespread and represented the lowest type of cooperative, but also that which could best serve as the basis for further development; (3) processing-producing cooperatives; and (4) work cooperatives, the highest type of producing cooperative. In Kardelj's opinion, it would be useful to unite the first three types of cooperative in a uniform type of general agricultural cooperative, which would coincide with the area of a village and would develop those activities for which the conditions existed [pp. 71-73]. In fact, this process had already begun: Boris Kidrić had posed the same demand at the Fifth Congress of the CPY, and the same idea had become the basis of policy on cooperatives in the following two years [45, p. 495].

General agricultural cooperatives engaged primarily in the purchase of manufactured goods for their members and in the buying up of agricultural products. In 1953, the turnover of the GACs amounted to a fourth of the country's total commodity trade [46, p. 114]. From the end of 1947 on, the GACs organized cooperative farms [zadružne ekonomije] on their own and rented land. It was then felt that cooperative farms should be created where the conditions were lacking for founding work cooperatives, and that they would be the basis for the later development of the latter. In Kardelj's opinion, "the peasant who participates in a cooperative farm is no longer only an individual owner; he is on his individual farm with one foot only and with the other he has already stepped over to socialist farming. This undoubtedly makes it easier for him to decide to go over to a work cooperative, which he assuredly will resolve to do one day" [14, p. 56]. From the organizational aspect, the cooperative farms corresponded to peasant work cooperatives of type I (as defined in the next section). However, their socioeconomic position was not particularly precisely defined, they did not receive adequate support in the form of credits and mechanization, and they had dispersed landholdings and little livestock. Hence, their yields were lower than on the peasant work cooperatives. In 1953, the number of cooperative farms as well as their area increased because of land obtained under the second agrarian reform.

Table 19

General Agricultural Cooperatives, 1945-53

	No. of cooper- atives	No. of members (millions)	Employed persons (thousands)	Total Area (thou- sand ha.)	No. of tractors (thou- sands)	No. of cattle (thousands)	Yields (q./ha.) Wheat	Corn
1945	4825	1.2	—	—	—	—	—	—
1946	8011	1.8	—	—	—	—	—	—
1947	6632	2.5	—	—	—	—	—	—
1948	8662	3.1	—	264	—	3.4	—	—
1949	9060	3.4	—	115	—	4.7	—	—
1950	8004	3.5	—	63	47	3.2	9.4	8.7
1951	7581	2.2	—	29	34	4.1	—	—
1952	6973	3.3	45	75	468	3.4	—	—
1953	7114	3.1	60	132	2024	6.2	—	—

Sources: SZS, Jugoslavija 1945-1964; M. Vučković, Zadrugarstvo (Zagreb: Zadružna štampa, 1957), p. 111.

The general agricultural cooperatives also held savings accounts and granted loans to their members,[5] processed agricultural products, and engaged in local production of quicklime, bricks, and such, handicrafts, and hotel and restaurant management. This diverse activity, however, was more of a hindrance than a benefit; it brought low incomes and absorbed the few experts available,

5. Cooperative savings banks ceased operation in 1960. In the following year, there began a process of standardizing the market — similar to the imposing of administrative control after the Liberation — by neglecting the specific characteristics of individual economic activities. Thus, for example, communal banks were formed in the communes and agricultural cooperatives also became account holders. Soon the communal banks began to disappear by integration into larger commercial banks and by reorganization, and the village was left without a suitable substitute for cooperative saving and credit. In 1958, cooperative savings deposits amounted to 4 percent of the working capital of the GACs on the average, and 20 percent in Slovenia, while in 1938 they amounted to 39 percent of cooperative liabilities [112, pp. 87, 89, 103].

who could not then devote themselves to advancing agriculture [47, p. 67]. Cooperative machine stations were also founded not only to cultivate the land of the cooperative farm, but also the land of the cooperative members. In 1953 there were 860 such stations, predominantly in Serbia [46, p. 119]. The number of GACs declined after 1949, for smaller cooperatives were merged. The number of cooperative members fluctuated, in particular because members quit the cooperative and later returned, and partly also because the substantial increase of the cost of shares in cooperatives led to the withdrawal of household members, so that ordinarily only the head of the family remained in the cooperative [47, p. 65].

M. Mirković has accurately expressed the conception of the general agricultural cooperatives that prevailed at the time: "The position of the GAC in the transitional period has transitional and temporary importance. They are to serve as a means and way of facilitating the transition to socialist agriculture. Hence, they themselves do not represent a pure and final form of cooperative in socialist agriculture. They organize, plan, and lead the activity of the peasants, who still farm on individual holdings, and they will be liquidated when their members become members of a higher type of cooperative, a socialist type: the peasant work cooperative" [20, p. 54]. Because of this, although rational analysis of the situation prompted the devotion of special attention to the development of agricultural cooperatives, and although political forums emphasized it and introduced it into programmatic documents, in practice agricultural cooperatives were neglected. The basic attention was devoted to that "real," "socialist" type of cooperative.

Peasant Work Cooperatives

Peasant work cooperatives (PWCs) represent a novelty in Yugoslav agriculture. They did not exist before the war, appearing spontaneously in the last year of the peoples' liberation struggle in Slovenia and Macedonia. In the beginning of 1945, they appeared in Vojvodina and Serbia [47, p. 43]. After the Liberation, they were founded by colonists and former partisans. By the end of 1945, thirty-one of these cooperatives — or communes for cultivation of the land, as they were called — had been founded. They still lacked rules and production-financial plans, but they were fired by the revolutionary élan of the people who created them. Legal regulations soon appeared. The agrarian reform law of

August 1945 regulated the founding of PWCs by colonists and others.
The following year, the Ministry of Agriculture prepared Model
Rules, which were changed in 1949, and in 1946 and 1949 laws
were adopted concerning cooperatives. The development of peasant work cooperatives is shown in Table 20.

The peasants brought all their land except the grounds around
their houses into the work cooperatives. They likewise brought
in their inventory and livestock, except that on the house grounds,
which were evaluated and later paid for. Four types of cooperative were anticipated by the Model Rules: type I — the peasant
would remain the owner of the land brought in and would receive
rent from the cooperative; if he left the cooperative, the same or
equivalent land would be returned to him; type II — the peasant
would remain the owner of the land, but he would bring it in as his
share, on which interest would be paid; type III — the peasant would
remain the owner of the land he brought in as his share, but interest would not be paid; type IV — the peasant would transfer his
land, except the house grounds, to cooperative ownership. Accordingly, in the first three types individual ownership remains, and
in the first two rent is kept as well; only in the fourth is ownership
collective and distribution according to work.[6] In April 1951, there
were 6972 cooperatives divided by types as follows: type I, 1018;
type II, 2179; type III, 3429; and type IV, 346 [47, p. 50]. The same
year, the peasant work cooperatives possessed 19 percent of the total agricultural area, and in Vojvodina close to 50 percent [47, p. 55].

In 1950, Mirković wrote: "The peasant work cooperatives represent the organizational type of collective ownership and collective cultivation of the land, and, accordingly, the basic unit of collective agricultural production.... At the same time, the PWCs
make possible the transition from small-scale commodity production with small and dispersed marketable surpluses to large-
scale commodity production in agriculture with large, concentrated
marketable surpluses" [20, p. 54]. Mirković saw the following
advantages in large-scale farming: better conditions for mechani-

---

6. In India after the abolition of the zemindars' holdings, two types of producing agricultural cooperatives were formed: in the first, distribution of income is carried out according to work performed and land and other resources
contributed; in the second, it is distributed exclusively according to work, while
resources are under common ownership [46, p. 30]. Accordingly, Yugoslav
types I-II correspond to the first Indian type, and type IV to the second. In
Peru, cooperatives that correspond to the fourth type are being created on nationalized large holdings by the agrarian reform which is now in progress.

Table 20

Peasant Work Cooperatives, 1945-53

	No. of PWCs	No. of coop. members (thousands)	Total area (thou- sand ha.)	No. of tractors (thousands)	Cattle (thousands)	Yields (q./ha.)	
						Wheat	Corn
1945	14	—	96	—	—	—	—
1946	280	75	122	—	—	—	—
1947	638	175	211	—	—	—	—
1948	1217	286	324	—	—	—	—
1949	6238	1707	1839	—	—	—	—
1950	6913	2129	2190	3.1	313	10.1	9.4
1951	6804	2004	2074	3.1	311	—	—
1952	4225	1505	1665	—	286	—	—
1953	1165	193	329	2.7	188	—	—

Source: SZS, Jugoslavija 1945-1964; Vučković [46, p. 134].

zation of production, more extensive division of labor and better organization of work, wider opportunities for combining production and crop rotation, regional specialization, adaptation to natural and economic-geographic conditions of production, and greater possibilities for net investment [pp. 54-55]. Mirković spoke of the law of the collectivization of land ownership and land cultivation, which is based on the liquidation of capitalist relations in agriculture and on the law of proportional development of individual branches of the economy (by which is clearly not meant mathematical proportionality, but the structure of interdependence). Mirković concluded: "The peasant work cooperatives must gradually encompass agricultural production and thus liquidate the remains of capitalism in the village; they must be the foundation and basic form of socialist farming in the first phase of creating socialist agriculture" [p. 56].

A year earlier, Todorović had examined in an article how to attain the goal just formulated. As was then customary, Todorović began his work by citing authorities. Marx and Engels had posed the demand for voluntary uniting of isolated peasant farms into large collective farms, with the many-sided financial, material, organizational, and political help of the socialist state. Lenin, in his cooperative plan, concretized that demand in the conditions of initial socialist construction in the USSR; and Stalin, in the period of final liquidation of capitalist elements in the village, when socialism was completely built up. The Central Committee of the

CPY proceeded from its own insights as well as the rich experiences of the USSR. The Fifth Congress confirmed this line and defined as further tasks: (1) aiding and developing agricultural cooperatives from the lowest forms (buying-selling cooperatives) to the highest forms (work cooperatives); (2) supplying substantial state financial aid to agricultural cooperatives; (3) increasing the area of cooperative land; (4) ensuring strict adherence to the principle of voluntary entry of peasants into cooperatives; (5) giving aid to cooperatives in the form of technical experts; (6) developing agricultural machine stations; and (7) preventing trade and speculation in land [48, p. 119]. Todorović directed his analysis to the first development task.

The buying-selling cooperative, as Kardelj had already stated, was the initial form, understandable and acceptable to all peasants. But it could not be the bridge leading peasants to the work cooperative. The unified agricultural cooperative of the general type was a further step in that direction. This cooperative not only supplies its members with consumer goods and sells their produce, but enables them to improve their farms by joint purchase of materials and mechanized equipment, organization of fertilizing stations, and so on. The general agricultural cooperative plans production for its area, makes contracts with industry for the production of industrial crops, builds cooperative workshops, and organizes the production of construction materials. It often assumes the responsibility of solving certain communal problems of the village, such as construction of cultural centers, electrification, organization of medical and veterinary services, and construction of water pipelines. Still another step further was the founding of cooperative farms and the use of cooperative mechanization to perform services for members [pp. 120-23].

The general agricultural cooperative has great educational importance. It should be the initiator of the work cooperative. It is a transitional form on the path toward the work cooperative, and therefore is temporary in nature. While the possibility of maintaining and developing capitalistic elements still exists in the GAC, even the lowest type of work cooperative is already on the track of socialist cooperative production and, on the whole, of socialist distribution as well. The work cooperatives of the lower type are calculated above all to draw middle peasants into collective farming. Rent is a concession to the middle peasant, made to facilitate his uniting of his farm with the small peasants in a work cooperative. However, "in the united chain of agricultural cooperation, only the peasant work cooperatives of the highest type, in which all the means of production are socialized, including land, and in which cooperative labor and cooperative appropriation, that is, accumulation, are carried out on the basis of cooperative means, are cooperatives of a pure socialist type. Such a cooperative is our goal in the socialist transformation of the village" [48, p. 129].

Todorović's conception — and it well represents the prevailing conceptions of that time — is perfectly logical and very plausible. Nevertheless, in practical application, the results were very far from those expected. But before we go on to the analysis of the failure, we should consider still another article by Todorović published in 1952, in which he analyzes the earlier unqualified socialist character of the work cooperative. Todorović states that the means of production in the work cooperative are no longer private property, but they still are not general social property. The cooperative members enjoy differential and absolute rent, which, of course, are not income from labor.[7] Todorović considers that cooperatives cannot be included in the state plan as can state-socialist enterprises (which is mistaken and represents a mortgage of the administrative method of planning) and adds: "The measures that the state undertakes for the inclusion of cooperatives in the general plan are either noneconomic, administrative compulsion, or of a state capitalist (monopolistic) character" [49, p. 76]. (This is empirically correct, but not because it was objectively necessary but because, owing to insufficient knowledge of economics, the alternatives were not known.) Such measures include the cooperatives in general economic construction, but do not move them toward general social ownership. Insofar as one persisted with them, the tendencies of state bureaucratic monopoly and private capitalist behavior among the cooperative members would be strengthened. Precisely this occurred on the Soviet kolkhozes — after which to some extent the work cooperatives were modeled; they were transformed into "some sort of peculiar mixture of a patriarchal family cooperative, forced labor camp of half serf, half hired laborers, [and] a collective small commodity producer...." Thus economic development was slowed down [49, p. 77].

---

7. Todorović explains the existence of absolute rent by the lower organic composition of capital in agriculture as a result of land ownership. This is a very widespread conception (see [57, p. 99]), but it is mistaken both empirically (organic composition can be higher in agriculture than in industry) and theoretically. Absolute rent is the result of monopoly that emerges from the limited amount of land as a factor of production (see [107, p. 400]).

Such a kolkhoz "played a decisive role in the formation and victory of a bureaucratic caste in the USSR and represents the incarnation of Stalin's ignorance of political economy and the height of his anti-Marxist practice" [p. 83].

The work cooperative is not the final socialist form. While in the development of state socialist enterprises the increasing linking of work with ownership — that is, the transfer of control over production and distribution from state organs to the direct producers — is basic, for work cooperatives the necessary process is in the reverse direction: the cooperatives should transfer a part of their rights to the state as the organ of society. In that way, "work collectives (workers) and cooperatives (peasants) come into the same socioeconomic position. The final result of such development will be the transforming of all means of production and land (and of state and cooperative property) into general social property under the management of the freely associated direct producers, and consequently the achievement of uniform ... production relations for all working people — that is, the abolition of class differences, the abolition of classes" [49, p. 85].

As was already mentioned, the internal organization of the work cooperatives was, on the whole, modeled after the kolkhozes. There were brigades and groups that received certain parcels of land for cultivation, along with the use of the corresponding inventory and livestock. A management board carried out the division into brigades and the appointment of the brigadiers (brigade leaders), and not the cooperative members themselves. Compensation for work depended on the fulfillment of work norms and labor days. The work norm represented the quantity of work that the average laborer could perform in a given time period. The fulfilled work norms were calculated in labor days according to the difficulty, expertness, and importance of the work. All jobs were divided into seven categories, and each fulfilled work norm was evaluated according to these categories as 0.5 to 2 labor days. Labor days were compensated in money and in kind, but their value was known only at the end of the year, as it was calculated on the basis of the general success of the cooperative. Thus, the cooperative members had no clear conception either of their incomes or of costs of operation. The labor day measured the input of labor and not the effect of production. Consequently, as V. Vasić observed [47, p. 46], the organization of work, instead of being based on economic interest, rested on administrative control and repressive measures. The recording of labor days — which was carried out by the appointed brigadiers — was tardy and inaccurate, which led to the favoring of some members of the cooperative and discrimination against others.

Table 21

Yields on Cooperative and Individual Farms,
1949-52 (quintals/hectare)

	Wheat		Corn	
	PWCs	Individual farms	PWCs	Individual farms
1949	14.5	14.0	18.6	16.3
1950	10.6	10.0	10.4	9.0
1951	13.5	12.6	18.4	16.6
1952	8.5	9.3	7.4	6.1

Note: GAC farms are included in PWCs.
Source: Vasić [47, p. 58].

Yields in the work cooperatives were barely above those on individual farms (see Table 21). But Vasić calls even this difference into question, for the house grounds, which had notoriously higher yields, were included in the cooperative sector. In addition, the cooperatives produced at higher costs. The development of livestock raising was particularly unsatisfactory.

Vučković cites the following comparative data on the number of livestock per 100 hectares of arable land [46, p. 135]:

	House grounds	PWCs	Orientational norm
Horses	7	10	8
Cattle	158	18	45
Sheep	402	76	60
Pigs	206	15	100-120

The data speak for themselves.

If, in addition to the above, it is also observed that political bodies constantly interfered in the operations of cooperatives, which hampered their work and checked initiative, that the cooperatives delivered their products at nonequivalent prices, and that the state could not provide them with help in equipment and agrotechnology, then it becomes clear that the entire cooperative system was extremely unstable and could be maintained only by crude state force.

At the end of 1951, Bakarić stated: "The truth is that in the internal organization of the work cooperatives we applied, on the whole, the Soviet system. But it is also true that this system of internal organization experienced its breakdown in our country..." [41, p. 302].

At the end of 1951 and 1952, some changes in internal organization were made. The cooperative members themselves elected the brigadiers and formed work groups. The president of the cooperative was no longer a permanently paid person. The labor day was replaced by money payment according to the result of work. Normal cost accounting was introduced, and personal incomes were given as money payments on account until the final reckoning. One of the first results was that the cooperatives, which earlier had constantly complained of a shortage of labor, suddenly discovered that they had labor surpluses [41, p. 335]. But these reforms were too little and too late. The system of work cooperatives began to collapse. In mid-1951, the gradual abolition of compulsory sale of individual agricultural products was begun, and that process was completed at the beginning of 1953. Conditions were created for the development of a free market. The peasants, who in Kardelj's judgment of 1953 entered cooperatives largely in order to obtain more from society and avoid obligations, now for the same reasons considered it more advantageous to return to individual operation (cited in Vasić [47, p. 53]). In addition, for many cooperatives, the legal minimum of three years had just then ended, which meant that members became free to leave. It can be seen from Table 20 that a large number decided to do just that. This was not an irrational choice, for as Stojanović states: "Small commodity production in agriculture has some advantages that helped it to maintain itself so long: greater interest of the producer in the results of his work, a better relation of the producer with the farm, greater thriftiness along with many personal sacrifices, greater possibility of faster reaction to various situations on the market, and so on. If these advantages are lost by cooperation, and the huge and far greater advantages that large-scale commodity production otherwise offers are not acquired only because the conditions for it are lacking, then the situation can be more difficult than in the case of small commodity production" [50, p. 69].

Practical Implementation of Economic Policy

It remains for us to consider the behavior of individual producers.

The mere formation of peasant work cooperatives led to the reduction of the number of livestock on individual farms, for the peasants expected that they would have to enter cooperatives and sold off — sometimes even slaughtered — their draft and breeding livestock. For the same reason, they made no investments in their farms. Besides, greater production would not have made much sense anyway, for the tax and purchasing committees carried away their entire surplus, and even more. "We do not lead the battle for harvests together with him [the peasant]," stated Bakarić in 1949, "but we leave that matter to him alone. Only we make it apparent to him that we will carry away in forced sale the greater part of his actual harvest, regardless of the pains he took" [41, p. 116]. The opportunities for earnings and employment outside of agriculture were great, owing to intensive capital construction and etatist inefficiency, and peasants took advantage of them. What is more, because of a scarcity of labor, the state from time to time mobilized peasants for various projects. The area under cultivation was less than before the war, and fallow area had increased. In the period 1947-53, fallow and neglected land took up 9 percent of the reduced arable land, compared to 5.4 percent before the war [47, p. 36]. Sowing plans were not carried out. In 1949, 81,000 hectares of land included in the plan remained unsown, and as a result 110,000 tons of wheat were lost [41, p. 120].

Since there is not even one published empirical study of the behavior of the individual peasant or of agriculture as a whole during that period, I will rely on one of my own studies from 1950 [51].[8] Since the study comprised Baranja, the largest agricultural district of Croatia, the results of the research can be considered representative. In addition, Baranja is interesting because, in mid-1950, 88 percent of the area was in the possession of the state and cooperative sector. A sixth of the agricultural population of Baranja was changed after the Liberation by colonization. As elsewhere, in 1949 the forced founding of work cooperatives began, and the number of farms in cooperatives grew from 15 percent in January 1949 to 71 percent of the total number of farms in June 1950. The middle peasants (5 to 10 hectares) most often entered into cooperatives, then the highest category of small peasants,

---

8. Although this study received an award at the May Festival of Zagreb University, it could not be published, for a number of critical observations were not in accord with the official optimism considered obligatory at that time. It hardly need be added that in the following three years these observations became generally adopted positions.

richer peasants, and, last, the smallest peasants. This was a positive phenomenon, for the middle and richer peasant brought more land and better inventory into the cooperative than the small peasant. There were similar tendencies elsewhere, which led to criticism of toleration of kulaks. To such criticisms, Bakarić replied in 1947 that "our economic system allows the possibility — and we then must work with all our might to make that possibility a reality — that there can coexist with our system the type of 'kulak' that can be included in it without damage to his interests, indeed with further personal prosperity. The only condition is that he fulfill his obligations and that we energetically suppress his eventual speculative demands at the expense of the other working masses, that we explain it to him and, by example, show him the right way" [41, p. 70].

In the first five-year period, yields in Baranja were lower than before the war for all the more important crops, and substantially lower for industrial crops. Since from 1946 on the yields constantly fell and, at the same time, the cooperative sector increased, it might be imagined that the founding of cooperatives was the basic reason for the decrease in yields. But that was not so. The basic cause was administrative planning. The Ministry of Agriculture put together plans in which the sowing of industrial crops was imposed, but the corresponding agrotechnical measures were not undertaken. The distribution of crops was determined by rote, and it was thought that the producers would somehow manage; the result was the exhaustion of soil and decrease in yields. Although the Ministry's plan was not so bad, the application was catastrophic. That is, in the district agricultural commissariat, the plan was broken down into the received sowing proportions allotted to local people's committees; these committees, in turn, broke down the plan in the same proportions by households and cooperatives. In addition, already allocated sowing tasks were frequently revised. The example of hemp is illustrative. Hemp greatly exhausts the soil, and therefore requires the use of manure. This presupposes a sufficient number of livestock, for which adequate fodder and other feed (for example, corn) are needed; but the area under fodder and corn was reduced precisely in order to increase the area under industrial crops. In the opinion of the cooperative members, they should have been asked what and how to sow. The plan should have been only a guideline, and it also should have been discussed previously. Obligations should have been given in quantities and not by areas, and elaboration of the plan should have been left to the cooperative members rather than quotas distributed to them in percentages. However, these logical and rational proposals could not be carried out in the etatist framework.

While poor administrative planning was the basic cause, the rapid founding of cooperatives also contributed to the lowering of yields, as can be seen from the fact that yields were somewhat lower in the cooperative sector than in the individual sector. On the other hand, the agricultural machine stations did not improve agrotechnology as was expected. In the race for fulfilling norms, the AMSs worked the land less well than the cooperative members. For example, deep plowing was often carried out in such a way that only the edge of a meadow was really deeply plowed. Then the tractor driver raised the plowshare, for the plowing goes much faster this way, less fuel and lubricants are used, and the norm is exceeded. The services of the AMSs were very expensive for the cooperatives and took half or more of the labor day. Because of this, the cooperative members tried to use the machines of the AMSs as little as possible.

The planning and carrying out of crop purchase had a particularly retarding effect. "The unreality of the purchase plan came from mistaken planning methodology: instead of proceeding from actual possibilities, these possibilities were construed from the pattern of the plan! Planning went approximately like this: first the obligations were determined on the basis of the sowing plan, and not of the actually sown areas; then needs were enumerated, that is, those quantities of grains the producer had a legal right to retain; the sum of the first and the second gave the quantity of production that had to be achieved! Of course this paper production often deviated from the actual. An extreme case ... shows that the fourth category of households in the Vardarac region, if all requirements were to be satisfied, would have had to grow 48 quintals of grain per acre! Such mistakes, clearly, are corrected, but it is impossible to correct these numerous situations completely ..." [51, p. 28]. In addition, crop purchasing was conceived by the authorities in Baranja almost exclusively as a measure for the forced founding of cooperatives. The plan of livestock purchase was substantially greater than the natural increase. The consequences were obvious. The number of livestock fell with the size of the holding, so that among the largest holdings there were, in all, one cow and less than four pigs to five households. In 1949, nonfarmers had more pigs on the average than peasants. "To strengthen the cooperative stock of pigs ... last year it was the practice that peasants could satisfy their obligations in the delivery of pigs also by giving pigs over to the cooperative in which they had entered instead of to the purchasing organs. This year officially this is not done, but the cooperative members have continued with that practice, for they say that the main thing is that one delivers over to the state, and the cooperative is also the state" [51, p. 42]. Indeed, it was thus. In an etatist system, cooperatives — as well as all else — were state institutions. Thus the failures of collectivization are basically explained.

Finally, we can once more concisely define the overall agricultural problem of that period. When, in an undeveloped country with peasant agriculture, the attempt is made to accelerate economic development, then one of the key problems is to accelerate the development of agriculture as well. If it is a socialist country and the desire is to avoid the development of capitalist relations in agriculture, then the small-holding structure must be conserved. The traditional small and middle peasant holding, however, is not capable of fast expansion. State farms represent a relatively small segment of agriculture and are not in a position to move the huge peasant masses. The Yugoslav political leadership and experts sought a solution in cooperatives. But imposed cooperation, no matter how rationally conceived, could not function well. Force and pressures discredited the idea of cooperation, which perhaps under other circumstances could have given substantially greater results.[9] Since police methods were not acceptable, a new solution had to be sought.

In this period, a book appeared that synthesized the basic attitudes toward collectivization in etatist construction Yugoslav style. This was Ekonomika agrara FNRJ [Agrarian Economics of the Peoples' Republic of Yugoslavia], by Professor Mijo Mirković. The conceptions and experiences of the succeeding period were reflected in the books of his student, V. Stipetić [1; 2].

---

9. It is characteristic that after the first spontaneous association into work cooperatives immediately before and after the Liberation — a spontaneity that was quickly ended by the heavy hand of state regimentation — experimentation with communist association ceased. American communes, Israeli kibbutzim, and similar communities in other countries remained unknown, and the one-time partisan ethos was forgotten.

11. COOPERATION: IDEAS AND IMPLEMENTATION

Discussion Themes

The bad experiences and final failure of collectivization of course prompted reflection and reexamination of earlier attitudes. The first reaction was a return to renewed examination of the Marxist texts. As early as 1950, Bakarić, in a study of land rent in the transitional stage, considered Soviet theory and practice in the light of the positions of Marx, Engels, and Lenin. Bakarić concluded that the Soviet nationalization of the land in 1917 "is the result of peasant striving for the creation of a small-scale peasant farm, and not the transition of agriculture from capitalism to socialism. In this form, differential rent also . . . belongs to the producer" [58, p. 125]. This nationalization "gave land to small producers, and later cooperatives, for perpetual use. It exempted land from commerce . . . but precisely greater commerce in land, greater opportunity of obtaining it, is the main sense of land nationalization . . ." [p. 96]. In studying the texts, Bakarić happened upon Engels's statement that handing over land rent to the state is equal to the elimination of individual private ownership [62, p. 575], but he still did not confront completely the far-reaching economic policy consequences of this fact.[10]

Immediately after the Liberation, primarily Stalin and Lenin were read and used, for they gave the pattern for concrete solutions to agricultural problems. After 1948 intensive study of the original texts of Marx and Engels was begun, and the cited work of Bakarić was one of the first results. However, Kautsky's Agrarian Question, published in 1899, and the most complete Marxist work in this field, was practically unavailable. In 1953, Kautsky's book was published in translation with a Foreword by I. Lavrač. In his Foreword, Lavrač quotes with approval W. Liebknecht's opinion that peasants will "voluntarily go over to cooperative farming, for isolated they will not be able to withstand the competition with large state farms, until finally they realize that the best form of farming is direct labor for the benefit of the proletarian state" [52, p. x]. A position of Kautsky cited later also has the same meaning: "The revolution for which Social Democracy strives

---

10. The consequence is that land can be economically nationalized without touching the right of ownership. It is sufficient to expropriate rent. The author of this study drew the same conclusion in another context in 1958 [107, pp. 402-6].

ultimately is not a <u>legal</u>, but an <u>economic</u> revolution, it does not represent an overturning in <u>property relations</u> but in the <u>mode of production</u>. Its goal is not the abolition of private property, but the abolition of the capitalist mode of production; it seeks the abolition of private property only insofar as it is a means for the abolition of the capitalist mode of production. The greatest difficulties that confront socialism do not lie in the legal, but in the economic sphere" [p. xxxiv].

The same year that Lavrač translated Kautsky, Stojanović completed a dissertation whose theoretical foundation was an intelligent adaptation of the positions of Marx, Engels, Kautsky, and Lenin. Although these authors later were often treated in textbooks and in a number of issues of the journal <u>Ekonomika poljoprivrede</u> [Economics of Agriculture], nothing essential was added. Stojanović saw the essence of the problem to lie in the question of how to achieve large-scale production while preserving the predominance of small peasant private ownership of the land. Would the process be the same as in the creation of capitalist large-scale agricultural production? Is there some special way or ways? [59, p. 11].

According to Marx, small commodity production constantly generates capitalism and the producers are stratified: a minority become capitalist producers, and the majority wage laborers. In agriculture, the same thing happens, only because of landownership capitalism penetrates slower than in industry. Because of this, small commodity production is maintained in agriculture even in very developed capitalist countries. Engels, as was already mentioned above (section 9), divided peasants into small peasants, who work themselves; large peasants, who are already capitalist producers; and middle peasants, who represent the transitional category. The task of the socialist state is to expropriate the holding of the large landowner and help the small peasant escape proletarianization, inevitable in capitalism, by combining with others to achieve large-scale production. Stojanović commented on the basis of Yugoslav experience, however, that in an undeveloped country the state lacks the material means to aid the rational joining together of peasants, and "because of general backwardness of the economy, individual production combined with various forms of cooperative association will for a long time be more profitable than the sort of collective production in agriculture that would immediately arise by the joining of backward, poor, dispersed farms" [59, p. 39].

Kautsky, after studying statistical data, criticized the conception that the entire development of capitalism in agriculture will be reduced to the suppression of the small holding by the large. In industry, concentration of capital can be carried out independently of centralization. In agriculture, this does not work: the ruin of many small farms is the precondition of the emergence of large-scale farming. This is why large-scale production in agriculture develops so slowly. In the period of primitive accumulation, centralization occurred through the forcible driving of peasants from the land. Later, this was done by mortgages — that is, by selling overindebted peasant holdings. A qualitative difference in technique between the large and small farm appears only in capitalist agriculture, and only then does large-scale farming achieve economic advantages. In socialist development, industry plays the key role. If the sugar mills, dairies, breweries, flour mills, and so on, are "united in one hand," then the producers of sugar beets, milk, hops, and grain, instead of partial workers of the capitalist enterprise, become partial workers of the state enterprise. Such socialization of production is much more important than mere membership in cooperatives.

Lenin observed that under capitalism the peasant must pay interest to the bank, taxes to the state, and a part of the surplus to the industrial capitalist in nonequivalent exchange, and thus his small commodity production becomes a part of total capitalist production, and the peasant himself remains only the formal owner of his means of production. After the victory, the working class will expropriate the holdings of the large landowners and will organize cooperative farming on their land. Agricultural cooperatives should be given larger loans even than those in heavy industry, for backward agriculture pulls back the entire economy. However, asked Stojanović, "industry very poorly developed, agriculture extremely backward, both with few possibilities for accumulation . . . who now should help whom when both need help? Fast construction by its own forces of such a very backward, semifeudal, poor country cannot occur without powerful exploitation of agriculture. Up to now the village in every backward country had to play the role of the basic source of accumulation if one wished to build up industry quickly. However, every more forceful drawing of accumulation out of agriculture necessarily had to be connected with the strengthening of central state power in a way that by no means can correspond to the socialist form of democracy" [59, p. 79].

In addition to the reexamination of economic policy and ideological positions, in this period the first work with measurements of economic phenomena appeared, which in the sphere of agriculture, as in other spheres of economics, would later allow a more rigorous and more scientific approach to the solution of problems. In his doctoral dissertation, Stipetić carried out measurements of agricultural production in Croatia for the previous seventy years [60]. Toward the end of this period, the same author also published the first study of supply and demand for agricultural products on the Yugoslav market [57].

From 1864, when Marx established on the basis of statistical data that the number of landowners in England and Wales had decreased by 11 percent in the previous decade, which meant that concentration of landownership had also increased by that amount [61, p. 354], it was taken as a fact among Marxists that the large holding pushes out the small.[11] The conclusion was drawn that the large holding is more efficient economically than the small, just as large-scale production is economically more efficient than small-scale production in industry. This conclusion obtained the force of an axiom on which all postwar discussions and economic and administrative measures in agrarian policy were based. Kautsky had already established, however, that the trends Marx observed in the 1850s changed in the last quarter of the past century, and not only did the rapid disappearance of the small farm fail to continue, but in some places the number of small farms even tended to increase [52, p. 130]. Kautsky explained this by the agrarian crisis in Europe, which occurred under the influence of overseas competition and struck capitalist farms more than independent peasant farms. This is approximately all that was known. We cited above one of Mirković's positions in which he tries to establish the advantages of large-scale agricultural production on the basis of ex ante analysis, without supplementing it with measurements (see pp. 104-5). Not until 1959 was the question addressed, when B. Milosavljević devoted the greater part of his dissertation to this matter [63]. Stipetić cited more recent statistical data in his textbook [1]. Both established that in the

---

11. In fact, independently of the statistical basis, the conclusion is methodologically incorrect: because of the increase in productivity of labor, the agricultural labor force declines, and abandonment of agriculture leads to the reduction of the number of holdings. But this still does not say anything about changes in the structure of holdings. The small holding is not defined by the amount of land, but by the amount of production relative to the available technology.

United States the total number of farms, as well as the area comprised of farms of less than 100 acres, rose until 1935, and then the tendency was reversed. However, even before the turning point, large farms — those with more than 500 acres — increased still faster, and their share of the total area rose from 32 percent in 1900 to 66 percent in 1964 [63, pp. 31, 33; 1, p. 84]. Now, it is characteristic that, in spite of centralization, farms remain family enterprises (although capitalistic) and are not transformed into corporations, which escaped the attention of Stipetić although it was observed by Milosavljević [63, p. 38]. Today in the United States, a family without hired help is considered able to work about 300 acres, and this area is constantly increasing (in the 1950s it was 160 acres). American farms are classified statistically into six groups according to the value of products sold. Even in the highest group, in which farms achieve sales of over $25,000 annually, there was no hired labor on a fourth of the farms in 1954, and on the average in this group, there were fewer than five hired workers per family worker [63, pp. 47-48]. Bićanić observed this phenomenon and explained it as the result of the deproletarianization of agriculture. In England, between 1871 and 1951, the number of farmer-owners increased by 12 percent and the number of hired workers fell by 46 percent. In France, from 1896 to 1946, the number of owners per 100 farms with hired labor increased by 30 percent and the number of hired workers fell by 15 percent. In the United States, between 1919 and 1950, the number of farmers fell by 36 percent and the number of agricultural workers by 43 percent [113, pp. 159-161]. It appears that technological progress in agriculture makes hired labor too expensive.

A tendency toward centralization is also observed in England [63, p. 63; 1, p. 90]. In Sweden, however, the number of holdings below 10 and above 100 hectares is falling [63, p. 67]. The same trend toward evening out, with the same limits, was also observed between 1935 and 1957 in Germany [63, p. 70] and to some extent in France [1, p. 90]. In the 1960s in Western Europe, between 67 and 98 percent of all farms comprised less than 20 hectares of land [8, p. 20].

It follows that in the Anglo-Saxon countries centralization is taking place, and in some European countries there is an evening out, while in both cases family farms dominate. To what extent is all this relevant to the Yugoslav situation?

In Yugoslavia, both processes are observed: evening out in the individual sector — the category of 5 to 8 hectares — and centralization in the collective sector, where the average size of collective farms has grown from 322 hectares in 1950 to 3500 hectares in 1969, when 88 farms larger than 5000 hectares possessed half of the area in the collective sector [2, pp. 88-89]. What conclusions should be drawn? Should centralization be continued? If so, should it be stopped at 3500 hectares? Or should one take as a norm the Soviet sovkhoz, which in 1962, on the average, included 28,300 hectares of agricultural land [64]? Or should greater attention be paid to the family farm? Statistical comparisons are merely the first step in seeking an answer to this question.[12] The axiom of unqualified enlargement has shown itself to be very problematic. A serious study that would treat this question from the standpoint of Yugoslav conditions has yet to appear. Yugoslav conditions, from the social standpoint, mean self-management, and from the economic standpoint, mean maximizing production per hectare until the reserves of labor are exhausted, and then maximizing labor productivity. (One should, however, note the research of D. Pejin, who established that in Vojvodina, during 1953-56, the most favorable size for agricultural estates from the standpoint of productivity and profitability was 1500 to 2000 hectares. In the next two years, this size fell, but in 1960-62 it increased to 3200 hectares [117, pp. 149-50].)

In the meantime, we can anticipate a finding of that future study. The basic economic difference between the average industrial and the average agricultural enterprise is that, for rationally organized agricultural production, substantially less total capital is needed (although perhaps more capital per worker) than for building an automobile or textile factory. In agriculture, nature carries out production and people only the preparatory and finishing operations, for which relatively little mechanization is necessary. A farm household can efficiently utilize this mechanized equipment — a tractor with attachments, and possibly a truck and com-

---

12. The literature cites as production units that correspond to the level of technological development in the near future: purely crop-growing holdings of 200 to 300 hectares; purely pasture holdings of 100 to 150 cows or 100 hectares of agricultural area; specialized holdings with small areas. In a memorandum of the Council of the European Common Market the following sizes are cited: grain growing and industrial crops on 80 to 120 hectares; milk production with 40 to 60 cows; meat production with 150 to 200 cattle; pig raising with 450 to 600 head [108, pp. 75-76].

bine — with its own labor.[13] However, just as in industry, in addition to small enterprises, there are large ones with which the former cooperate, so also in agriculture family farms do not exclude, but rather presuppose, the existence of agroindustrial combines and estates as well as a whole network of institutions that enable the system to function efficiently and without slowdowns. What should be done is to define precisely the function of each component of the system.

Formation of a Concept of Cooperation

After the new 1954 decree on agricultural cooperatives, which made the organization somewhat more flexible, there was a further reduction in the number of cooperatives, due to mergers. The cooperatives continued to engage primarily in trade and increasingly in crop purchases, and then in hotel and restaurant management and handicrafts, while in 1954 the income from agriculture amounted to only 9 percent [36, p. 105]. Since the decline of the peasant work cooperatives meant the end of an orientation toward that cooperative form, attention gradually began to be directed to agricultural cooperatives. At the end of 1955 and the beginning of 1956, these cooperatives began to enter into certain business arrangements with individual peasants beyond the earlier buying and selling relationships.

At the same time, the study of Marxist texts, discussed in the previous section, led in 1956 to the posing by H. Hasanagić of the question: If, in the capitalist system, peasant farms function as parts of that system, why could not the Yugoslav socialist economy include the small commodity producers in a similar way without touching their ownership of the land? [65, p. 65].

---

13. Well-known agricultural economist Georgescu-Roegen observes that "there is no parallelism whatever between the laws of scale in agriculture and industry. Someone can grow wheat in a pot and raise chickens in the yard, but no enthusiast can make an automobile merely with the tools from his workshop.... Second, the role of the time factor is entirely different in the two activities. We can shorten the time for weaving a yard of cloth by machines, but until now we have not been able to shorten the breeding time in livestock raising or (more importantly) the ripening period of plants." In addition, in agriculture the natural rhythm must be observed, while in industry something can be done tomorrow instead of today. Finally, in contrast to the numerous new materials and sources of energy in industry, in agriculture we continue to rely on plants and animals, which is reflected in differences in the change of yields with the increase of the volume of production [114, p. 5].

The solution was obvious: socialization — but of production, rather than of land — should be carried out not by nationalization of the land or by the joining of land in cooperatives, but by the use of social means of production on individual farms on the basis of contracts and without touching the peasants' private ownership of the land [66, p. 69]. As early as April 1957, this idea was incorporated into the Resolution of the Federal Peoples' Parliament on the Prospective Development of Agriculture and Cooperatives, and the means for its implementation was found in the agricultural cooperative. Through their mechanized equipment and personnel, the cooperatives should make possible the rapid increase of production on the peasant holding while differentiating the functions of the peasant as owner and as producer: the producer makes progress, and his ownership is not touched. Thus cooperation was born as a specific system of production cooperation between collective and individual farms.

The following year, this economic policy orientation was fixed in the new Program of the LCY:

Increasing agricultural production and its socialist transformation are only two sides of a single process. Every prospect of advancing agriculture through capitalistic development and the enrichment of some agricultural producers at the expense of others in our conditions is economically and politically impossible. The policy of the League of Communists of Yugoslavia in the sphere of agriculture consists of the gradual socialization of the process of production in agriculture through the development of means of production in the framework of the present socialist agricultural organizations and other socialist forms that may arise in the development of that process and without forcible intervention in individual ownership of land. . . . The general farming cooperative is one of the suitable forms by which small owner haphazardness will gradually be surpassed and large-scale socialist production be developed. In its activities the general farming cooperative should develop those forms of production cooperation that essentially increase production. . . . The decisive material-economic stimulus for various forms of the teaming of the individual peasant with the cooperative should be the material interest of the individual agricultural producer and the economic interest of the commune that invests social means in the development of agriculture. This individual economic interest will convince the peasant of the advantage of the large-scale socialist farm over the backward, small, and unorganized one [67, pp. 212-14].

On the basis of this political line, investments in agriculture were substantially increased (see Table 12) and a third of these investments were made through the general agricultural cooperatives.

In 1959, Kardelj's book on socialist policy in the village appeared; in a sense, it completed the formation of the cooperative conception [68]. Kardelj started from the position that the basic means of production in social ownership make possible the growth of the economic strength of the socialist sector to the extent to which those means are more profitably employed in agricultural production, regardless of the ownership of the land. That is, these means, by their economic role, "create a certain system of economic relations in the village and productive interdependence, which become the main factor in the gradual transformation of individual farms in the sense of their gradual inclusion in the social production process, by which inevitably the form of private land-ownership also must begin to change" [p. 15]. This goal is attained by cooperation, which represents "every form of productive cooperation of socialist economic organizations — agricultural estates, peasant work cooperatives, general agricultural cooperatives and their farms, and in certain cases even industrial and trade organizations — with individual peasant farms, which prepares, establishes, begins, or develops elements of the social process of production on socially organized ... complexes of land and which enables socialist economic organizations to become the carriers of production in such a process, on the basis of social investments and social basic means of production" [p. 151]. This approach requires certain concessions, as, for example, paying rent to the peasant owner. But this concession is incomparably more acceptable than the alternatives: capitalist stratification of the village, expropriation, or Stalinist collectivization [pp. 154-57].

Kardelj further expected — and this is, in fact, a repeat of the conceptions of the earlier period — that the farms of the GACs would represent the socialist core about which large-scale farming would gradually form, for the cooperative farms would expand by purchase and renting of land [pp. 227-28]. The cooperatives themselves would operate differently under different conditions:

1. Under conditions of backward agriculture and its own underdevelopment, the cooperative would engage predominantly in buying and selling and giving expert and technical aid to the peasant.

2. The more developed cooperative would engage in crediting, contracting, and offering services in mechanized land cultivation.

3. Well organized and equipped cooperatives would approach joint cultivation of the land with the peasant.

4. If under condition 3 the mutual relations were established so that the cooperative was the owner of the output and the peasant was paid rent and wages for labor in money, then it would be in fact a work cooperative [pp. 234-35].

However useful, cooperation is nevertheless only a transitory phenomenon. By its own development it will create the conditions for its disappearance, for it will gradually be replaced by increasingly developed socialist relations. When "on some 30 to 40 percent of the arable land a modern technological process of agricultural production is established that will give socialist productive and other economic factors the absolutely ruling role in the sphere of production and market for agricultural products ... [then] the problem of the further broadening of socialist relations in agriculture will lose that social and political severity that it has today" [pp. 296-97].

These attitudes represent a significant and positive evolution in relation to the conceptions of the previous period. Life will confirm this judgment by the exceptional acceleration of agricultural production (see Table 12). However, the presence of the old centralist vision of socialism in which the individual agricultural producer is treated as a necessary evil is still felt. He is no longer an enemy of socialism, but neither is he its integral element. Hence, it is necessary to restrain and control him. It can be expected that the limitation of this conception will soon appear also as a limitation to the further expansion of Yugoslav agriculture.

Agricultural Cooperatives and Cooperation

Although in principle every collective farm can organize cooperation with the peasants — and, for example, many agricultural combines founded economic units for cooperation — nevertheless agricultural cooperatives emerged as the main instrument of cooperation. The number of agricultural cooperatives constantly and rather rapidly declined, mainly because of forced mergers. The number of cooperative members also fell, for, as was already mentioned, only the heads of households remained members to avoid payment for additional shares. In 1956, 47 percent of agricultural households were enrolled in cooperatives [47, p. 96]. The volume of activity of the cooperatives, measured by number employed, land area, and number of tractors, increased rapidly during the entire period. The turning point in agrotechnology came in 1957, when the input of artificial fertilizers per hectare of arable land sharply increased and, with it, yields as well. Increasing investment is reflected in production jumps, a rise in the number of tractors, and land purchase.

131

Table 22

General Agricultural Cooperatives, 1953-64

	No. coops.	No. members (thousands)	No. employed (thousands)	Total area (thousand ha.)	No. tractors (thousands)	No. cattle (thousands)	Use of fertilizer (kg./ha.)
1953	7117	3.1	60	132	2.0	6.2	—
1954	6538	2.0	—	145	10.5	10.5	58
1955	6066	1.4	69	149	2.7	13.4	140
1956	5576	1.3	77	181	4.1	12.4	—
1957	5472	1.5	80	203	6.3	15.4	732
1958	5242	1.4	87	290	10.2	26.9	603
1959	4817	1.6	99	429	15.0	70.0	695
1960	4086	1.5	110	635	16.4	123.0	560
1961	3228	1.4	113	691	16.7	99.6	506
1962	2816	1.4	116	752	18.1	107.1	747
1963	2438	1.4	114	899	19.1	107.8	826
1964	2096	1.5	118	962	19.0	119.3	776

Source: SZS, Jugoslavija 1945-64; SGJ-1962; SGJ-1965.

To summarize what has been said earlier, cooperation between cooperatives and peasants, in essence, consists in the peasants' bringing in land, manpower, and inventory and the cooperatives' assisting with mechanization and providing materials and expert management of operations. The following forms of cooperation developed [2, p. 106; 47, pp. 168-87; 23, p. 125; 66, pp. 105-28]:

1. In providing services to peasants, the cooperatives supply high-quality seed, artificial fertilizers, chemicals for plant protection, and services in land cultivation with their mechanized equipment. Services are also provided to nonmembers, but members obtain them somewhat cheaper, usually by 10 percent.

2. Crediting consists of the assumption by the cooperative of the obligation to deliver materials or breeding stock to the credit user, or to carry out certain work operations. In crop raising, the period for credit repayment is usually the time of the harvest. Credit can also be partly repaid in kind.

3. Contracting is an agreement by which the peasant obligates himself to take artificial fertilizer in prescribed quantities and selected seed or livestock, to use the machine services of the cooperative, and to apply protective chemicals, and, upon completion of the production process, to deliver a certain quantity of output to the cooperative.

4. Land renting enables cooperatives to extend the areas of their

farms. Land is usually rented out by mixed and aged households that lack adequate manpower to work it.

5. Joint production means that the cooperative and peasant jointly contribute labor and resources, jointly bear risk, and share the incomes obtained. In practice, several subforms have developed:

a) Cooperation on the basis of guaranteed yields. The cooperative carries out complex cultivation of the land on certain of the peasant's parcels on credit, and the peasant obligates himself to carry out the necessary agrotechnical measures according to the advice of an expert. The cooperative then guarantees a certain yield. If this yield is not obtained, the cooperative compensates for the difference; if it is exceeded, the cooperative and the peasant share in the surplus in certain percentages. In this type of joint production, the risk for the cooperatives is rather high, so this sort of agreement is avoided.

b) Cooperation on the basis of joint investment and division of income. The cooperative cultivates the land and gives the peasant materials or livestock and feed. The peasant performs all the planned operations with the labor of his household. The total income is divided proportionally to the share in the costs of production with or without prior calculation of rent.

c) Cooperation on the principle of division of the increased yield above the average yield. The cooperative credits the peasant with services and material and shares in the achieved increase of yields, receiving from 10 to 35 percent.

d) Three-way cooperation. The participants are a farm with a land surplus, a farm with a labor surplus, and a cooperative that serves as the organizer of the undertaking.

Special mention can also be given to cooperation in long-term plantings (e.g., trees) and so-called complex cooperation in which the peasant enters his entire farm in the arrangement.

Vasić, expressing a widespread opinion, terms the first four types lower forms and the last a higher form of cooperation. This is a remainder from the prevailing mentality during the period of lower and higher forms of peasant work cooperatives, in which the higher forms naturally are more socialist and more desirable. In a survey carried out in 1962, D. Vukčević established the following shares for individual forms of cooperation: contracting, 42.3 percent; services, 33.7 percent; credit, 17.0 percent; renting, 4.7 percent; and joint production, 2.3 percent [66, p. 128]. It follows that again — as with the PWCs — the "more socialist" forms are least represented.

Vukčević also tried to determine the motivation of peasants and cooperative management in participating in cooperation. In 32 percent of the cases, the peasants answered that for them the main reason for entering into cooperative relations was the lack of draft animals and implements as well as of money for the purchase of special seed and artificial fertilizer. Another 25 percent of peasants turned to cooperatives because of the application of new methods of production with the aim of achieving higher yields. Finally, another 23 percent of those surveyed cited both reasons as an explanation. This accounts for 80 percent of all those surveyed [p. 132]. Among cooperative managements, the most favored form of cooperation is contracting (44 percent), followed by crediting (22 percent), while 15 percent declared themselves for joint production [pp. 134-35]. The reason for such positions is the desire to achieve the greatest material benefit for the cooperative (42 percent of responses) or the belief that the cooperative must apply those forms that the peasant most willingly accepts (31 percent) [p. 138]. With respect to the achieved results, in joint production 43 percent of the cooperants emphasize, in the first place, improvement of the quality of land and the achievement of higher yields, while 23 percent state that they derived no benefit whatever. In contracting and crediting, 81 percent of the cooperants consider the increase in yields to be the basic result [p. 151]. In services, 77 percent of those surveyed emphasized above all the improvement of land quality [p. 156].

The maximum cooperation was attained in 1964-68, when nearly half of all peasant households and about 20 percent of their sown area were included [69, p. 64]. It is interesting that cooperation is more widespread in the developed than in the undeveloped regions. In 1960, on the average 24 percent of peasant households in Yugoslavia were participating in cooperation. By republics, the figures are: in Montenegro, 6.9 percent; Bosnia-Herzegovina, 8.6 percent; Macedonia, 14.5 percent; Croatia, 22.3 percent; Serbia, 31.8 percent; and Slovenia, 44.2 percent [70, p. 11]. Households with over 5 hectares of land, which in addition also have the most members capable of working, participate in cooperation most frequently and for the longest periods [109, p. 496].

Table 23 shows the already mentioned increase of yields during this period. The characteristic ordering of yields according to category of farm, which is narrowly correlated with the amount of investment, can also be seen. Peasant work cooperatives caught up with the agricultural estates, but general cooperative farms

Table 23

Yields on Yugoslav Farms, 1954–73 (in quintals/hectare)

	1954	1956	1957	1958	1959	1960	1962	1964	1966	1968	1970	1973
Wheat												
Combines and estates	9.0	15.4	23.5	24.6	39.4	32.8	32.0	27.0	40.1	35.6	29.8	43.0
Peasant work cooperatives	9.6	15.4	22.1	22.6	41.8	35.4	30.5	22.1	—	—	—	—
GAC farms	7.9	—	21.7	20.1	34.3	26.1	24.1	23.7	34.3	28.6	27.0	—
Individual farms in cooperation	—	—	22.8	14.1	29.4	23.8	18.4	19.4	29.2	23.8	19a	—
Individual farms not in cooperation	—	9.5	15.2	11.5	16.5	14.4	14.2	—	—	—	—	—
Corn												
Combines and estates	18.5	21.5	37.8	41.1	50.3	46.1	49.8	54.1	57.9	53.8	56.5	52.7
Peasant work cooperatives	17.8	22.7	35.7	40.2	48.7	46.9	46.9	54.2	52.4	—	—	—
GAC farms	11.3	—	33.0	33.4	39.6	38.4	38.7	47.3	52.4	47.5	38.6	—
Individual farms in cooperation	—	—	39.4	21.4	37.2	34.1	30.3	41.7	45.7	40.7	25a	—
Individual farms not in cooperation	—	12.7	20.8	14.6	23.2	20.7	17.3	—	—	—	—	—
Sugar beets												
Combines and estates	149	153	283	253	321	357	322	374	448	448	403	—
Peasant work cooperatives	168	196	275	246	320	269	386	—	—	—	—	—
GAC farms	117	—	245	231	256	287	247	335	409	393	353	—
Individual farms in cooperation	—	—	218	202	254	263	210	265	327	312	—	—
Individual farms not in cooperation	—	160	229	184	345	238	190	—	—	—	324a	—

Sources: SZS, Jugoslavija 1945–64; SPK [71, pp. 118–19]; SGJ–1963; SGJ–1965; SGJ–1974; Vasić [47, p. 115]; SGJ–1971; Leković [78, p. 838]; Čukanović [112, p. 145].
a. 1969, all individual farms.

attained perceptibly lower yields. Here too, however, the lag is only one of several years; general cooperative farms achieved greater yields toward the end of the period than did estates in the initial years. Similarly, relatively little lag is observed between the farms of cooperating peasants and general cooperative farms. However, peasants not cooperating lag more substantially, except in sugar beets. The general success of cooperation can be measured by this difference. (The real difference is somewhat less, for cooperation is more developed in regions with more fertile soil.)

Before proceeding to the analysis of tendencies in the development of agricultural cooperation, we must consider the cooperative's self-management structure. Until the 1954 decree on farming cooperatives, the agricultural cooperative was uniformly organized, and the cooperative was managed by an assembly and a management board elected by the assembly from among the ranks of the cooperative members. Cost of membership shares was minimal (100 dinars until 1952). Workers in the cooperative plants could be elected to the cooperative leadership only if they were members. After 1954, a cooperative could be organized in several ways, and the right of membership was automatically acquired by every worker or employee permanently employed by the cooperative or by any of its plants. In addition, the founding of a cooperative council, which could replace the assembly, was permitted and later became obligatory. In the self-management bodies, workers had to be represented in at least the same proportion as the number of persons employed in the collective in relation to the total number of cooperative members. In 1965, 20 percent of the cooperative council members and 23 percent of the management board members were workers [72, p. 13]. The authority of individual bodies was regulated more precisely by the decree on farming cooperatives of 1958. The assembly was comprised of all cooperative members and adopted the rules and production plans. However, the assembly lost almost all importance in favor of the cooperative council, which performed the same functions as the workers' council of an enterprise, including the election of the management board and the appointment of managerial personnel. The management board was an executive body like its counterpart in the enterprise. Now the workers and employees were represented in the management board by 44 percent of the members, and the peasant cooperants by only 56 percent [72, p. 22]. In the etatist period, 80-90 percent of peasant households were enrolled in GACs. In the second half of the 1950s, the percentage fell below 60 [72, p. 56]. With the development of cooperation, however, formal membership became practically pointless, for the cooperatives ceased to differentiate between members and cooperants. The evolution was completed with the law on agricultural cooperatives of 1965. The assembly appears now only on the occasion of the founding of the organization; the remaining self-management organs function in the same way as those in the enterprises. Membership in the cooperative is acquired through collaboration with the cooperative, which means that cooperants become members of the GAC [73]. In 1964, 47 percent of cooperative members, 4 percent of cooperants, and 47 percent of workers and employees were elected to cooperative councils [74, p. 87].

At the end of its evolutionary path, the agricultural cooperative, to some extent harmonized with the overall system of self-management, differs essentially from the traditional cooperative. The material base is comprised of nondistributable funds in which shares account for less than 1 percent. Thus the traditional security becomes pointless. Ristorno, or division of profits proportional to purchases, does not exist. De facto membership is acquired by founding a more lasting business relationship with the cooperative. By this alone, cooperants can also enter the cooperative's management bodies. Accordingly, a cooperative — like an enterprise — represents a self-managed economic organization in which the means of production are socialized and the producers exercise control of the production process. In a certain sense, this is a broadened agricultural machine station under the control of the workers and peasants who make use of its resources. The final result of the evolution is both specific and original.[14]

In daily operation, the cooperatives struggle with many difficulties. One of the most unpleasant is business uncertainty and the constant arbitrary administrative interventions of various political bodies: "Cooperative farms, tractors, livestock for breeding, and other things are taken away or transferred, often without compensation, to other economic organizations, institutions, or organs. What is worse, there are cases where cooperatives continue to pay installments and other obligations connected with the confiscated

---

14. New institutional forms are also appearing elsewhere in the world. In some Far Eastern countries — Thailand, Malaysia, Taiwan, Japan — consolidated farming has appeared. Here several small peasant farms are joined into a larger unit; the peasants retain ownership, but join together for the sake of more efficient cultivation and management [115, pp. 114-15].

fixed capital, common welfare assets (cooperative centers . . .), and for other things" [74, p. 91]. On the other hand, because of the unplanned equipping of cooperatives under outside influence, capacity is chronically underutilized. Employment of inexpert labor is imposed. Performance of services for certain enterprises or institutions at fixed prices is "recommended." Election of a smaller number of representatives of cooperative members and cooperants to the cooperative council is sought in order to prevent "peasantizing" [seljakovanje] [74, p. 91]. In the name of all-solving enlargement — most often motivated by losses — cooperatives are merged without much reflection, which removes the cooperative center from the local producers. (In addition, P. Milenković maintains that the larger cooperatives are both less productive and less profitable than the smaller ones [110, p. 911].) Or they are joined to estates and agroindustrial combines and thus lose independence. While in 1960 cooperation was almost exclusively carried out by cooperatives, in 1968, 70 percent of the area under cooperation fell to cooperatives, and 30 percent to other economic organizations [69, p. 65]. The old mentality of the etatist patron is clearly observable. It is therefore no wonder that, in 1961, 30 percent of the GACs conducted business with a loss. Half of all losses fell to GAC farms [66, pp. 11-18]. In 1964, a third of agricultural organizations — of which the GACs represent the overwhelming majority — operated with losses, and another third were on the borderline of profitability [75, p. 488].

Special problems appear in livestock cooperation. Such cooperation could activate the resources of cooperants — lodging space, livestock, feed — and land is not a condition of production to the same degree as in crop raising. Since a labor-intensive activity is involved, cooperation in livestock raising is especially recommended [70, p. 14]. However, the livestock market is extremely disorganized and unstable, which discourages cooperatives from forming more lasting and secure connections with individual producers. Cooperation in cattle raising suffered particularly great damage, for the production process is more long term. Because of uncertain conditions of production and marketing, here also cooperation had to be reduced to short-run crediting and promotion of somewhat improved peasant production [71, p. 125].

When in 1960 rebates for agricultural machines were further reduced, cooperatives tried to compensate by charging higher prices for services. But then the peasants began to acquire draft animals and to compete with the cooperatives in providing services. This was an indication of the new problems the cooperatives would encounter in the next period.

Peasant Work Cooperatives, Agricultural Combines, and Estates

After 1953 the peasant work cooperatives matched the yields of the agricultural estates (see Table 24), as well as their average size [2, p. 88]. However, in the self-management framework, the difference between an agricultural estate and a peasant work cooperative with a nondistributable land endowment was practically lost. Consequently, many of these cooperatives transformed themselves into estates or GAC farms. On the other hand, cooperatives with preserved landownership — even though there were no longer model rules with lower and higher forms, but cooperative members themselves could regulate their obligations — showed themselves to be unstable, while economic policy did not pay particular attention to them. Thus, for both reasons, the number of PWCs constantly and rapidly fell; there were 1165 in 1953 but only 7 in 1966, with a total number of employees of 1188, when

Table 24

Agricultural Combines and Estates, 1953-64

	No. farms	Employed persons (thousands)	Total area (thousand ha.)	No. tractors (thousands)	No. cattle (thousands)	Use of fertilizer (kg./ha.)
1953	666	—	432	—	56	—
1954	848	58	574	3.4	67	79
1955	914	63	586	3.7	72	124
1956	883	58	603	4.4	70	238
1957	776	56	637	5.7	92	548
1958	713	63	640	7.4	141	776
1959	559	82	663	9.8	242	752
1960	475	93	798	11.0	303	687
1961	469	101	894	13.3	321	576
1962	469	110	904	14.7	294	803
1963	348	121	1096	16.7	246	990
1964	300	139	1144	19.1	306	870

Source: SZS, Jugoslavija 1945-64.

the statistics ceased to report them separately [119, p. 9].[15]

Greater aid was provided to agricultural estates than to other agricultural organizations, for they were to serve as a practical example of the advantages of collective large-scale farming. Here also, however, as on the GAC farms, investments were made that were not thought out, and almost all the estates worked with losses; only after 1956 did they gradually free themselves from these losses [40, p. 333].

After 1953, on individual estates manufacturing plants were constructed or the estates were integrated with whole food products factories. Thus the formation of agroindustrial combines came about. In 1966, the combines had greater capital intensity than industry on the average, and possessed half of the total area of the collective sector. In Marković's opinion, combines ensure the linking of production flows, turnover of materials, processing, and final turnover, and therefore he considers that such a concept "could be carried over to the organization of all of agriculture" [76, p. 26].

The rapid reduction in the number of farms, along with the increase in area, led to a rapid increase in average size. Although concentration of production was pressed in the entire economy, nowhere did it come so much to expression as in agriculture. Not one study subjecting this process to serious analysis has been published, however. Stipe Šuvar expresses a general opinion when he says that "one of the first and basic conditions of industrialized, highly productive agriculture becomes the centralization and concentration of land in large productive farms, which will have a high organic composition of social capital, scientific organization of work and production, highly specialized producers, and production in large series" [77, pp. 10-11]. Šuvar sees in this the basic sense of socializing land and then examines the process by which this occurs.

From 1945 to 1964, the land under social ownership increased 3.2 times. At the end of the cited period, 30 percent of that land had been acquired under the agrarian reform of 1953, 24.6 percent by purchase, and 23.0 percent from other sources [p. 18].

Šuvar observes a substantial decline in the value of land and

---

15. At the same time in France, for example, producing peasant cooperatives were founded in which the peasants combine land, livestock, and machines. In 1963, there were 1000 such cooperatives, which Stipetić considers "have in greatest part a socialist character" [1, p. 91].

ascribes it to the rapid urbanization of the peasantry [p. 27].[16]
However, the influence of various restraints on the sale and use
of land should also be emphasized. In any case, cheap land facili-
tates purchase. Since the individual holding, in Šuvar's opinion,
succeeds less and less in satisfying social needs, "the unpost-
ponable task is posed before the social community of mastering
this development by organizing production on it and taking over
land that is abandoned and alienated, or that would be alienated
under certain conditions" [p. 56].

Finally, it is of interest to observe a phenomenon that, up to
now, has not been analyzed in published scholarly works. If the
profitability of production is defined as the ratio of accumulation
(allocations to funds, interest on loans, and insurance premiums)
to fixed (present value) and working capital, then the profitability
of individual forms of production can be calculated (unweighted
average) for the period 1964-68 from data processed by Pjanić
and others [118, Table 55]:

Agroindustrial combines	6.4%
Agricultural estates	6.8
General agricultural cooperatives	8.0
Peasant work cooperatives	9.6
Industry and mining	9.6

The largest and best equipped — the combines — are least profitable. The politically written off peasant work cooperatives
achieve the best results, which are equal to the industrial average. It is symptomatic that this phenomenon has not been subjected to scholarly analysis and that there has been no expert and
political discussion of it.

12. THE SEARCH FOR A NEW WAY AFTER 1964

The Crisis of Cooperation

The institutional development of agriculture began in the etatist
period with the authoritarian sponsorship of the state, and was

---

16. The price of land is lower in the fertile plains than in the livestock-
raising mountain areas [89, p. 455]. While before the war the price of land
amounted to thirty years' rent, in the 1960s it fell to the level of four or five
years' rent [104, p. 78].

continued in the following period with a partnership between state organized and aided collective farms and the peasants. The latter showed themselves to be incomparably more efficient economically. But in the course of a decade, the new conception to a large extent lost stimulative power, and social practice uncovered numerous gaps. It could be expected that in the next developmental phase the initiative of the direct producers and self-organized agriculture would be manifested without the administrative tutelage of the state. A conception of such a policy still is not formulated, however, and, for the entire period after 1964, a search for new ways, along with a slowing of agricultural expansion in the framework of a general slowing of economic growth, is characteristic.

The new period began with the economic reform of 1965. The reform had two features: on the one hand, a series of administrative obstacles to the freer development of the market, a market without discrimination and administrative arbitrariness, were removed; on the other hand, the conviction prevailed that producers should be left to themselves and that a laissez-faire approach is most suitable. The price reform reduced agricultural subsidies to the lowest level in Europe [88, p. 22]. Prices of artificial fertilizers and equipment increased relatively speaking, and they are now used less.[17] The freer market led to a 10 to 30 percent increase in land prices [89, p. 461], and land purchase was slowed. All these phenomena were reflected very differently in the agroindustrial combines and cooperatives.

Owing to the higher prices, agroindustrial combines and estates decreased their input of fertilizers and purchase of tractors, and because of the generally greater pressure of competition, they also decreased the number employed. These reductions were in good part compensated by the use of complex fertilizers (with a higher content of active substances), heavier tractors (with increased effectiveness), and better organization of work, so that yields were maintained. But there were no longer jumps in production. The number of livestock stagnated, and agricultural area increased by approximately the same as it declined in cooperatives. Thus, after 1964, the increase in area under social

---

17. The amount of various commodities that had to be produced in 1967, as compared to 1964, in order to purchase 1000 kilograms of mineral fertilizer were as follows: wheat — 44 kilograms vs. 28 kilograms; corn — 69 kilograms vs. 39 kilograms; sugar beets — 237 kilograms vs. 162 kilograms. For one 35-horsepower tractor, it was necessary to produce: wheat — 28.1 tons in 1967 vs. 28.5 tons in 1964; corn — 42 tons vs. 37.6 tons [85, pp. 24-25].

ownership was halted. Price increases for agricultural products along with reductions of tax burdens and increase of production led to the elimination of losses in the first two years. The opening of price scissors along with the slowing of production expansion led to a new explosion of losses. About half of all losses fell to agroindustrial combines, and a third to cooperatives [88, p. 73; 28, p. 849].

Table 25

Agricultural Combines, Estates, and Cooperatives, 1964-73

	Number of farms	Employed persons (thousands)	Agricultural area (thousand ha.)	Number of tractors (thousands)	Standard head of livestock (thousands)	Use of fertilizer (kg./ha.)
Agricultural Combines, Estates, and GAC Farms						
1964	296	139	1017	19.1	323	878
1966	278	146	1145	20.6	341	954
1968	272	105	1200	17.5	292	841
1970	269	118	1321	17.6	321	625
1973	306	94[a]	1512	17.5	—	599
Agricultural Cooperatives						
1964	2096	118	836	19	147	776
1966	1712	106	890	17	125	804
1968	1403	76	762	12	71	710
1970	1102	68	618	8	75	532
1973	832	26[a]	463	6	—	496

Sources: SGJ-1971; Statistički bilten broj 716; SGJ-1974.
a. In agricultural activities.

While stagnation of combines was noted, a drastic contraction of cooperatives occurred which began to resemble the decline of the peasant work cooperatives a decade earlier. Land areas and the input of artificial fertilizers per hectare were reduced by a third, and the number of cooperatives, number of employed persons, and number of tractors and livestock were halved in only six years. The reasons for these phenomena must be examined in more detail.

A freer market meant, above all, the liberation of the agricultural producer from the various forms of economic discrimination to which he was subjected. One such form was the administrative prevention of the purchase of tractors and equipment. "It was considered that the peasant holding must disappear at any price in the new socialist society ...," comments Stipe Šuvar, "and when the attempt at half-forced collectivization did not prove fruitful, it was maintained that equipping the peasant holding with machines (no matter how many) carries in itself the danger of restoring capitalist tendencies in the village and agriculture!" [79, p. 125]. Expressing this notion, D. Mutapović in 1956 cited the existence of peasant tractors as one of the important proofs of possible capitalist tendencies in the village [111, p. 101]. Three years later Edvard Kardelj set forth the following position, which was consistently applied in economic policy during the next several years:

The second essential administrative measure — that is, besides the limitation of the use of hired labor — is the ban on purchase of equipment for large-scale production, such as tractors and similar machines. These machines, even on a property of 8 to 10 hectares, which is our maximum, are not profitable. They can serve only for providing services to others or for some nonagricultural activities. In other words, these machines, if they appeared to a greater extent in private hands, could become the source of strengthening capitalist tendencies in the village. In any case, by tolerating such a state, we would encourage antisocialist tendencies in the village and create obstacles to the implementation of our own socialist policy in the village. Today agricultural producers own about 3000 tractors. ... I think that this private stock should not be touched, but neither should its increase or renewal be permitted [68, pp. 310-11].

An echo of the same idea appeared seven years later — when practice had already begun to deny it — in an article by B. Radovanović of the Agricultural Faculty in Zemun. He considered the demonstrated interest of the peasant in the tractor not as a sign of the vitality of and prospects for the family farm, but the consequence of the lack of development of the socialized sector. As soon as the socialized sector is strengthened and a surplus of agricultural products begins to appear on the market, the peasants will begin to free themselves of the unprofitable machines. "The more production for the market is developed, the less the family farm fulfills the conditions for survival. Since its disappearance is an economic law, it would be unreasonable to help it in the purchase of major means of production. To aid it in this would mean nourishing in it illusions of the possibility of survival of the small commodity producer, or strengthening the chains that bind it to small-scale production and low productivity, that is, to a low standard of living" [90, pp. 429-30]. In contrast to Kardelj, however,

Radovanović does not advocate preventing the purchase of tractors.

Kardelj and some other politicians and economists who took such positions neglected to answer several obvious questions. If the peasant farm is incapable of developing large-scale production, as it is maintained, then to what purpose is the administrative ban of such production? And if large-scale production could be organized on the peasant farm without the use of hired labor, why would that be antisocialist? If 10 hectares is too small an area for rational production, why isn't the maximum increased? And if a larger maximum would require hired labor — which is improbable — why couldn't two peasant households join together to jointly acquire a tractor? Life has slowly begun to give answers to these questions. Finally, the presumed "economic law" and "lower productivity" should be documented by analysis of the empirical data of a country on a higher level of general and agricultural development than Yugoslavia.

Even in the 1963 Constitution, individual work in agriculture was equalized with the work of a collective [80, p. 487], but the possibility of limiting the possession of machines was left to legislators. Many communes introduced prohibitive taxes on tractor purchase. The number of tractors increased slowly on individual farms until 1960 (see Table 13). However, communal assemblies soon perceived that by such practices they prevented the development of production on their own territory, and pressures were relaxed. The peasants began to buy the worn-out tractors of collective farms, and after 1964, regardless of regulations, new equipment as well. In 1967, a law was passed liberalizing the purchase of tractors by peasants. From then on, the peasant holding began to be rapidly equipped with modern equipment. From 1960 to 1969, the number of peasant tractors increased almost eight times, and the arable area per tractor fell from 1817 hectares to 223 hectares on the average and to 111 hectares in Slovenia [81, p. 20]. This is now judged as a positive phenomenon, and S. Sivčev of the State Chamber of Commerce of Serbia advocates the stimulation of this process by extending credit as well as by legalizing the existing forms of spontaneous association of peasants to achieve their economic interests [82, p. 133].

Earlier the agricultural cooperatives also often realized losses on the mechanized equipment intended for cooperation. These losses were increased by the reduction of rebates on equipment. However, before the reform the cooperatives had a monopoly on crop purchase and the supply of villages in their "operational area," and could cover these losses out of large price differences. Now this monopoly was abolished and prices for services had to be increased. Thus the peasant tractors became competitive. As early as 1967, B. Dimković observed: "A real danger already exists! In the grain-growing regions, one sees the joining of several more prosperous farms into so-called wild cooperatives for the sake of joint purchase of mechanized equipment for cultivation of the land" [83, p. 175]. Dimković feels that these producers could be attractive to a cooperative and that mutually beneficial cooperation could be established. But in practice the cooperatives have increasingly limited themselves to their own area and oriented themselves to trade.

In the materials prepared by the Committee for Agrarian Policy of the Presidency of the League of Communists of Yugoslavia for the First Conference of the LCY, it is stated that socialized farms and cooperatives "have participated and contributed to the development of overall agricultural production in three ways: by increasing area, intensifying production in their own facilities, and engaging in production cooperation with individual producers, they have influenced the penetration of modern technology and the production of individual producers" [84, p. 13]. In all three areas there was stagnation and even regression after the reform. The Committee explains this as a reaction to the economic and legal intervention of the state without the adequate development of the self-managed positions of the producer in the village — the cooperative was neither treated nor behaved as an economic organization, but as the means of expression of social interests conceived in a particular way. For individual products, collective farms were guaranteed higher prices than peasants. In 1969, when purchasing a tractor, a peasant still paid a special sales tax, from which he was exempt if he bought the tractor through a cooperative [85, p. 44]. The cooperative official charges a peasant a fee for the sale of livestock and sometimes has not even seen that livestock. The trade markup is high and is used to cover losses, as well as to pay the huge administrative apparatus.

Because of this, "the conviction is created in the producer that the cooperative deceives him" [84, p. 14]. Monopoly did not stimulate businesslike behavior. And when the conditions were changed, the cooperative fell into a crisis. A certain number of cooperatives sought an out through integration and business connection with the processing industry and larger trade enterprises. These cooperatives then began to bind more permanently to themselves those producers who could produce for the market. Various associations of individual producers for the production of certain commodities began to be formed [84, p. 30]. In a larger number of cooperatives, a psychosis of insecurity or disorientation was created. Investment was reduced, tractors were sold to peasants, experts were dismissed [86, pp. 4-5].

The cooperative had been formed as the instrument of cooperation. Cooperation had enjoyed the state's special material support in the form of premiums, rebates, prices, refinancing losses, and so on. The basic task of cooperation was to produce as much agricultural products as possible. The attempt was made to include as many peasant farms as possible by contracting, as large an area as possible, and application of as much artificial fertilizer and selected seed as possible without any petty analysis of the economic effects. When noneconomic interventions were eliminated by the reform and the cooperative reduced to the position of an economic enterprise, the whole construction began to collapse — and all the faster, since in the meantime Yugoslav agriculture had increased production so much that, for the first time since the war, difficulties in marketing appeared and supply exceeded demand.

In cooperation, the cooperative behaved as a distinct monopolist. "To the cooperants...," states Sivčev, "it remained to accept the conditions offered or to desist from cooperation. Most often the contracts were not the fruit of negotiation with the producers, but were contracts between an economically strong work organization with large capital and a large work collective and a cooperant lacking such possibilities.... The absence of sufficiently harmonized interests leads to the violation of contractual obligations: In boom periods the individual producers usually violate the agreements; and in downturns, the work organizations. Hence, with the exception of some organizations that take into account the interests of the individual producers, these producers accept the organization as a business partner but not as their own organization, regardless of the title it bears" [87, p. 7].

The much-promoted "highest" form of cooperation — joint production — failed the test of practice, just as the onetime "highest" form of work cooperatives. "Studies have shown, almost without exception, that the trend of cooperation went in the direction of the disappearance of the form of joint production..., the reason...was that this form of cooperation did not give the economic effect that should incite its further development; that is, it did not

give the peasant increased income, nor the cooperative the necessary accumulation." The organization is complicated and control
expensive. "The complexity of joint production is felt especially
in organizing production itself, in record-keeping, in caring for
and fertilizing plantings, and still more in dividing income between the peasant and the agricultural cooperative. This complexity causes a substantial increase in production costs, which,
along with rent payment, in the majority of cases makes this production unprofitable for the agricultural cooperative. On the other
hand, it excludes the peasant from the work process and reduces
his gross income, which in many households is equated with net
income; so, although it increases personal income, joint production is unacceptable to him" [23, p. 131]. To this it should be
added that the cooperant succeeded in attaining the same yields as
the cooperative when the latter organized the production process.

With respect to self-management, a tendency toward ever-
increasing limitation of the cooperants manifested itself. Fewer
and fewer peasants were elected to self-management bodies. Sivčev judges that the participation of cooperants in management was
most often reduced to the advisory right of voting [87, p. 11].
S. Filipović states that the decisive positions in the cooperative
were assured to the narrower work collective as the representative of society and the promoter of social goals and interests. Because of this, there was no obstacle to prevent the work collectives from hypertrophizing themselves by utilizing "primarily . . .
inexpert labor" and allowing "clan relations [to infiltrate] into
them and [provide] a livelihood for many social welfare cases or
people devoted to the order, and so on. This, on its part, contributed to halting self-management and the level of self-management relations. Such a situation did not derive and develop on the
basis of the acquisition and distribution of income but on the basis
of a model of the planned proportions of representatives of the
collective and of the cooperants. In such conditions, in determining the composition of representatives of both parties, account
was taken primarily of the individual's political relationship to the
cooperative and to society, so that some self-management bodies
contained not the best cooperants, but 'our' adherents, or peasant
demagogues imposed by the cooperants, who, in such a context,
'fought' for the interests of the cooperants and individual producers. This inflamed the conflicts between the cooperative collective and the cooperants . . . developed them and provoked disagreements, and above all checked and deformed self-management

forms and relations, reducing them to fiction and pseudo-self-
management. In such a situation, the feeling was generated among
the cooperants that a 'state' organization was what was involved
and that as much as possible should be ... extracted and obtained
from it" [97, p. 640]. Radovanović observes that cooperants had
no opportunity to participate in self-management precisely where
they were most interested, in the economic units that engaged in
cooperation. This led to various deformations: the bribing of
tractor drivers, poor care and irrational use of machines, and so
on. "Because they have no right to decide on the use of the means
of production nor on the distribution of the income of the economic
unit for cooperation, the cooperants depend on the subjective measures of those who work in the cooperative and particularly in that
economic unit, and they are uncertain with regard to the time and
quality of the services rendered. The reaction of individual agricultural producers to the insecurity and dependence in using cooperative machines is manifested also in the increased desire and
striving to buy large machines" [90, p. 427].

The Debate over Possible New Solutions

The crisis of the cooperatives and of cooperation evoked a lively
debate. Various opinions emerged; they could, however, be reduced to two basic positions. According to the first, the agricultural cooperative has no future. It should be reduced to what it,
in fact, is in essence — an economic enterprise, although sui
generis. Then the need for forming the traditional peasant cooperatives naturally appears. According to the second position,
the agricultural cooperative should be revitalized, above all by
more adequate participation of cooperants in management.

Throughout the entire postwar period, political forums strongly
resisted the self-initiated association of peasants in traditional
cooperatives. Such cooperatives were termed wild, and their formation was prevented. Bakarić explained the reasons for that resistance as early as 1952:

In our country, there was a tendency to force the League of General Agricultural Cooperatives to follow in the footsteps of the old Yugoslav prewar leagues,
which founded their activity on helping the peasant as a private owner, on helping to maintain his holding. This ... usually then developed so that the richer
peasant received greater benefit from the cooperative. I am not against such
things happening today too, but to orient all one's policy in this direction means
strengthening in the peasants the illusion that they can live well on their small

plots. And such illusions, if we continue to put them into the peasants' heads, will make it harder for them to pull themselves out of their poverty, will make it harder for them to create new employment, new production in the village itself. It will be harder to carry out those social transformations that must be carried out in the village [41, p. 330].

No one, however, ever tried to explain why plots would have to remain small, why the rise in productivity and the standard of living on the individual holding would be an illusion, why the experiences of prewar Yugoslavia would have to be repeated, and why the basic social transformations — which consist of the elimination of exploitation and the establishment of self-management— would not be possible. Two decades later, Bakarić's position was echoed by the Committee for Agrarian Policy of the Presidency of the LCY. Since the First Conference of the LCY adopted this position, let us cite the argumentation in its entirety:

Certain demands that the farming land maximum be changed and that cooperative ownership be reintroduced lack justification, for they have in view only some economic effects and do not take sufficient account of the long-term goals of our agrarian policy. In our agriculture, it is no longer such a problem to increase production, but the basic question is that of self-management socioeconomic relationships. The goal of agrarian policy is not the isolated individual farm, and a solution should not be sought through changing the size of the farm, but through its inclusion in large-scale production, increase of income, and socialization. Agriculture is an area in which economic and political currents and social problems mingle in a specific way, in which longlasting and planned work on overcoming all that has accumulated over decades is necessary, and this cannot be left to chance. Under our conditions, that way must be through association, cooperation — that is, socialization and self-management socioeconomic relations.... To be sure, the agrarian maximum is not some essential socialist principle, but a historically conditioned means of encouraging socialist processes. We could also do without it, but then progressive development would be hindered and illusions would be created about the possibilities of the "farmer's way" in the development of agriculture [84, p. 45].

As we can see, all the old questions remained unanswered, and the "illusions" without explanation. Only the extremely problematic implication of the possibility of conflict between increasing production and the development of social relations is new.

The cited attitudes checked the free examination of alternative solutions, so such examinations are rare. In a 1971 study of the relationship of the peasant farm and integrative processes in agriculture, S. Popović of the Institute for Agricultural Economics set out from the correct — although rarely understood — position that the peasant mode of production cannot develop into a separate social system, but is subordinate to the prevailing system: in capitalism, to the capitalist mode of production, and in socialism, to the socialist mode. Popović then comes to the conclusion that, in the nature of things, in large organizations individual producers can have only the role of an advisory body, no matter how democratic the form of their participation in management bodies. Self-management of cooperants according to the same principles as among workers sets up a political form without economic content. What is more, in relation to socialized farms, peasant farms represent nonunified and economically weaker units that can become the object of exploitation. The peasants can defend themselves by forming cooperatives for the purchase and use of major means of production, purchase of materials, and sale of their products, and for erecting small manufacturing workshops (dairies, smokehouses, refrigerators, etc.). These cooperatives would resemble the traditional cooperatives as regards shares, security, and profit sharing, and would differ in that employed persons would also be members or would participate in self-management. These cooperatives could, of course, also be work cooperatives. However, all this would not mean a renaissance of cooperation, and the cooperatives that would be founded would be led to integrational connections with large enterprises in the food industry and trade [91, pp. 747-54]. Similar positions are taken by M. Župančić of the Institute for Village Sociology in Zagreb [120] and S. Šuvar [116, p. 4].

The number of works concerned with revitalization of the agricultural cooperative is greater. S. Mitić states that the rapid enlargement of the area of agricultural cooperatives until 1963 had negative effects — which we have already cited — because the cooperatives were centralistically organized. But after that year, there was a decentralizing of cooperatives into economic units, so certain advantages could be drawn from enlargement. Thus economic units could be founded for which the conditions were lacking in small cooperatives (livestock feed factories, incubator stations, mechanical workshops, slaughterhouses). Self-management rights should, of course, be transferred to the economic units [92]. Radovanović considers that one such economic unit should be cooperation. The cooperants would manage the resources of this economic unit together with the unit's members [93, pp. 377-78; 90, p. 431]. M. Kovačević shares the same conception, in that he considers that the assembly of cooperative members should be reestablished as the body guiding general development [94, p. 620].

P. Milenković contributed the most elaborated study of the new organization of the agricultural cooperative. There are basically three alternatives: (a) the cooperative could become an economic enterprise; (b) it could be formed as an association of peasants; and (c) it could develop into an association of direct producers. Under the first alternative, the cooperative would lose a part of its present functions, for it would be organizationally separated from the peasants and would become only the organization of the work collective. Under the second, it would become less important as a socialist organization, for its exclusive goal would be the strengthening of the individual farm (it is not explained why this would be unsocialist). Therefore, the third alternative is the only acceptable one. But then the peasant should no longer be the economic partner of the cooperative, but the direct carrier of production in the activity that concerns him as a producer. And this means that cooperants should be sovereign in their economic unit. In order to be able to make decisions about the resources in cooperation, the peasants must participate in the formation of these resources by bringing in either their own means of production or money contributions. Until now, the peasant was only the external partner of the cooperative; relations were short term, and they always had to be established anew by new contracts. Instead of partnership with the cooperative through major social resources, mutual production relations of the peasants with social resources or their own resources or some combination of the two should be established and developed. Accordingly, it is not a matter of the cooperation of the peasant with the cooperative, but of the associated labor of the peasants within the structure of the cooperative. The economic unit for cooperation delegates its representatives to the cooperative council in proportion to its contribution to the cooperative's income, just as do other economic units. Both cooperants and the unit's personnel participate in the income of the economic unit for cooperation after deducting costs and allocations to the funds of the unit and the cooperative. S. Čukanović advocates a similar solution [112, pp. 186-88].

One of the themes which was still discussed in this period was the role of cooperative leagues. After the war, "basic" [osnovni] leagues were formed — district, state, and the main cooperative league of the Socialist Federal Republic of Yugoslavia — with obligatory membership of all cooperatives; in the second half of 1956, business leagues with voluntary membership were formed [112, p. 83]. The task of the business leagues was to provide services to cooperatives, processing or finishing their products, and managing sales, purchasing, and export for the cooperative's account. The leagues were formed rapidly and reached a maximum in 1958, when there were 340 of them throughout the country [112, p. 85]. At that time, Kardelj judged these leagues to be essential as a form of business association in agriculture and as a means of influencing agricultural development. "Such a role... cannot be performed by some organizations outside the economic relations in which the cooperatives develop and work, but only by the type of organization to which the cooperative is linked by its economic interest. And these are precisely the business leagues..." [68, pp. 245-46]. However, as early as 1960 the business leagues disappeared. That year a law was passed on association and business collaboration in the economy, and it was held that the cooperatives could associate themselves in the same way as all other enterprises. Many business leagues merged with agricultural cooperatives, and some became the core of business associations which were joined also by food-processing, trade, and other enterprises. In 1962, unified chambers of commerce were formed, and the basic cooperative leagues became councils of the chambers. Several other changes were made with the obvious perception that something was not right organizationally and that agriculture cannot simply be included in a general pattern. In 1967, Milija Kovačević of the Board for Cooperatives of the Federal Chamber of Commerce (FCC) stated that almost no one concerned himself with the trends and problems of agriculture and the village comprehensively and seriously, and that therefore cooperative councils needed to be reestablished [94, p. 622]. The following year, this was one of the official proposals of the Board for Cooperatives of the FCC, along with another that the leagues of agricultural cooperatives be included in the corresponding chambers [95]. But a year later, Radovanović expressed criticism of this proposal. The leagues as spiritual pastors watching over the cooperatives' work were long since surpassed. Guidance of the cooperatives was performed through the market. Cooperative leagues were also unnecessary from the viewpoint of expert and business aid to cooperatives, for these were obtained through the professional and business associations that had just replaced the surpassed earlier business leagues [93, p. 378].

As always, life began to judge these debates. In Slovenia and Dalmatia, business cooperative leagues were founded with an accent on developing production and business integration. In

Vojvodina, the chamber of commerce prepared propositions for a law on association of agricultural producers which, in addition to agricultural cooperatives, also anticipated two forms of peasant cooperatives. Terminology also changed. Peasants became "farmers" [poljoprivrednici]. In the "peasant amendment" to the Croatian Constitution, it is provided that farmers can join in various organizations of associated labor, and the latter, in turn, can form cooperative leagues.

Let us conclude. Postwar discussion on the institutional construction of socialist agriculture was — and still is — burdened by inherited ideology and uncritical interpretation of prewar experiences. From this sprang numerous disagreements, misunderstandings, and confusion of problems and categories. In this connection, it is sufficient to observe two basic and most frequent mistakes. One originates in the centralistic vision of socialism that was developed in the last century and then (brutally) applied in the Soviet Union and some other countries. Although Stalinist collectivization had long since been rejected, a burden remained in the conception that the individual producer is in some way an antisocialist element and that by various state measures — earlier administrative, and later more economic — he should be driven into a collective pen where he will be under control. However, if self-government is the essence of socialism, then the individual farm offers an ideal opportunity for the implementation of that principle. Every enlargement means removal from direct control and an increase in the danger of bureaucratic deformations. The criteria for an adequate solution are not preconceived models, but institutional forms that enable the maximal long-term increase of production. To find these forms, a certain amount of social experimentation is essential — of which there was more in Yugoslavia than anywhere else. Accordingly, the empirical material on the basis of which effective solutions can be constructed, has already been gathered.

The second error follows from the constant confusion of legal and economic ownership. If society does not collect differential (and absolute) rent — which today is in good part the case — then there is no essential difference between the combine and the peasant farm. Both the work collective and the peasant draw rent from the land and in that way privatize it. If, however, rent is absorbed into social funds — which can be achieved by a suitable tax policy — the combine and the peasant are again in the same position, but this time deprived of economic ownership of the land.[18]

The agricultural cooperative experienced a crisis, for it was an artificial combination of two different institutions: of the enterprise that should maximize its business result and of the agricultural station that should educate and help the backward to adopt modern agrotechnology without charging the full value of the services rendered. As soon as abundant state aid was eliminated, the cooperative freed itself of its development component and transformed itself into a pure business organization. At the same time, the agricultural stations "vegetate and cope by themselves" [84, p. 37].

The following institutions in Yugoslav agriculture were or are being created through agricultural development up until the present:

1) the individual peasant farm, which provides the greater part of production and where the greatest reserves lie for further increasing productivity of labor and yields per hectare;

2) combines and estates, which excell in modern agrotechnology and the achievement of marketable surpluses;

3) agricultural cooperatives, which provide services to peasants with their modern equipment and organize trade and other activity;

4) peasant cooperatives or organizations of the associated labor of farmers, which make possible the application of modern agrotechnology and marketing of products without the use of hired labor and state tutelage;

5) agricultural stations, which represent transplanters of superior agrotechnology developed with the aid of scientific organizations;

6) manufacturing and trading enterprises of the agroindustrial complex, which develop cooperation with agricultural producers in the same way as the large final producers do with their cooperants;

7) cooperative leagues and chambers, which make possible the business association and integration of agricultural producers in general economic and social currents.

These seven institutions represent a unique system of socialist agriculture. The system still is not completely built up, still does not encounter complete understanding among authoritative social factors, and still does not function efficiently. But there is little doubt that this system is also vitally capable of creating a way out of the temporary institutional crisis that occurred after 1965.

---

18. It is of interest to point out Stipetić's research on the trend of rent in modern agriculture [98]. Contrary to the expectations of the classical economists, rent per unit of area is falling and its share in agricultural income is falling still faster. In England, this share fell from 24 percent in 1878 to only 4 percent in 1952, and in France from 26 percent in 1901 to 9 percent in 1947.

LABOR-MANAGED ENTERPRISE IV

13. SELF-MANAGEMENT

Self-management is undoubtedly the most characteristic of Yugoslav institutions. Further developed into social self-government, it is the pivotal institution of the Yugoslav socioeconomic system. Moreover, Yugoslav social scientists are quite unanimous in the belief that, without self-government, socialism is impossible [1]. Thus the fate of socialism depends on the feasibility and efficiency of self-government. In this section, we will be concerned only with self-government as applied to business firms, which is usually denoted as self-management.

Self-management is not a Yugoslav invention. The development of this institution can be followed from the beginning of the last century [2, ch. 5]. Every social revolution from the Paris Commune onward attempted to implement the idea of self-management. At the very beginning of the Revolution in Yugoslavia, in 1941, workers were assuming control over factories in various places [3, p. 30]. With the establishment of central planning, the idea of self-management suffered a setback. As early as 1949, however, it was revived; by the end of that year, workers' councils were created as advisory bodies in 215 major enterprises, and in June 1950 the law was passed inaugurating the era of self-management.

For more than a decade, the basic organizational principles of self-management remained unchanged. All workers and employees of a firm constitute the work collective [radni kolektiv]. The collective elects a workers' council [radnički savet] by secret ballot. The council has 15 to 120 members elected originally for one year and more recently for a two-year period. The council is a policy-making body and meets at intervals of one to two months. The council elects a managing board [upravni odbor] as its executive

156

organ. The board has 3 to 11 members, three-quarters of whom must be production workers. The director is the chief executive and is an ex officio member of the managing board.

As soon as it was established, self-management met with criticism and skepticism. Both came mostly from abroad. It was said that self-management would erode discipline and that workers would distribute all profits in wages, thus reducing the growth potential of the economy. In 1955, B. Ward suggested that workers had no real choice in the election of the council and that actions reportedly taken by the councils might represent rubber stamping [4; 5]. In evaluating these criticisms, one may point out that, regarding labor discipline, an International Labor Organization mission found in 1960 that "while the self-government machinery for labor relations has curtailed the former powers of the supervisory staffs, it would not appear to have impaired their authority. ... It has undoubtedly strengthened the position of the collective vis-à-vis the management, but it does not appear to have underminded labor discipline" [6, p. 203]. As to growth potentials, the rate of accumulation remained high, with a chronic tendency toward overinvestment and a high rate of growth. Elections are supervised by courts, and all candidates approved by the majority of the workers are included in the voting list. The safeguards against the creation of a managerial class are the workers' majority in the managing board and the provision that members of self-managing bodies may be elected only twice in succession.

The real difficulties were encountered elsewhere. The original organizational scheme proved to be too rigid and all three of its components had to be revised extensively. It soon became evident that the director's position was not quite compatible with the new arrangement, and directorship came to be "one of the most attacked and criticized professions in the country" [7, p. 137]. In the etatist period, the director was a civil servant and a government official within the enterprise. He was in charge of all affairs in the enterprise and responsible exclusively to the superior government agency. In the self-management system, the director became an executive officer of the self-management bodies, while at the same time continuing to represent the so-called public interest at the enterprise. This hybrid position has been a constant source of conflicts. At first the director was appointed by government bodies. In 1952, the power of appointment of directors was vested in the commune (local government). In 1953, public competition for the director's office was introduced, and the representatives of the commune retained a two-thirds majority in the selection committee. In 1958, workers' councils achieved parity with communal authorities on the joint committees authorized to appoint and dismiss directors of the enterprises. The present state of affairs is that the director is appointed by the workers' council from among candidates approved by the selection committee on the basis of public competition. He is subject to reelection every four years, but may also be dismissed by the workers' council. The director must be relieved of duty if the enterprise has been placed under receivership [44]. Since the appointment of the director does not depend exclusively on the will of the collective — as is the case with all other executives — he has been considered a representative of "alien" interests in the firm. There have been constant attempts to reduce his power, which makes his position ambivalent and reduces his operational efficiency. On the other hand, as Gudrun Lemãn remarks, the director is expected to play the triple role of local politician, manager, and executive [39, p. 28]. In this context, the managing board was supposed to exercise control over the work of the director and the administration. Involved in problems of technical management and composed of nonprofessionals, the managing board often proved to be either a nuisance or ineffective. For professional management, the director had to rely on the college of executive heads [kolegij], which was his advisory body and subordinated to him [42]. Thus two fundamentally different organizational setups were mechanically fused into one system. The director's office provided a link between them — that is, between the self-management organs and the traditional administrative hierarchy.

Finally, in any somewhat larger firm, a single workers' council was not sufficient if there was to be real self-management. In 1956, workers' councils on the plant and lower levels were created apart from the central workers' council. In large firms, there may be three layers of self-management. Even this was not enough, for hierarchical relations between workers' councils at various levels were not compatible with the spirit of self-management. "The self-management relation in its pure form is polyarchic and not democratic," explains D. Gorupić, "the democratic relationship represents a domination of the majority over the minority. . . . The polyarchic character of the self-management relationship is revealed in equal rights of members of a certain community" [8, p. 16].

In 1959, an interesting new development began with the creation

of so-called economic units [ekonomske jedinice]. The enterprises were subdivided into smaller units with a score or several
scores of workers. Since a year earlier the enterprises became
more or less autonomous in the internal division of income, it was
thought that a strong incentive could be built into the system if
economic units recorded their costs, took care of the quality of
output and the use and maintenance of machinery, and distributed
their incomes themselves according to certain efficiency criteria.
In an interesting study, Gudrun Lemân, a German student of Yugoslav self-management, argues that economic units resulted from
the endeavor to eliminate dividing lines between three fields of
activities: policymaking, managing, and executive work [40, pp. 38-
39]. Soon, economic units began to practice collective decision
making on all sorts of matters. It became advisable to enlarge
economic units so as to comprise individual stages of the technological process or separate services. Economic units were transformed into work units [radne jedinice]. The hierarchical self-
management relations within the enterprise called for a revision.
Important self-management rights (distribution of income, employment and dismissals, assignment to jobs) were transferred to work
units. Direct decision making at meetings of all members of the
work unit became the fundamental form of management. In this
way, the work unit provided a link between the primary group and
social organization. It was both a well-defined technoeconomic
unit, meeting the requirements of efficient formal coordination,
and the basic cell of workers' self-government [13]. As has already been mentioned in section 3, in constitutional amendments
and later in the Constitution of 1974, work units evolved into basic
organizations of associated labor [43].

Work units, several workers' councils and managing boards,
many commissions and committees — all this made the formal
organization of a labor-managed enterprise rather complicated
and inefficient. In order to make such a formal system work, it
had to be simplified in practice, and this was done in various informal ways. That, in turn, meant further limitations on competent professional management and a further reduction of efficiency.
Workers' management is passing through an efficiency crisis
caused by the need for a radical transformation of inherited organizational structures. After all, workers' management meant
a fundamentally new principle in running enterprises, and it would
have been surprising if that did not require painful adaptations and
deep changes in social relations. I must add, however, that the

conclusions in this paragraph, though based on widely held beliefs, cannot be substantiated in a more rigorous way because no adequate empirical research has been undertaken so far.

Although the crisis has not yet been overcome, matters have begun to be gradually sorted out. A constitutional amendment passed in 1969 made it possible for enterprises to drop managing boards and to experiment with various organizational schemes. Trade unions, authorities, and workers have come to realize that certain developments were based on erroneous beliefs concerning various management functions in a labor-managed enterprise. Perhaps the clearest analysis of the mistakes made came from a sociologist, J. Županov [9]. Županov distinguishes among self-management [samoupravljanje], management [upravljanje], and executive work [rukovodjenje]. The last mentioned is a partial activity intended to carry out a decision made within a policy framework. The integration of all decisions into a consistent framework is the task of management. But management means only technical coordination, while coordination of various interests, the making of basic policy decisions, is a task of self-management. Self-management means social integration, the formulation of common goals, which is a precondition for efficient operational work of the management. The confusion between management and self-management generated tendencies to transfer more and more formal coordination to bodies whose task was social integration. As a consequence, satisfactory social integration was not achieved, while nonprofessional management meant lower efficiency [33]. S. Bolčić reminded me that this inherently complex problem was complicated even further by a rather naive ideology contained in legislation and political propaganda which advocated direct participation in administrative work as an indispensable means of safeguarding the interests of the workers.

Another consequence of inadequate social organization inside and outside of the firm is the appearance of informal decision-making groups. Their existence severely distorts equality in participation, which is the basic goal of self-management. Although the power distribution in a Yugoslav firm is substantially more egalitarian than in either a Western capitalist or an Eastern etatist firm, virtually all researchers agree that the power structure is still to a great extent oligarchic [46, p. 68; 47; 49]. Neca Jovanov quotes a research survey conducted in Slovenia, where in 1971 the ranking of various groups according to the amount of influence on the state of affairs in the firm appears to be as follows: (1) general manager; (2) department managers; (3) workers' council; (4) managers of work units; (5) collective executive bodies; (6) foremen; (7) the League of Communists; (8) trade unions; and (9) workers [49, p. 536]. Other researchers found that experts have an equally restricted amount of power as workers [47, p. 1015]. This finding contradicts the general image of the power position of the so-called technostructure and indicates that power is based primarily on the position in executive hierarchy. On the other hand, Janez Jerovšek reports the important finding that social integration in a firm is dependent on the level of education of all employees. He explains this by saying that "the educational level of all employees in a firm is closely connected with the adaptability of the work organization, its openness, as well as its ability to receive and absorb external influences and information inputs; in other words, the education of all employees makes it possible for the organization to be internally structured so as to meet the requirements of the environment" [48, p. 1047].

For a long time the main attention in the sphere of self-management was given to the acceptance or rejection of decisions. It remained unnoticed that the decision-making process has five different phases: (1) initiative or the definition of the problem; (2) the preparation of the decision or elaboration of variants; (3) the decision itself or the selection of a variant; (4) implementation; and (5) control [50, p. 520]. Since four of the five phases were left to the domination of the executive hierarchy, it is little wonder that a skewed distribution of power emerged. Only after the adoption of the 1963 Constitution and various constitutional amendments in 1969 did the establishment of supervisory committees and workers' control begin to take care of phases four and five.

How are the problems encountered to be solved?

Gorupić [10] and the Institute of Economic Sciences [11] see the solution to lie in a fusion of professional competence and self-management. The enterprise may be considered as an association of work units. The professional managers of the work units are no longer appointed, as in the traditional setup, but are elected by their associates. In this way, they represent the interests of their primary groups, while at the same time they are also professionally competent. So elected managers make up a managing board that is both an executive organ of the workers' council and a professional management body. Decisions are made collectively. Since most of the decisions affecting the daily lives of workers

are made and implemented within economic units and by the workers themselves, executive work becomes more and more purely
organizational and loses its order-giving character [7, p. 118].
Businessmen proved amenable to this approach [38]. As might
have been expected in a country like Yugoslavia, as soon as these
ideas had been clearly formulated, practical experimentation began, and the Constitution was promptly amended.

Before closing this section, let me note another interesting phenomenon: the development of the so-called autonomous law. Enterprises appear as law-creating bodies. Their self-management
organs pass charters and rules governing the organization of work,
the composition and responsibility of self-management and other
organs, the distribution of income, and the conduct of business.
The autonomous law-creating power emanates directly from the
Constitution; the rules and regulations are legally binding on all
persons to whom they are addressed within an enterprise, and disputes are settled by the enterprise organs, except in some specific cases. In this way, "a continual narrowing of the area of
state law and corresponding broadening of the area of so-called
autonomous law characterizes the entire process of regulation of
social relations in Yugoslavia" [12, p. 1].

Wherever there is law, there is also breach of law. For a long
time, people believed that workers' councils and, in particular,
management boards could efficiently control the activities of the
executive apparatus. Eventually it was realized that this was not
so, and, as was mentioned above, supervisory committees emerged.
Similarly, it was believed that the mere existence of the workers'
council guaranteed that the rights and interests of every individual
would be safeguarded. If one was offended, one appealed to one's
colleagues in the workers' council and the wrong was redressed.
It turned out that human groups functioned differently. Often trade
unions had to intervene to defend a powerless individual. Later,
special complaints and grievances committees were established.
Eventually it became clear that a more systematic approach to
the entire question of self-management legality was necessary.
The Constitution of 1974 established specialized courts of associated labor [sudovi udruženog rada]. When internal conciliation
and arbitration fail, these courts deal with conflicts involving the
financial interests of constituent units of a firm, the exit of a
work unit, the consistency of the autonomous law, and the rights
and duties of members of work organizations. The Constitution
also created the post of special self-management ombudsman, a

public attorney for self-management [društveni pravobranilac samoupravljanja]. He is nominated by the appropriate assembly and is expected to protect the self-management rights of individuals and of social property. He is empowered to initiate legal processes in courts and also to take certain cases before the assembly. The self-management attorney functions at all three political levels: federal, state, and local [51, pp. 158-59].

14. ENTERPRISE

The introduction of self-management in 1950 implied the dissolution of the centrally planned, administratively run economy. The enterprise was to become independent and autonomous. Individual enterprises needed some guidance and coordination. Therefore, so-called higher business associations [viša privredna udruženja] were set up to replace former state directorates and to preserve continuity in the organization of the economy. The governing councils of the new bodies were composed of representatives of workers' councils of the constituent enterprises. But higher business associations tended to operate along the same administrative lines as former directorates and were therefore dissolved in 1952. A period of laissez-faire ideology followed. Isolated enterprises were expected to engage in free competition on the market. Attempts to form larger business units and multiplant firms were frowned upon as contrary to genuine self-management and as signs of regression to disguised state control. In spite of that, the system worked well because a special sort of administrative coordination was still effective. The chief coordinator was the National Bank, implementing the targets of the plan. The bank ran a specially designed bookkeeping operation for every enterprise, distributed the incoming money to various accounts (for wages, taxes, different enterprise funds), determined the amount of necessary working capital that was to be provided on a credit basis, and so on [14, pp. 11-20]. Although the control was monetary, the value proportions were derived from physical targets.

After 1952, the process of decentralization was not arrested at the level of the enterprise, but went below it. It was already mentioned that in 1956 the formation of plant workers' councils began and in 1959 the first economic units appeared. The internal cohesion of the enterprise was reduced, and it looked as if it were broken up into its component parts. At the same time, various monetary and nonmonetary administrative controls were gradually being removed. In 1954, the enterprise assumed control of its fixed capital. Fixed assets could be bought and sold without asking for permission. Investment auctions were tried out. In 1958, the enterprise gained control over the internal distribution of income, and two years later the trade union control of wages was removed. The stage was set for a genuine market economy.

As soon as all preconditions for classical free competition of numerous small enterprises were met, it became clear that such an economy would not work very efficiently in the second half of the twentieth century. Since the state refrained more and more from coordinating economic activities, some other agency or agencies had to take over that function. This is why the process of integration was initiated. Working collectives themselves had to resume economic coordination in a state that was withering away. The circle of organizational development seemed closed. The process was started by a fully integrated, state-managed economy, passed through a period of radical decentralization, and is now moving toward another stage of full integration in the form of a labor-managed economy.

There are various forms of integration. The simplest is an agreement for business cooperation intended, for instance, to achieve specialization of production programs of two or more enterprises. Next comes contractual technoeconomic cooperation resulting in joint production, sales, or procurement of raw materials. If business relations are numerous and complicated so that it is impossible to regulate everything in advance in a contract, the enterprises form a separate body called a business association [poslovno udruženje]. Business associations first appeared in 1958. By 1962, half of all manufacturing enterprises were already members of such associations. In 1967, there were 290 business associations, including ten enterprises on the average [15]. The next, more integrated form consists of firms known as affiliated enterprises [združeno poduzeće]. Such firms are run according to commonly accepted business principles, while constituent enterprises retain operational independence. The latter disappear in another form, the merger. In a seven-year period, starting in 1959 when the process began, the total number of firms was reduced by one-half through mergers. It is characteristic, however, that nine-tenths of these mergers were effected within the boundaries of the same or neighboring communes, and only 1.2 percent were interstate mergers. In the same period, the number of banks was reduced from 378 to 108. Special status was given to so-called unions of enterprises [zajednice privrednih organizacija] created for railways, electric power generation, and postal and communication services. Membership in these unions is obligatory. Finally, there are economic chambers, organized territorially and associated in the Federal Economic Chamber. The chambers have a dual role: they help their members in various ways and they also perform a public function, mediating between the state and business interests. Membership is obligatory.

Mergers and various forms of business cooperation may mean monopoly. That is why a sort of antimonopoly legislation appeared as well. It is explicitly forbidden to limit free competition in production or sales to any enterprise outside the business group concerned, and government inspectors are expected to take care that there is no sharing of the market or connivance with regard to prices. No serious research on possible monopolistic practices has been undertaken as yet, so it is impossible to present an evaluation here. But it must be borne in mind that the Yugoslav economy will behave differently from other market economies. Workers' management implies a spontaneous public supervision of business conduct, and so classical forms of collusion characteristic of private monopolies are hardly to be expected. J. Dirlam [34, p. 3854] finds that the degree of output concentration is higher in Yugoslavia than in the United States; J. Drutter [35] establishes the nonexistence of a correlation between profits and output concentration, and, similarly, H. Wachtel [36] finds no correlation between wages and output concentration. In spite of a considerable number of mergers in the period from 1959 to 1963, the degree of concentration actually decreased [3].

A new enterprise may be founded by an already existing enterprise, by a government agency, or by a group of citizens. The founder appoints the director and finances the construction. Once complete, the enterprise is handed over to the work collective, which elects management bodies. As long as all obligations are met, neither the founder nor the government have any say about the operations of the enterprise. Enterprises are also free to merge or divide into parts. If a work unit wants to leave the mother enterprise and the central workers' council opposes the move, a mixed arbitration board composed of representatives of the enterprise and of the communal authorities is set up. In all such cases it is, of course, implied that mutual financial obligations will be settled.

Since the capital of an enterprise is socially owned, the fundamental obligation of the enterprise is to keep capital intact. If it
fails to do so for more than a year, or if it runs losses or fails
to pay out wages higher than the legal minimum for more than a
year, the enterprise is declared bankrupt or the founder undertakes to improve its business record. In the latter case, self-
management is suspended and replaced by compulsory management [prinudna uprava], a form of receivership administered by
officials chosen by the commune [16]. Bankruptcies are rather
rare because the commune is obliged to find new employment for
workers and so prefers to help the enterprise as long as possible.

If integration processes are to proceed efficiently, the organizational forms must be extremely flexible. Thus, since 1967, it
has become legally possible for two or more enterprises to invest
in another enterprise and then share in profits. Similar arrangements were adopted in joint ventures with foreign capital [17; 18].
In an open economy such as the Yugoslav one, foreign capital is
welcome provided it does not limit workers' self-management.
Therefore, direct investment is impossible, but joint ventures are
encouraged. The basic motivation for a Yugoslav firm to enter
into close business cooperation with a foreign partner lies in the
desire to secure access to the know-how and sales organization
of the foreign firm. In this way, the Yugoslav firm tries to achieve
international standards in technological efficiency and to expand
its market.

Theoretical analysis of the behavior of the Yugoslav firm has
only begun. Oddly — or understandably — enough, the pioneering
work was done by a foreigner, B. Ward of the University of Cali-
fornia at Berkeley. In his 1958 paper on the "Illyrian" firm [19],
Ward argues that rational behavior will require maximization of
income per worker. In the Marshallian short-run, one-product,
one-factor case, this leads to some queer consequences: an increase in wages leaves output and employment unchanged; an increase in fixed costs increases output and employment; and an increase in product price reduces output and employment. In a similar analysis eight years later, E. Domar shows that by generaliz-
ing the production function to include several products and several
factors and by introducing the demand curve for labor, the results
are changed and begin to resemble the traditional conclusions
about the behavior of the firm [20]. Proceeding along similar
lines, D. Dubravčić comes to the conclusion that in a labor-
managed firm there will be a strong tendency to use capital-

intensive technology [21]. The empirical evidence does not give unequivocal support to this conclusion. While on the one hand there is a chronic hunger for capital and enterprises use every opportunity to invest, Yugoslav enterprises are also full of redundant workers. Instead of postulating what should be rational, the present author observes the actual practice of Yugoslav enterprises, which fix wages in advance for the current year and at least once a year make corrections (positive or negative) depending on the income earned. If this behavioral rule is used in the analysis, the results are again the same as in the traditional theory of the firm [22]. The last in the controversy, Dubravčić, points out that comparative analysis is really not legitimate because it is assumed that a capitalist firm maximizes an absolute magnitude (profit), while a socialist firm is expected to maximize a relative magnitude (income per worker). He suggests a symmetrical treatment on the basis of the entrepreneurial input, which is capital in the capitalist case and labor in the socialist case. If a capitalist firm maximizes the rate of profit (profit per unit of capital), it will behave in exactly the same way as Ward's Illyrian firm with entrepreneurial inputs being interchanged. In both cases, firms will economize on the entrepreneurial input, and this will lead to capital-intensive techniques in a socialist firm and to labor-intensive techniques in a capitalist firm [23] — a nice and almost humorous result.

This brings us to the problem of entrepreneurship in a labor-managed firm. If an entrepreneur is a risk-taking and innovating agent — as Knight and Schumpeter would say and most economists would agree — then the work collective qualifies for the role [24, ch. 6]. In fact, the work collective is generally treated as an entrepreneur. However, doubts were voiced as well. Županov argues that the practice of fixing wages in advance means that they are not a residual in the income distribution, as is profit in a capitalist firm, and that this sets up a barrier to entrepreneurial behavior. He quotes the results of empirical research which finds that, in work units, only managers and professionals are prepared to bear risks, while other categories of workers and employees generally are not. Bolčić drew my attention to the fact that workers are behaving rationally when they are prepared to bear risks only to the extent that they are able to control business operations. That is why managers are both prepared and expected by others to bear risks to a much larger extent. Such an explanation was spelled out explicitly by workers in a case quoted by Lemân [39, p. 40].

In another piece of research undertaken in Zagreb in 1968, it was found that all groups were more prepared to share in losses if output was diminished than if income was reduced while output remained the same or even expanded [25]. On the other hand, it is an empirical fact that wages vary pretty widely depending on the business results. Wachtel quotes data on the issues discussed at workers' council meetings: two-thirds of agenda items are concerned with general management issues (labor productivity, sales, investment, cooperation with other enterprises, management work) and only one-third with direct worker issues (personal income, vocational training, fringe benefits) [36, p. 58]. Variable wages derived from profits amount to 8-14 percent of standard wages, on the average [36, p. 100].

15. THE OWNERSHIP CONTROVERSY

In Marxist sociology, ownership relations are the basic determinants of social relations and thus of the socioeconomic system. The class that owns — that is, has economic control over — the means of production rules the society. For a long time, and in most instances even today, it has been maintained that private property generates capitalism and state property socialism. In fact, the percentage of the national capital owned by the state has been taken as the most reliable measure of the degree of socialism achieved. It follows that a socialist economic policy must be oriented toward overall economic control by the state and must be hostile toward private initiative.

As already noted, the view described above was generally accepted in Yugoslavia until 1950; since then it has been thoroughly revised. It is now pointed out that at least three reasons can be cited why the dogma of the identity between private ownership and capitalism and between state ownership and socialism is false: the artisans of medieval towns were private owners but not capitalists; in ancient Oriental kingdoms, state ownership was frequent and yet that had nothing to do with socialism; in fascist countries, the state extensively controlled social and economic life, while these countries were obviously capitalist [2, ch. 4]. Yugoslav scientists are now quite unanimous in the belief that state ownership may be a useful device to initiate socialist reconstruction, but is otherwise as alien to socialism as is private ownership. The present position is well summarized by J. Djordjević: "state ownership

of means of production creates a monopoly of economic and political power and ... makes possible the unification of economic and
political power under the control of a social group personifying
the state." Thus "the essense of classical [class] ownership is
not changed. ... As the holder of the title to property, it [the
state] disposes with the producers' labor and its results, on the
basis of which surplus labor is appropriated by groups which have
their own interests in keeping their commanding functions and thus
retaining power and their social status and prestige" [26, pp. 81, 79].

If state ownership fails to promote socialism, what is a feasible
alternative? The Yugoslav answer is, social ownership. But the
answer to the next question — what precisely is social ownership? — is not so easy and simple. The legal experts agree that
social ownership implies self-government, that it is a new social
category, that, if it is a legal concept, it does not imply the unlim-
ited right over things characteristic of the classical concept of
property, and that it includes property elements of both public and
private law [27, p. 5]. In practically everything else, there is disagreement. A. Gams and a number of other writers maintain that
social ownership of property also implies rights of property, since
property implies appropriation, enterprises are juridical persons,
and the basic ingredient of the juristic person is property [28,
p. 61]. Article 8 of the Constitution says that the disposal of
means of production in social ownership and other rights over
things will be determined by the law. S. Pejović talks about the
right of use, which is somewhat wider than ususfructus because it
makes possible the sale of capital goods, but is narrower than ownership because the right of disposal is not absolute [30, p. 29]. A
diametrically opposite view is expressed by Djordjević and most
other writers, who maintain that social property represents a negation of property rights [26, pp. 84-90]. Djordjević quotes Part II
of the Basic Principles of the Constitution to support his view:
"Since no one has the right of ownership of the social means of
production, no one — neither the sociopolitical community [1] nor
the work organization nor an individual workingman — may appropriate on any property-legal ground the product of social labor,
or manage and dispose of the social means of production and labor,
nor can they arbitrarily determine the conditions of distribution."

Legal writers differ as well according to whether they stress

---

1. Territorial political units such as a commune, a district, an autonomous
province, a state, and the Federation.

the public law or private law component of social property. Further disagreements relate to the subjects of law (state, society as a real community of people, several subjects, no subjects). Next come disagreements on whether social property is a legal, economic, or sociological concept or is nondefinable in these terms because it relates to quasi-property. And if it is a legal concept, it may be so in various ways. By applying the calculus of combinations, we can easily find the number of possible theories. It seems the available possibilities have been efficiently exploited, for Marija Toroman [27] was able to describe thirteen different theories.

The legalistic controversy was somewhat less interesting than the one among economists and sociologists that followed. I. Maksimović distinguishes economic substance and the form of property [52, p. 7]. Bajt draws attention to the fact that the legal owner and economic owner may be two different persons. The former holds legal title, but the latter derives the actual benefit from the use of a thing [29]. In this sense, social ownership implies the nonexistence of exploitation, which in turn implies the distribution of income according to work performed. If a person or a group of persons are earning nonlabor income, they are exploiting others, and, insofar as this happens, social property is transformed into private property. Thus self-management per se is not a sufficient condition for the existence of social property.

The institution of property undergoes gradual disintegration even under capitalism. Shareholders are legal owners, but management exerts real economic control. That is why I prefer to replace the traditional concept of property by a more fundamental concept of economic control [2, ch. 15]. The latter always means "control over labor and its products," which is Marx's definition of capital as a social relation [31, p. 167]. In this respect, legal titles are irrelevant. If artisans or peasants possess no monopoly power — which in an orderly market system is likely to be the case — then they represent no alien elements in a socialist society. And there can be little doubt that they practice self-management. The present writer and Bajt came to the conclusion that individual initiative is not only compatible with but is an integral part of a socialist system. In fact, the process of production can be organized individually or collectively, and that is why Bajt talks about two forms of social ownership: individual and collective.

Agreement about the matters mentioned so far is quite universal by now. Differences in view appear when intermediate cases are considered. Yugoslav law makes it possible for artisans and inn-keepers to employ three to five workers. V. Rašković [32, pp. 106-7] and many others consider this to be a form of exploitation, a remnant of the old society, something that is alien to the system but that has to be tolerated at the present level of development. In support of this view, Rašković argues that the employer would not hire workers if this were not profitable for him. It may be argued in reply, however, that a worker, by choosing an individual employer instead of a firm, reveals that he finds such employment more profitable for himself. Such a line of reasoning leads clearly to an impasse. To resolve the question of whether workers may be hired by individual employers and, if so, how many, a sociological argument has been advanced as a criterion. As long as an individual employer himself works in the same way as his employees and has not become an entrepreneur who merely organizes the work of others, employees may be considered as (often younger) associates in the work process, direct personal relations of a primary group are preserved, and the alienation phenomena of wage labor relations are not present.

Discussion of the scope and role of individual work was invited by political bodies, and very soon decisions were made following more or less the ideas expounded above. Individually organized production became a constituent part of a socialist economy. (The private sector — which Yugoslav economists prefer to call the "individual sector" in order to avoid various connotations of the attribute "private" — accounts for 29 percent of GNP, and this percentage has not changed much in the last twenty years.)

MARKET AND PRICES

16. PRICE POLICY

Price policy represents an incessant series of attempts to control the famous law of value (supply and demand relations). Its history is instructive, since it provides an insight into the working of various institutional arrangements.

Administratively Set Prices

Immediately after the war, with the economy totally destroyed, there was an extreme scarcity of all goods. The prime purpose of economic policy was to prevent profiteering and to generate output by any means available. This was the period of "profitability at all costs" [1, p. 143].

Prices were determined on the free market only for a few luxury products. Mostly prices were set on the basis of actual costs incurred and could vary from one producer to the next. The price offices would examine each case and make the relevant decisions (a procedure known as normiranje cijena). This was not a very efficient procedure. Since actual cost was taken as given, there was no incentive to economize on inputs. Wages were fixed, and products could always be sold. In order to minimize risk, producers tended to inflate costs in their price proposals. To keep prices down, the price offices tended to apply linear reductions to proposed prices. The authorities and the businessmen began to play hide and seek, which is so characteristic for an administratively controlled economy.

The launching of the First Five-Year Plan in 1947 required a system of uniform prices [jedinstvene cijene]. Uniform prices were determined by the planning authorities and were expected to be rigidly stable. The aim was to provide a link between the physical and the value part of the plan, to exert control over the implementation of plans and to avoid the administrative costs of frequent price changes. Prices were formed by adding the average rate of profit to the average cost for a product. The less efficient producers had planned losses, the more efficient ones extra profits; in both cases, differences were settled with the budget. Through the establishment of the system of uniform prices, the law of values was considered to be subject to efficient social control [2, p. 143].

It soon became evident that uniform prices did not equilibrate supply and demand. There was chronic excess demand. Private producers (peasants and artisans) held a large share of the market, and their incomes could not easily be controlled. Most consumer goods were rationed. These goods were sold at the existing uniform prices, and the quantities available were not sufficient to satisfy the needs of the entire population at the lower uniform prices. By the end of 1947, the first quantities of consumer goods were supplied to the free market at higher uniform prices [više jedinstvene cijene]. These prices were derived from the existing uniform prices by applying multiplication factors varying from 2 (for potatoes and beans) to 6.5 (for garments). The resulting trading profit was absorbed by the budget. In 1948, about 45 percent of consumer goods were supplied at higher uniform prices [3, p. 376]. In this way, it was hoped, excess money incomes would be absorbed.

In agriculture, a system of compulsory deliveries [obavezni otkup] was applied. Peasants were obliged to sell most of their products to the state at prescribed low prices. They could not buy all the industrial products they wanted for the money they obtained. Thus, they tried to reduce deliveries and substitute their own consumption for money incomes. The government reacted by creating a market for industrial goods at higher uniform prices. Peasants reciprocated by evading compulsory deliveries and supplying more goods to the free peasant market, the only section of the market where prices were equilibrating supply and demand. These prices tended to rise rapidly, so the government decided to substitute a carrot for the stick: in 1948, it introduced linked prices [vezane cijene]. Under this system, agricultural prices were linked with industrial prices in such a way as to establish the prewar parity. Peasants sold their products to the government at lower prices and, in return, obtained coupons which enabled them to buy industrial products at prices that were about 16 percent lower than commercial prices [4, p. 141].

Local markets were less rigidly controlled. After 1949, local enterprises could in principle sell their products at commercial (higher uniform) prices. Trading establishments that were supplied by two different producers — national and local — were now unable to sell commodities at one single price. And so sliding prices [klizave cene] were invented. Under this sytem, the selling price slides in a span determined by the lowest and the highest supply price. These prices were approved by the local authorities. Thus two different markets were created: one for enterprises that traded at lower and higher uniform prices, and the other for retail trade and the population, in which prices approached free market prices.

The system of linked prices did not work very well. The supply of industrial goods was inadequate and richer peasants began to speculate with coupons. In 1950, only some agricultural products could be sold at linked prices. More of the peasants' products went to the free peasant market, whose counterpart in the state sector was the system of sliding prices. Higher uniform prices, as they were administratively set, were lagging behind the free market prices. The output of consumer goods was stagnating, and even falling, while incomes were rising [5, p. 49]:

	1948	1949	1950	1951	1952
Consumer purchasing potential	100	128	125	245	327
Retail trade in real terms, excluding peasant trade	100	100	94	70	77

The widening gap between supply and demand could be controlled by either administrative or economic means. The government chose the latter. In the transitional year of 1951, eight different price categories coexisted [4, p. 143]. Sliding prices were superseded by higher prices for consumer goods. Rationing was abolished. Consumer goods prices were left to be regulated by the market. Producer goods prices were increased one to twelve times and then frozen for about half a year. In 1952, compulsory deliveries of agricultural products were abolished. By the second half of 1952, all prices were freely formed with the exception of those for a few goods (bread, sugar, electric power, etc.) for which ceiling prices were established.

Development of the Market

The strategy of the 1951-52 price reform can be summarized
as follows: (a) an increase of prices high enough to absorb all excess money incomes; (b) an increase in retail prices of manufactured consumer goods relative to agricultural prices high enough
to generate the capital accumulation necessary for fast growth;
and (c) a smaller increase in producer goods prices in order to
stimulate investment and the expansion of department I (producer
goods industries). The first two goals were achieved with remarkable success. As a result, industrial producer prices were kept
stable over a period as long as a decade. The third strategy
proved to be deficient and generated a lot of trouble.

While the general index of industrial producer prices declined
for almost three years, prices of certain raw materials (ferrous
and nonferrous metallurgy, building materials, wood products)
rose. That is why in 1954 ceiling prices were set by the government for a number of raw materials, and the next year the list of
controlled intermediate goods was further extended. In 1955, industrial producer prices rose by 5 percent. This led to the creation of the Federal Price Office in that same year. Since then, a
system of administrative control of prices has been gradually developed. The essential features of this control are as follows:

1. The government sets fixed prices for electrical power, cigarettes, transportation, sugar, oil, salt, and some other commodities.

2. The government sets ceiling prices for metallurgical products, coal, petroleum, and some other goods.

These two categories of prices are changed only at infrequent
intervals. But when they are changed, the change is rather drastic.

3. Control on the basis of prior price registration is the most
frequent kind of control. This type of control was introduced in
1958. Producers intending to raise prices are obliged to notify
the Federal Price Bureau thirty days beforehand. If, within this
period, the Bureau does not veto the price increase, it can be effected. The principal criteria for placing a product under control
are: (a) its importance to the standard of living or to production
costs of other products; (b) scarcity on the market; and (c) the
monopoly position of the producer [6].

4. Control of trade margins is implemented by republics for
wholesalers and by local authorities for retailers.

5. The instrument of price freeze was used on only two occasions, in 1952 and in 1965, during two price reforms.

6. Agricultural prices are placed under a special regime. Guaranteed prices are applied to stable food products. This means that the Federal Food Reserve Board is obliged to purchase all quantities of the products offered for sale and to pay the guaranteed prices. Minimum prices apply to milk and industrial crops. This means that if these products are bought, at least the minimum prices must be paid for them. An industrial crop is normally not grown unless the producer has a prior contract with the buyer. Prices used in such cases are agreed-upon prices.

Industrial prices have been most heavily controlled. In the last decade, this control was exercised over the following percentages of the value of industrial output [1, p. 282; 7, p. 113; 8, p. 6; 78, p. 21]:

1958	31.2%	1965	70%
1962	67.0	1968	46
1962-65	60.0	1970	43

The time series of prices, given in Table 26, may give an idea of how efficient price policy and price control were.

Table 26

Changes in Price Levels in Percentage per Year

	1952-63	1964	1965	1966	1967	1968	1970	1973
Producer prices in manufacturing and mining	+ 0.9	+ 5	+ 15	+ 11	+ 2	0	+ 9	+ 13
Agricultural producer prices	+ 8.6	+ 24	+ 43	+ 16	−3	−4	+ 15	+ 25
Retail prices (including services)	+ 3.9	+ 9	+ 29	+ 23	+ 7	+ 4	+ 10	+ 19

Sources: SZS, Jugoslavija 1945-1964; SGJ-1969; SGJ-1974.

After 1961, the administrative control of prices was increased and so was the inflationary pressure. What, in fact, happened?

The most frequent form of price control — prior price registration — could not be adequately applied to new products. By making small changes in the design of a product, an enterprise could transform it into a new product and so would evade price control. In 1964, almost 25,000 new products were launched. Low and rigidly controlled prices of raw materials made their production unprofitable and thus depressed the output; in agriculture, prices were particularly depressed. That is why, in 1964, prices were raised administratively in agriculture, the food-processing industry, energy generation, and nonferrous metallurgy. Next, differential taxation, a system of premiums and subsidies, and administrative interventions in foreign trade all tended to preserve and even increase price disparities [10]. As a consequence, individual enterprises conducted their business under highly unequal conditions. Producers whose prices or wages were lagging behind tried to catch up with their neighbors. The Federal Price Bureau received 12,800 requests for price increase in 1961 and 69,000 requests in 1964 [7, p. 107]. But the most important reason for the break in price trends in 1961 lies elsewhere. Until 1961, personal incomes were quite efficiently controlled by fiscal and nonfiscal means (trade unions). That is why prices were quite stable (except in agriculture) and administrative controls relatively few [9, pp. 37-41]. In 1961, income controls were abolished. Very soon a cost-push inflation occurred, and, despite increasing administrative control, prices went up. A few years later, the Institute of Economic Sciences suggested that the Federal Price Bureau relax administrative price control and focus its attention on income control [8, p. 41]. The suggestion was not followed, and instead monetary policy was used as the chief anti-inflationary weapon.

By 1965, the economy was ripe for another radical price reform. In March, prices were frozen and a tax reform was carried out. Various subsidies were drastically reduced and the tax burden of enterprises alleviated. In the next few months, a new price structure was prepared. In July, the dinar was devalued; new prices were introduced and frozen. Relative prices of certain raw materials, intermediate goods (electric power, petroleum, ferrous and nonferrous ores and metals, chemicals, timber products, and agricultural products), and transportation services were substantially increased. World prices (as registered in exports or imports) were taken as a basis for the new price structure to allow the rapid integration of the Yugoslav economy into the world economy. World prices were corrected upward or downward by taking into account the capital accumulation needs of various industries and other specific aims or requirements. A new customs tariff was to iron out these differences. Prices for about two-thirds of industrial and most agricultural products were formed on the basis of this principle. Prices of commodities and services sold almost exclusively on the home market were fixed at a level that would ensure normal business conditions [78, p. 16].

Price stabilization proceeded rather slowly, as can be seen from Table 26. The lifting of price controls went even slower. In 1968, prices appeared stabilized, but almost half of all industrial prices were still under control. Disparities between controlled and uncontrolled prices began to emerge. The output of certain industries tended to become depressed. In 1969, prices began to rise again. The experience of 1964 seems to have been repeated. The reform of 1965 eliminated the worst price disparities, but subsequent price controls created new ones. The price game was far from won.

There has been lively discussion about the appropriate type of price for a labor-managed economy. This discussion hardly touched the classical controversy of marginal cost versus full cost pricing. Since marginal cost pricing requires government intervention, the lack of interest in this procedure among Yugoslav economists is understandable. On a more theoretical level, it was pointed out that allocational efficiency (as represented by marginal cost pricing) is inferior to growth efficiency (as represented by full cost pricing, which makes possible the business autonomy of an enterprise) [11, ch. 2].

The price debate was centered around the problem of how the price is to be formed. It started in 1950, when B. Kidrič opted for the "value price" [12]. In 1952, in his last writing before his death, Kidrič describes the value price as the price consisting of costs of production (including wages) and accumulation (gross profits) calculated as proportional to wages. These prices were actually tried out in practice in 1953 and 1954. Kidrič compared the rate of accumulation principle with the traditional average rate of profit principle (profit proportional to capital invested is characteristic of Marx's price of production) and came to the conclusion that only the former was appropriate for a labor-managed economy. In his view, the average rate of profit principle "represents a contradiction to socialist planned management of the economy," and leads to "a kind of cooperative capitalism" [13, pp. 42, 46]. A decade later, M. Todorović, who was to become the Secretary of the League of Communists, came to the opposite conclusion. He maintains that in a system of commodity production, including its socialist variety, in which fixed capital is used, prices must take the form of prices of production. Since capital is socially owned and production is planned, the use of prices of production cannot lead to the same consequences as in the laissez-faire framework of liberal capitalism [14, pp. 60, 65, 78].

Strange as it may sound, there is no basic disagreement between

Kidrič and Todorović. The difference between their views reflects primarily the difference in the degree of economic sophistication. In 1952, Kidrić's view was commonly accepted — by Todorović as well — while today hardly anyone would be prepared to support it. Todorović's theory of the specific price of production (specific because social planning is one of its basic ingredients) as an equilibrium price in the Yugoslav setting has been accepted by a certain number of economists (Z. Pjanić, V. Rakic, I. Maksimović [15]) but by no means by all. In 1964, in a heated debate in Sarajevo, another group of economists — M. Kovač, J. Sirotković, S. Dabčević, T. Vlaškalić — expounded the theory of "income price" [16]. In their view, the Yugoslav enterprise maximizes income in relation to suitably defined inputs. Other economists were busy inventing new types of prices: gravitational (M. Mesarić [17]), normal, actual social reproduction price (F. Černe [77, p. 233]), and so on. M. Radulović was able to describe six different price theories of this sort [1, pp. 299-326].

Price theory is closely linked to distribution theory, which we shall consider in the next section.

17. DISTRIBUTION POLICY

It is not quite common to talk about distribution policy. One is accustomed to speak about wages <u>policy</u> and distribution <u>theory</u>. However, as we proceed, it will become evident that in the Yugoslav setting the distribution policy is also a meaningful concept.

Wages Policy

In the administrative period 1945-52, workers were government employees classified in a certain number of salary categories according to their skills. Salaries were paid out of the state budget; enterprise income was paid into it. Directorates set work norms whose overfulfillment brought an increase in pay. Managerial personnel received premiums for the fulfillment of the government plan. The range for various salary levels was 1:3.5 [18, p. 6], as compared with 1:16 before the war [50, p. 56]. The lack of material incentives was compensated by moral incentives such as public praise, the trophy flag, or the title of shock worker or innovator. In the postrevolutionary atmosphere, these were very powerful.

After several years, the lack of material incentives became a serious obstacle to efficient production. Because of postwar scarcities and an egalitarian ideology, by 1953 the salaries of office employees in industry were reduced by one-third and those of civil servants by one-half relative to workers' wages and to the prewar levels [19, p. 81]. Nonwage income (fringe benefits) was higher than wage income. Since 1952, both trends have been reversed. Trade unions advocated higher skill differentials. Economists urged an increase in the share of discretionary income (income after taxes and contributions left to the free disposal of an enterprise) in order to increase productivity [31]. H. Wachtel finds that interskill differentials increased until 1961 and then began to fall. The average income ratio between the highest and the lowest paid job is now 1:4 [19, p. 82], but in 1 percent of firms it is as high as 1:9 or more [80, p. 140]. M. Janković estimates that wage income increased to 65 percent of total workers' income in 1956 and to 73 percent of total income in 1967 [20, p. 159]. The idea was to leave to the market the job of determining the appropriate income differentials and to stimulate efficiency by increasing the discretionary part of workers' income. The latter was also thought necessary in order to curb centralist distribution of income. As far as consumption was concerned, the Gini coefficient of concentration was reduced from 0.37 in 1938 to 0.19 in 1968 [80, p. 207].

Since 1952, it has been the task of workers' councils to determine wage differentials and work incentives. The distribution of income between the enterprise and the community was settled in a very simple way. The expected income of the enterprise and the corresponding wage bill were determined on the basis of the social plan. The difference between gross income (depreciation excluded) and wages was termed accumulation and funds (AF). The ratio between AF and wages was called the rate of accumulation and funds. This rate was applied to actual gross income earned in order to derive wages. It was mentioned in section 16 that the AF rate was considered an appropriate socialist substitute for the rate of profit, and that was its theoretical justification; whatever the merits of this argument, the practical effects were good. The AF rate helped to bridge the institutional gap between complete administrative control and relative autonomy of the enterprise. It also induced workers to economize on labor. In 1953, employment in manufacturing and mining increased by 5 percent, and labor productivity by 6.2 percent. In 1954, when the AF system was abandoned, employment increased by 13 percent and labor productivity fell slightly.

The AF rates were, of course, not uniform. The 1952 plan envisaged a rate of 19 for agriculture and of 582 for manufacturing and mining. This difference reflected the goals of the price policy already described: industrial prices were inflated in order to facilitate the collection of investment resources. However, even within manufacturing, different industries had widely different rates. In industries with high rates, there was no incentive to reduce costs. Since the rates could not be established very precisely, some collectives began to earn high wages. The government reacted by introducing a tax on the surplus wage fund (the difference between the standardized and the achieved wage bill). Since the standardized wage bill was the product of the average wage rate and the number employed, the enterprise increased the employment of less skilled workers — often fictitiously — in order to reduce the tax base. The government reacted by differentiating taxation according to skill categories. Enterprises countered by changing the skill structure artificially, declaring their workers to have higher skill.

The AF rates clearly were not a very refined instrument of economic policy. They were introduced in the belief that they could be standardized for all enterprises within an industry group. Soon, however, individual rates had to be prescribed for each particular enterprise. This implied direct administrative interventions, which were at variance with the basic intentions of the new system. In 1954, the AF system was replaced by a system known as accounting wages, which lasted for the next three years.

Yugoslav economists had been complaining for some time that in their economic calculus enterprises do not consider capital services as a cost item [21, p. 142]. This was a natural result of the fact that capital was given to enterprises free of charge. This practice was discontinued in 1954, when a capital tax of 6 percent was introduced. This tax was considered as a price for the socially owned capital and was also levied on capital invested from enterprise funds. Apart from that, the enterprise was obliged to pay normal interest rates on credits granted by the bank. Profit and turnover taxes were also introduced, and the latter became the chief instrument of accumulation. In this way, instruments of economic policy became more varied and more flexible.

The new system implied a division of the wage fund into two components: accounting wages and wages out of profit. Accounting wages were derived by applying prescribed wage rates to skill categories, with actual working time taken into account. Again skills were fictitiously increased. Working time as a basis of accounting led to a disregard of work norms. The next year, wage schedules [tarifni pravilnik] were introduced. Wage rates were determined by the social plan. Wage schedules of individual enterprises represented a kind of collective agreement between the enterprise and the trade union and local government [18, p. 11]. Differential efficiency was accounted for, and a part of profit was used as a premium for improvements in quality, reduction of costs, and so on. Since profit was taxed (the rate of taxation was 50 percent), enterprises tried to reduce profit by increasing wage rates and reducing norms. Government commissions for wages were unable to prevent this from happening.

In 1957, the First Congress of Workers' Councils was held. The Congress asked that the autonomy of the enterprise be widened. This primarily implied greater independence in income distribution. The division of income into wages and profit was considered inappropriate and reminiscent of wage-labor relations. In order to meet these demands, the income distribution system was changed in 1958 and a compromise reached. The wage schedules remained and were still subject to the approval of local authorities and trade unions. The enterprise income was treated as a single whole and was distributed by workers' councils into wages and contributions to various funds. The difference between income and accounting wages (called minimum personal income) was taxed progressively. The wages in excess of the basic pay were also progressively taxed [22, pp. 98-99].

Progressive taxation was very much resented. And so was the outside tutorship as far as wage differentials were concerned. In 1961, both were abolished. Workers' councils became completely independent in determining wage rates and distributing income. Progressive taxation was replaced by a flat 15 percent levied on income. In 1965, even this tax was abolished.

Changes in wages policy implied drastic changes in relative factor shares. If we divide value added into gross wages (wages and taxes levied on wages) and gross rentals (depreciation, interest, net profit, and taxes levied on capital), the percentage share of the latter in manufacturing and mining varied as follows [23, p. 41]:

1952	10%	1961	54%
1953	11	1963	53
1955	74	1964	50
1957	77	1965	48
1959	67	1966	46
1960	62	1967	45

Percentage shares of gross wages of course represent the complements to 100 percent of the figures quoted for rentals. In the AF system, depreciation was the only capital cost. The introduction of profit and capital tax into the system of accounting wages increased capital cost drastically. The gradual reduction and final elimination of profit taxes (which implied a relative increase in wage tax) reduced the share of gross rental to somewhat more than half of the value added. Price changes were superimposed on these changes. The increase in food and service prices after 1960 increased nominal wages; the abolition of various subsidies at the same time — and, in particular, after 1964 — made possible a reduction in taxation, which to a certain extent offset the effect of wage increases. The net effect was to lower the share of gross rental below 50 percent. For an enterprise to adapt to these changes required an extraordinary effort on the part of the management. But enterprises did react. Simultaneously with increased capital charges, the capital coefficient (the ratio of gross fixed capital to gross material product) in manufacturing and mining fell from 3.6 in 1955 to 2.5 in 1964 [23, p. 51]. If enterprises are market oriented and if the production function is linear homogeneous (which proved to be an acceptable approximation), the elasticity of output with respect to capital in the last decade must lie somewhere in the region of 0.45 to 0.62. The actual elasticity coefficient turns out to be 0.48. This is taken as one indication that the economy was following market rules [23, p. 42].

While wage systems with wage schedules and progressive taxation were applied, real wages lagged behind productivity increases and producer prices were stable. From 1958 on, real wages began to increase faster than labor productivity, and the discrepancy between the two series was particularly widened in the cyclical trough in 1961-62 and after 1964 [24, p. 627]. The peculiar movements of prices that followed were considered in section 10. Another peculiarity was established by Wachtel: interindustry wage differentials continued to increase, and interindustry wage structure appeared as a function of average productivity, which explained 80 percent of the variance [25]. Sofija Popov found a high correlation between the rate of growth of industrial output and productivity of labor ($r = 0.86$) [24, p. 622]. If all these bits of information are put together, the following interpretation begins to emerge.

Trade unions announced the principle that wages should increase in proportion to productivity. This principle was widely accepted, and it is a sound principle when applied to the economy as a whole. If applied to individual enterprises, however, it generates great troubles. In a rapidly growing economy, various industries expand at widely different rates (the petroleum industry at 19.2 percent, the tobacco industry at 5.1 percent per annum in the period 1952-66). Thus, rates of growth of labor productivity are bound to differ very widely (11.7 percent and 1.2 percent, respectively, for the industries mentioned above). Thus wages must differ and differentials must increase with time (money wage rates increased 12.8 times in the petroleum industry and 8.3 times in the tobacco industry during 1952-66) [24, p. 630]. M. Korač found that, in 1966, wage rates for the same category of skill in the highest paid and the lowest paid industry group were in a ratio of 2:1 [26, pp. 130-33]. All this is, of course, in flagrant contradiction to the principle of distribution according to work. That is why A. Bajt remarked that the principle of remuneration according to productivity actually denied the principle of remuneration according to work performed [38, p. 363]. Deviations of productivity income from labor income have been analyzed by the present author. They represent (after deductions for other factor costs) a form of rent which I call the rent of technological progress [27]. The faster the rate of growth, the more important this rent becomes. A comprehensive empirical study undertaken by S. Popov and M. Jovičić showed that differentials in productivity growth represent the most important source of inflationary pressure [79].

Rašković [75, p. 230] and others suggested that the principle of distribution according to work be replaced by a more appropriate principle of distribution "according to the results of work." It is not the process of work as such but its results that must be rewarded. Rašković noted that the grossly imperfect market in Yugoslavia meant exploitation of one group of collectives by another, more privileged group [75, p. 218].

The meaning of the principle, "according to the results of work" has been stretched by B. Šefer in a rather curious fashion. Šefer notes that, in developed capitalist countries, free market wage determination has been replaced more and more by a policy of "equal pay for equal work." He feels that such a policy is inapplicable in Yugoslavia because workers bear business risks; that is, they share in both profits and losses. Work cannot be remunerated automatically; it must be socially recognized, which happens at the market where the exchange determines the result of work. The principle "equal pay for equal work" could be implemented only in a system of state ownership and state management of the economy [76, pp. 74-75]. Thus, Šefer, Korać, and a certain number of others in fact argue that this principle, which is considered Marxian, can be implemented in a capitalist or etatist setting, but not in a self-government system. The fallacies of this laissez-faire reasoning are obvious: market imperfection provides no criteria for the social recognition of a person's work; the redistributive effects of market imperfections can be eliminated also by means other than the etatist ones.

Other Issues

Differentials due to variable entrepreneurial abilities of various work collectives are superimposed on income differentials due to technological and other rents. Šefer quotes data for Belgrade enterprises in 1967, when pay rates for the same jobs in various enterprises differed by as much as 1:3 or 1:4 [28, p. 434]. It is clear that such extreme differences generate enormous inflationary pressure. There is also an additional consequence. Capital-intensive enterprises are able to improve their personal income position by distributing part of profit in wages. That is why wage rates are positively correlated with capital intensity. Yet, if profits tend to be reduced, enterprises become more and more dependent on outside sources for financing their investment. This generates new difficulties, which we will consider in section 19.

Apart from technological rent, the classical forms of rent were both discussed in the literature and applied in practice [29; 30]. Agricultural rent is absorbed, in principle, through taxation according to cadastral revenue. Mining rent represented a separate item of income of mines and crude oil producers for several years. However, it was determined in a rather arbitrary way and generated regional differences. Consequently, it was resented by the enterprises and was eventually abolished. All urban land belongs to communes, and urban rent is used to finance communal investment.

J. Dirlam [87], an American student of Yugoslav economic affairs, points out that the Yugoslav system can be viewed as one in which labor employs capital, instead of a system in which capital employs labor, as is the case under capitalism. The social ownership of capital requires a somewhat different approach to capital charges in the labor-managed enterprise as compared with its capitalist counterpart. The floor and not the ceiling is set for depreciation rates. Profits need not be taxed, and instead payroll taxes are suggested [9]. A tax on capital is primarily an instrument for allocating resources and not necessarily a device for collecting revenue for the government. The revenue from capital taxation has been used by the government to finance major investment projects and also to finance the fund for underdeveloped regions. Resentment against these redistributive activities of the federal government has been growing. Capital tax was reduced from 6 to 4 percent in 1966 and to 3.25 percent in 1970, and eventually the capital tax was abolished. Many economists disagree with this decision. Some argue that the abolition of capital tax, which represents the price for the use of social capital, will initiate the transformation of social ownership into collective ownership. D. Gorupić and I. Perišin argue that the price of a product should contain the element of growth [32, p. 124]. This can be achieved if accumulation is determined by the social plan in the form of interest on capital used. But this money must not be expropriated by the state; it ought to remain with the enterprise, earmarked for investment. Thus, this internal interest is to be treated in the same way as depreciation. In order to cope with business fluctuations, minimal depreciation cum accumulation must be determined in a cumulative fashion [33, pp. 12, 13]. I. Lavrač maintains that the accumulation-protecting interest rate may be differentiated according to industries and regions [34]. S. Popović suggests that the compensation for the use of social capital will provide the bulk of development resources. After all factors of production except labor are paid their shares, the remaining net income is to be distributed among workers. Additional accumulation can be derived only from this private income, which means that workers remain owners of that part of capital [35]. A similar position is taken by F. Černe, who maintains that the participation of workers with their own means in the development of the enterprise — which implies receiving adequate interest or dividends — would stimulate rational behavior of workers and management bodies [36, p. 21]. M. Samardžija, on the other hand, argues that this is both economically irrelevant and socially dangerous. Contemporary shareholders participate in the profits of their corporations in only the small percentages that accrue to dividends. Attempts to make workers co-owners must end in the establishment of a separate group of owners of means of production within the society [37, pp. 145, 303].

We have thus reached the point at which general principles of an adequate distribution policy may be discussed. There seems to be considerable agreement on two issues: (1) as great a part of the income generated as possible should remain under the direct control of the working collective; (2) only labor income should be distributed in wages. These two principles imply a sharp division of income into two components — labor income appropriated by individual workers and nonlabor income belonging to the society but remaining under the control of the working collective and used exclusively for investment purposes.

To be able to divide net income into its labor and nonlabor parts, we need a theory of factors of production. In this respect, Bajt follows the traditional approach and defines factors of production as sources of productive services. He enumerates five such sources: labor, entrepreneurship, invention, land, and capital [38, p. 351]. The first three generate labor income, although normally a small proportion of income from inventions is appropriated by inventors. This theory leads Bajt into difficulties when he has to explain monopoly income. He then argues that in a market economy monopoly participates in income; monopoly does not add to output but only to the income of all factors [38, p. 357].

In order to avoid the shortcomings of the traditional theory, the present author defines factors of production as types of forces that influence the generation of output. Factors have to be priced in such a way as to lead to the optimal allocation of resources. This means achieving maximum output from given resources or minimum input of resources for a given output. There are four factors: labor, entrepreneurship, capital, and monopoly. The first two generate labor income (wages and profit), the latter two generate nonlabor income (interest and rent). Creative, organizational work as well as routine work generates labor income. The income due to the activities of the working collective as a whole represents entrepreneurial income. Capital services are priced in the usual way and have already been discussed. A few more words need to be said about the morphology of rent. Rent is the price of monopoly in the sense that it represents the surplus over the minimum supply price of resources. Land rent appears in three forms described by Marx (differential rent I and II and absolute rent); there are also mining rent and a somewhat special urban rent. The rent of technological progress — due to the fact that certain industries expand faster and enjoy economies of scale, or participate more in general technological advance, or both — has already been described. Bajt adds the rent from market monopoly, which he defines as a situation in which selling prices are above normal and buying prices are below normal [39, p. 93]. After land, natural resources, technology, and market monopolies are accounted for, the remaining part is a monopoly in the narrower sense. Except for the last, the prices of the monopoly factors may, in principle, be determined either by the market mechanism (land and mines) or by economic analysis (technology and market). As far as the latter is concerned, progressive taxation may in practice prove a more efficient procedure. If taxes are designed so as to be generally considered just, they will not affect the supply of resources, and this is how, in fact, we defined rent [11, chs. 3, 4, 6].

Actual business practice and legislative measures do not quite follow the principles discussed above. The productivity-wage practice leads to the appropriation of a considerable part of nonlabor income. The same consequence follows from the fact that mining rent is included in an undifferentiated income and that there is no progressive taxation. In 1968, the new law on distribution of income in the enterprises included income from capital invested in other enterprises in the undifferentiated income of the collective-investor. P. Jurković promptly called that a rather dubious theoretical solution [40, p. 50]. In general, the distribution of income according to work performed is still a goal to be reached.

18. FOREIGN TRADE POLICY

Background

The prewar trade structure was rather simple. Food and other agricultural products represented about one-half of total Yugoslav exports. One-fifth of exports consisted of wood, and almost an additional fifth of nonferrous ores and metals [4, p. 408; 42, p. 144]. Thus, close to 90 percent of export earnings were provided by these three sectors producing raw materials and semimanufactured goods. Immediately after the war, the development strategy consisted in (1) expanding the exploitation of natural resources in these three sectors, and (2) using the export proceeds to finance imports of equipment and other producer goods. It was also expected that (3) the Soviet Union would provide great help in speeding up economic development. The second part of the program was carried out successfully; the share of consumer goods in imports was reduced from 22 percent before the war to only 11 percent in

the period 1947-51 [43, p. 59]. The first and the third parts encountered unexpected difficulties.

Due to a decline in per capita agricultural production and rapid
industrialization, agricultural export surpluses were reduced, and
so was the total volume of exports. It soon became fashionable to
explore the question of whether Yugoslavia was not becoming a
permanent net importer of agricultural products [44]. The nationalization of foreign property imposed a new burden on the balance
of payments. On the other hand, reparations for war damages
were to a large extent left unpaid, by West Germany and Hungary,
in particular. Immediately after the war, about 75 percent of foreign trade was conducted with the Soviet Union and its East European allies. In 1947-48, the trade shares with these countries
were stabilized at around 50 percent in exports and 42 percent in
imports. In mid-1948, the ominous Resolution of the Cominform
signaled the end of good relations. By 1949, the Soviet group reduced trade to one-third, and in 1950 it was canceled altogether.
The Soviet Union and its allies applied a total boycott to all relations with Yugoslavia.

Thus, the country was completely cut off from the East. It was
separated from the West as well. It did not enjoy the facilities
mutually provided by Western countries to each other. It was not
included in the Marshall Plan; it remained outside GATT. In short,
it was isolated in a hostile world. The five-year industrialization
plan — imbued with so many hopes — had only been initiated when
suddenly the contracts were broken and supplies of equipment and
materials ceased to arrive. Trade was declining:

	1948	1949	1950	1951	1952	1953	1954	1955	1956	1965
Exports	100	79	74	64	87	80	102	99	122	328
Imports	100	95	86	114	115	106	103	130	142	311

Sources: SZS, Jugoslavija 1945-1964, p. 77; SGJ-1959, p. 121.

Foreign exchange reserves dropped from 43 percent of the value
of imports in 1937 to 12 percent in 1948 and 4 percent in 1952 [45,
p. 186]. Personal consumption was declining. Defense expenditures amount to 20 percent of national income. Two severe
droughts, one in 1950 and the other in 1952, proved unexpected
allies of the Cominform and reduced agricultural output to 25 percent below the prewar average. The situation looked hopeless.
That is why Stalin expected surrender.

Yet this nation was not accustomed to surrender; it was more at home in fighting back. And it did so for the first two years, struggling practically alone. Investment plans were changed, trade was channeled toward the West, even the economic system was changed. From 1951 on, foreign economic aid began to flow, mostly from the United States. It consisted primarily of food, raw materials, and military supplies. The aid amounted to 38 percent of total imports in 1951, and over the next decade was gradually reduced to zero.

The crisis was soon overcome and the economy entered a period of unprecedented growth. The heavy capital investment of the First Five-Year Plan began to materialize in rapid expansion of industrial output. The new agricultural policy soon generated phenomenal growth of agricultural output. Exports were catching up with imports. In 1954, the first trade contacts were established with the East European countries. After the conciliatory visit of Premier Khrushchev to Belgrade in 1955, normal trade relations were established, and a precious outlet for increasing exports was found [53, p. 40]. In the decade that followed, exports increased by 3.3 times — that is, at a rate twice as high as in the world as a whole.

These developments were too good to last long. In 1957, the Common Market was born in Rome. Two years later, the European Free Trade Association (EFTA) was created in Stockholm. Practically all West European countries became members of one or the other trading group. East European countries belonged to Comecon, created in 1949 but actually operating since 1954. Yugoslavia found herself isolated again. At first it did not matter very much. But gradually intrazonal trade in all three areas began to increase rapidly and to depress trade with third parties. This was true in particular for the Common Market, the most important trading partner of Yugoslavia. At present, Common Market countries account for 30 percent of Yugoslav exports, 38 percent of imports, and two-thirds of financial transactions. What makes this trade so vulnerable is the fact that between one-third and one-half of Yugoslav exports to Common Market countries consists of agricultural products. Regular and variable import tariffs in the Common Market amount to 50 percent of the Yugoslav export prices, on the average, and for beef even up to 60 or 70 percent, which clearly cannot encourage exports. Variable protection rates, when first announced to GATT, were said to be an exceptional instrument, with the customs tariff remaining the basic one. In fact, however, variable rates amount to 2.5 times the regular tariff; they are changed daily, weekly, or quarterly and represent a permanent instrument of total protection [46;47].

Yugoslavia reacted to the new situation by trying to increase her trade with the developing countries. This attempt met with limited success. Imports from developing countries increased to a maximum of 14.1 percent of Yugoslav imports in 1964, and there has been a permanent balance of payments surplus with these countries [48]. Next, close relations were established with GATT. At first an observer, Yugoslavia became an associated member of GATT in 1959, when it also enacted the Customs Law. In 1961, a temporary customs tariff was passed, and the next year Yugoslavia became a temporary member of GATT. In 1965, a new, permanent customs tariff was enacted, and a year later full membership was granted by GATT.

Comecon was also approached. Its members absorb almost one-third of Yugoslav trade. In 1964, Yugoslavia became an observer in Comecon. Special agreements were also negotiated with the Common Market.

India and the United Arab Republic account for one-third of Yugoslav trade with developing countries. In 1966, the heads of the three countries initiated a scheme that became known as Tripartite Cooperation. The agreement, ratified in 1968, covered 500 products to which preferential rates of 50 percent became applicable, and envisaged industrial cooperation as well. It was also suggested — this time by economists and not by politicians — that a Danubian trading area be formed [50, p. 33]. If that proved possible, it was hoped that the area could be extended north and south. The occupation of Czechoslovakia rendered that idea utopian for the time being.

Attempts to develop economic relations with as many countries as possible and the foreign policy of an uncommitted nation enabled Yugoslavia to establish trade with 120 countries. Trade was not only geographically dispersed, it was also diversified in terms of products exchanged. As a result, a theory of "capillary trade" emerged. V. Pertot [52] argues that small quantities reduce marketing difficulties, and S. Obradović [53] adds that highly diversified trade reduces risks of business fluctuations. Empirical research lends some support to this hypothesis. P. Mihajlović finds that the concentrated prewar export was very much dependent on external business fluctuations, while no such dependence appears to exist after the war [51, p. 77]. Capillary trade also has its drawbacks. Obradović points out that it increases marketing costs and approvingly quotes Bičanić, who maintains that export concentration is a precondition for a permanent export position on the world market [53].

Rapid growth after 1955 led to profound structural changes. The share of exports of commodities and services in social product increased from about 13 percent to more than 20 percent. The Yugoslav share in world trade doubled but, at still less than 1 percent, provided a justification for the capillarity theory. The share of the three traditional natural resource sectors in exports was reduced from 90 to 50 percent [42, p. 144]. Raw materials and manufactured goods changed places in the structure of exports (from 55:6 in 1939 to 13:50 in 1968). The once self-sufficient peasant economy is now only a matter of historical interest. It has been replaced by a relatively open industrialized economy participating actively in the development of the world market.

Prologue

Rigid central planning in the period 1945-51 implied state monopoly in foreign trade. The domestic market was completely cut off from the outside world. The rate of exchange was just an accounting device without economic meaning. Export and import trade was conducted at prescribed domestic prices. The Fund for Price Equalization, created in 1946, compensated exporters for the differences between the domestic and export prices. Each transaction implied a separate foreign exchange rate. This was consistent with the principle of profitability at all cost applied in the home market. Exporters were obliged to surrender their foreign exchange proceeds to the National Bank, which, in turn, supplied importers with what they needed. Foreign trade enterprises acted as agents for the Ministry of Foreign Trade and were obliged to implement import and export plans. Plans were defined in physical terms, and so traders were not interested in prices and other trading conditions. The system was simple and consistent, but not very efficient. Yet, in the turbulent postwar years, it did the job for which it was designed.

The most important event in those years was the Cominform economic boycott. At that time, details about the operations of mixed Soviet-Yugoslav companies became publicly known and stirred great indignation. A certain number of these companies were created with the proclaimed aim of helping to develop the country. Capital was invested in even shares and profit was divided evenly; but the Russians appointed their own people as general managers, insisted on preferential treatment, and objected to Yugoslav financial control. All this reminded people too much of their prewar experience with foreign capital, and mixed companies were gradually liquidated. The problem was more complex than that, however; economic relations among socialist countries were at stake.

In an interesting 1949 article, M. Popović, then a member of the government and later the President of the Federal Assembly, explained the position that had been taken [54]. If a less developed and more developed country meet in the world market, they will exchange commodities with different labor contents. The more productive country will get back more labor than it gives away. This implies exploitation. Further, if in mixed companies profit is divided according to capital invested, a principle of distribution alien to socialism is introduced, and, as a result, exploitation appears in yet another form. "According to socialist principles," says Popović, "the entire surplus value, that is, the entire profit obtained by the society after it had sold the commodity on the world market, belongs to the proletariat, which has created that value..." [54, p. 108].

As was not quite unexpected, Russian negotiators reacted to such theories rather laconically: "Torgovlja — torgovlja, a družhba — družhba" [Trade is trade and friendship is friendship]. But to Yugoslavia, then but a year or two past the Revolution, socialism meant immensely more than trade; to put the two on equal footing was profoundly shocking. Economic relations among socialist countries were seen as relations of various regions within one country. Developed socialist countries had an obligation to grant aid to the less developed ones in order to speed up their growth and enable them to reach the same level of development in the shortest possible time [53, p. 39; 54, p. 70].

These were not abstract ideas; they were applied in relations with Albania. Yugoslav and Albanian partisans fought together during the war, and relations between the two countries were very close. As a more developed country, Yugoslavia sent experts and material supplies to Albania. Tariffs were abolished and monetary units were given the same nominal value. Attempts to design a single system of prices failed because productivity differences between the two countries were too great. But they continued to trade at their interval prices, which meant that Albania exported at Albanian prices and imported at Yugoslav prices (the latter were somewhat lower than the Albanian, on the average). In this substitution of world market prices by respective domestic prices, Popović sees the elimination of the exploitation characteristic of the world market mechanism [54, p. 128]. In fact, however, this conclusion does not necessarily follow. To find out whether and how much Albania gained, one would have to calculate the entire trade in Albanian, Yugoslav, and world prices and compare the value aggregates. And in order to make exchange equivalent in labor terms, one would have to apply input-output analysis. Another policy measure had much more obvious implications. Albania was granted interest-free loans for an unspecified length of time. This was an early anticipation of the now familiar aid programs for underdeveloped countries.

Bulgaria was another country with which Yugoslavia expected to eliminate tariffs and possibly even form a confederation. Yugoslavia waived Bulgarian reparation obligations for war damages, and after the Bled agreement in 1947, hopes ran high in both countries. A few months later, Stalin launched his attack, and soon all achievements were forfeited, all hopes buried. Former friends became enemies.

The Cominform economic boycott and the need to finance the five-year plan compelled Yugoslavia to establish contacts with the world capital market. Ideological considerations and unpleasant experience with Western capital before the war and with Soviet capital afterward made joint stock companies and mixed companies an undesirable form of import of foreign capital. Loans remained the only available alternative. But loans may also unfavorably affect the economic and political independence of a country. To prevent this from happening, V. Guzina, in a paper representing the common opinion of the time, suggested that foreign trade be conducted according to the economic plan, and that a specified volume and structure of exports be secured [55, p. 71]. Guzina also held that autarchy was both impossible and undesirable, and favored development of an open but controlled socialist economy. These ideas were characteristic of foreign trade policy in the next decade.

Three Steps Toward Free Trade

By the middle of 1951, the new economic thinking had reached the foreign trade sector. As usual, market experimentation began with agricultural products. Exporters of certain agricultural commodities were allowed to sell their foreign exchange proceeds at a price obtained by multiplying the official rate by a factor of 7. This foreshadowed the new official rate determined on January 1, 1952, at $1 = 300 dinars (the old rate was $1 = 50 dinars). Exporters were granted a retention quota of 50 percent with which they could finance imports of their own choice and sell imported commodities at free prices.

The transition from complete state monopoly to a system of free trade was not a simple affair. Various alternatives were discussed. In an important article early in 1952, D. Avramović, now a staff member of the World Bank, argued that a fixed exchange rate and, in particular, its exclusive use, cannot be established in a socialist economy. In order to secure the minimum volume and the necessary structure of exports and imports — that consistent with production and investment targets — the fixed exchange rate should be replaced either by physical allocation of goods or by a system of multiple exchange rates. The latter is more consistent with a socialist market economy. Since foreign prices constantly fluctuate, and since a full employment economy with a high rate of growth needs stability, there ought to be an Equalization Fund to absorb too violent fluctuations. Thus, not only are multiple exchange rates necessary, but rates should also be allowed to fluctuate. The capitalist principle of a fixed exchange rate cum business fluctuations must be replaced by a socialist principle of multiple fluctuating exchange rates cum economic stability and growth [56].

Most of these ideas were soon tried out. In July of the same year, the system of seventeen price equalization coefficients was set in operation. Coefficients, applied to export prices calculated at the official exchange rate, ranged from 0.8 for exports of agricultural products to 4.0. Low coefficients were applied to imports of equipment and raw materials to keep their prices low.

A high degree of liberalization was envisaged in foreign trade, but, in comparison to the liberalization of the home market, the liberalization of the foreign trade system proved to be a much tougher job. First of all — and again in contrast to the home market — the price of foreign exchange was set too low. Even in 1951 the actual average export exchange rate was 354 dinars to 1 dollar, and in 1952 it increased to 585 dinars, which was almost twice as high as the official rate. The average import exchange rate lagged behind appreciably ($1 = 440 dinars). Cheap imports exerted pressure on the balance of payments. The foreign exchange reserve of 4 percent of imports made economic interventions impossible. It was no wonder that the newly created foreign exchange market, DOM (Devizno obračunsko mjesto, or Foreign Exchange Accounting Place), did not work. At first, exporters were obliged to sell only 55 percent of their foreign exchange to the bank; the remaining 45 percent, representing their retention quota, could be used for imports of their own choice or sold to importers at the DOM. As early as October, the retention quota was lowered to 20 percent, which meant the death sentence for DOM. In the next year, DOM rates soared to a level 6.8 times higher than the official rate. Average actual exchange rates went up as well.

In 1954, a series of desperate attempts were made to save the system. The accounting exchange rate was increased to 632 dinars to 1 dollar. Coefficients were revised and applied to DOM rates, and not to the official rate. A steep tax on the gains at DOM was introduced. A number of other complicated procedures were applied. DOM rates were brought close to the new accounting rate, for which the authorities aimed. Yet importers of raw materials could no longer compete at DOM for foreign exchange, so separate sales were organized for them. This reduced the amount of available free foreign exchange to something like 1 percent of the demand. The retention quota was reduced to only 1 percent. Prices of foreign exchange soared and by 1960 reached a level 12.3 times as high as the official rate. The National Bank replaced exporters as the only seller of foreign exchange [45, pp. 301-15].

The first free trade attempt failed because the initial price for foreign exchange was set too low, initial reserves were too small, the share of the free market in foreign exchange supply was too small, and disparities between home and foreign prices were too great. It would have been rather difficult, remarked V. Meichsner, to find anywhere else in the world relative prices such as existed in Yugoslavia in 1955: one typewriter ribbon (2800 dinars) equals a pair of shoes equals two yards of woolen fabric equals one-third of an average employee's monthly salary equals a two-day full board in a first-class hotel in a tourist resort equals fifty-six haircuts equals the monthly rent of a five-room apartment [57, p. 193]. At that time, three different foreign exchange regimes coexisted: the official rate, the regular rate, and the separate DOM rate. Meichsner suggested that the number of coefficients be gradually reduced to only two, one for industrial and one for agricultural products. In 1957, M. Frković calculated deviations of actual exchange rates of various product groups from the average actual rate of $1 = 779 dinars. It turned out that industrial exports and food, equipment, and invisible imports were subsidized at rates between 21 and 35 percent, that there were export taxes between 16 and 21 percent for agricultural, wood, and invisible exports, and a protection rate of 105 percent for consumer goods imports [58].

By 1960, it had become clear that the foreign trade system needed a thorough revision. D. Čehovin evaluated the situation by citing three points. Enterprises were stimulated to press for an increase in coefficients, not to compete on the world market. Coefficients had ceased to be passive equalization instruments and were in fact transformed into active devices for increases in price disparities. Finally, profitability calculation was made practically impossible [43, p. 125]. Ž. Mrkušić noted that, in an economy where exports are price elastic and imports are not, there will be a constant tendency for export exchange rates to move away from the import rates. That required physical restrictions on imports [45, p. 297]. Both did happen. Higher export exchange rates were bound to produce inflationary pressure — by means of the money supply — as was already warned by Avramović [56, p. 24].

The recession that started in 1960 made things worse and prompted authorities to undertake a reform in 1961. This time, an ample supply of foreign exchange was secured by foreign loans. But the other two mistakes of the 1952 reform were committed again: the new accounting rate was set too low (750 dinars to 1 dollar; the actual export rate in 1960 was 981 dinars and in 1961 went up to 1021 dinars [63]), and price disparities were corrected in only a few cases.

The strategy of the reform can be described as follows. Multiple exchange rates were abandoned and coefficients were replaced by a customs tariff. Instead of exchange rates varying between 500 dinars and 1200 dinars to 1 dollar, there was to be a single 750 dinar rate, with no protection for agriculture and lumbering, a 10-40 percent protection for consumer goods, and a 17-60 percent protection for equipment and other industrial products. Export was free and was supported by premiums and tax reductions. Exporters were supposed to sell foreign exchange to the National Bank, but in most cases they could buy back 7 percent of the amount sold for their own needs. About one-fifth of imports was liberalized, and for the rest commodity quotas or foreign exchange allocations applied.

The deficiencies of such a strategy soon became apparent. Exports were retarded, imports accelerated. In order to keep the balance of payments deficit under control, import restrictions were multiplied, and in 1964 tariff protection was increased from 20 to 23 percent. Exports were stimulated by making foreign exchange allocations conditional upon export sales. Export premiums and tax reductions were rapidly expanding. Soon the old system of multiple exchange rates reappeared with all its inefficiencies [59].

The situation was made worse by the fact that about one-half of Yugoslav foreign trade was oriented toward clearing currency countries, most of it toward Comecon. Both import and export flows with the Comecon countries are much more unstable than with the convertible market [71]. Both import and export prices are higher on the Comecon market than on the world market. Besides, it is easy to export to this market, while it is difficult to import from it, and vice versa for the convertible currency market. As there was one single exchange rate for both markets, the consequences should be obvious. Importers were oriented toward convertible currency countries, exporters toward clearing currency markets. The balance of payments deficit with the former increased rapidly, while there was an unabsorbed surplus on the trading account with the latter. A boom in 1964 produced unbearable pressure on the balance of payments. In the same year, the cycle was reversed. The recession helped to induce authorities to undertake another reform in 1965.

This time, the structure of domestic prices was radically readjusted, as explained in section 10. The actual export rate of exchange in 1964 was 1050 dinars; it was expected to increase to 1200 dinars in 1965, and the new official rate was determined at $1 = 1250 dinars. Thus two fatal mistakes of the preceding two reforms were avoided.

An additional element of the strategy consisted in lowering tariff protection from 23.3 percent to 10.5 percent, with the traditional differentiation of rates from 5 percent for primary commodities to 21 percent for consumer goods [61]. The necessary supply of foreign exchange was secured through the cooperation of the International Monetary Fund.

The ambitions of the reform were great. D. Anakiovski, one of the directors in the Federal Planning Bureau, describes the objectives of the reform as follows. The Yugoslav economy was to be integrated into the world market. Trade was to be gradually liberalized and the dinar made convertible. Exports were to rise relative to imports, which would permit the buildup of substantial foreign exchange reserves. The balance of payments deficit was to be eliminated [60, p. 71].

The new foreign trade regime became operative in 1967. About
one-quarter of imports was liberalized and retention quotas
remained at 7 percent in most cases. For the rest, there was a
complicated system of inducements and restrictions. In order to
achieve a proper regional distribution of trade, a category of imports from the convertible area was made conditional upon the purchase of a specified amount of clearing currency [62]. Export
premiums and tax subsidies were abolished. Tight money policy
was to keep prices stable, reduce internal demand, and compel
enterprises to export.

Once again, the new regime failed to produce the results expected. After an initial burst of exports and a contraction of imports which in 1965 produced a small balance of payments surplus,
imports began to expand faster than exports. Internal demand was
checked, but so were exports. A balance of payments deficit reappeared and was increasing. Unpleasant clearing currency surpluses were accumulated. Import restrictions were multiplied.
Export inducements were reintroduced. Differential exchange rates
were back. The dinar was stable on the tourist market — dinar notes
could be bought at rates close to the official one at all foreign ex-
changes — but a quiet devaluation was proceeding under the surface.
None of the objectives quoted by Anakiovski was achieved.

The ways in which the free trade reforms were carried out did
not indicate an impressive professional competence. But in this
respect Yugoslavia is not quite so unique in the present world.
The most popular method of policymaking seems to be trial and
error. It has its drawbacks, but, if applied with sufficient persis-
tence, it also produces useful results. So far, I have been examin-
ing deficiencies. Let me now briefly evaluate the results. Since
1952, the span between extreme actual exchange rates (resulting
from actual revenues of exporters and actual payments of importers) has been considerably narrowed. Actual exchange rates have
become quite a bit more stable. The positive difference between
the actual export and actual import exchange rates of 303 dinars
in 1955 was transformed into a negative difference of 100 dinars
in 1967. Government interventions in foreign trade operations
have been reduced in every respect. About one-fifth to one-fourth
of imports has been firmly and completely liberalized, either directly or by means of retention quotas and other arrangements.
The tourist dinar is a stable and convertible currency. The stage
is set for the last assault — if there is such a thing as "last" in
economics — on free trade and convertibility.

The Yugoslav Economic System

The What-to-Do-Next Controversy

The misfortunes of the third reform were not quite so unexpected. Ž. Mrkušić, A. Čičin-Šain, and other economists evaluated various government objectives as unattainable given the policy pursued. Soon a lively discussion developed focusing on three themes: protection, the nature of exchange rates, and convertibility.

I. Fabinc argued that every protection policy ought to be associated with a development program. Developing countries encounter serious bottlenecks in output capacities and shortages in material and financial means. Therefore, unlike developed countries, whose protection policy aims at changing the structure of prices and incomes, developing countries must have a protection policy oriented toward changes in the structure of production. The main objective of tariff policy is to protect national production by creating a desirable differentiation of internal prices as compared with prices on the world market. There are, however, three important tasks that a tariff policy cannot perform. It cannot regulate the volume of imports, it cannot achieve the desirable structure of imports, and it cannot regulate a regional distribution of trade [64; 65]. One must find other devices to do these three jobs.

Evidently, administrative interventions of the government are one possible alternative. However, this is not acceptable as a dominant alternative in the Yugoslav setting. Next, a proper exchange rate system could do at least part of the job. This system may be based on one single rate, or on multiple rates; the rate or rates may be pegged or may be fluctuating. Out of these elements, four main combinations and a number of variations may be formed. On the one extreme, there will be a single pegged rate and, on the other, fluctuating multiple rates.

In the debate, the Institute of Foreign Trade noticed an inconsistency in the traditional approach. The policy of a single rate usually imposes the elimination of multiple rates on the export side, while on the import side they are retained in the form of a customs tariff. In fact, however, the economic justification for multiple rates is the same for both components of foreign trade [59, p. 75]. Ž. Mrkušić and O. Kovač of the Institute of Economic Studies suggested that the pegged rate be made flexible by applying exchange rate ingredients such as tax reductions, preferential transportation rates, and the like. But they find direct export subsidies unacceptable, presumably because they fear a proliferation of arbitrary government interventions [63, p. 34]. As far as the import

200

side is concerned, Fabinc noted that fixed customs rates do not prevent their flexible application (by an appropriate definition of the customs value or the introduction of point clauses) [64, p. 38]. Other devices — such as a customs registration tax — are available as well. Thus, even if the single fixed exchange rate is chosen as a basis for the system, the prevailing expert opinion favors making it flexible in both senses: it ought to be changeable in time and differentiable with respect to the fixed standard. The justification for this approach had already been provided by D. Avramović in the 1952 paper cited earlier: a planned economy cannot tolerate for outside economic conditions and fluctuations to be automatically transmitted to the internal market. This was now reiterated by U. Dujšin, who advocated not only flexible but also fluctuating rates [66, p. 593]. Mrkušić pointed out that if one wants to keep the balance of payments in equilibrium, either the exchange rate or internal prices will have to be continually adjusted. Since internal stability is obviously the first priority, the flexibility of the external value of money follows as a natural consequence [74].

The government had chosen to base its policy on the pegged rate. This decision now came under attack. A pegged rate implied government interventions, which were resented. Fluctuating rates, on the other hand, involved risks of instability, which the government was not willing to assume. Čičin-Šain thought that these risks could not be so great, that fluctuating rates required much smaller reserves and much less stringent conditions in terms of financial discipline, organization of the market, and so on [67]. A few years earlier, G. Macesich, an American economist of Yugoslav extraction, had also argued in favor of fluctuating rates. He believed that "such a system would serve to integrate the country's economy more effectively with the world's economy by quickly indicating to planners when mistakes in the planning have been made. The correction of mistakes would not have to depend on intermittent changes in rigid official exchange rates" [72, p. 202].

Mrkušić, on the other hand, argued that fluctuating exchange rates would generate speculation and would be destabilizing. He cited the Canadian twelve-year experimentation with fluctuating rates, which ended with trade restrictions for about one-half of imports [73]. Čičin-Šain suggested that speculation could be avoided if enterprises were obliged to sell foreign exchange as soon as it was earned. Capital movements would clearly require separate control.

Fluctuating exchange rates implied the existence of a foreign exchange market. The government feared that this might mean repeating the failures of the DOM. On the other hand, enterprises and business chambers were pressing for higher retention quotas. The prevailing expert opinion seemed to be in favor of the market, even if not for all currencies. Since the country ran a chronic surplus on its trading account with the clearing area as a whole and with most of the individual clearing currency countries, it seemed advisable to start market operations with those currencies [50, p. 34]. That would mean fluctuating rates for about one-half of the foreign exchange proceeds. The next phase might be trading in convertible currencies, and finally a proclamation of the external convertibility of the dinar.

Čičin-Šain examined the pros and cons of approaching full convertibility by means of external convertibility — that is, by satisfying Article VIII of the IMF agreement — or by means of internal liberalization. He was in favor of the former, and cited the following three reasons: (1) the dinar may become a reserve currency, which would mean an interest-free credit for Yugoslav imports; (2) clearing countries may find it advisable to liquidate their clearing deficits in order to accumulate convertible dinar balances; and (3) the financial prestige of Yugoslavia would increase. He felt, however, that the reasons are not particularly convincing. Even if fully convertible, the dinar would probably not be held as a reserve currency in any substantial amount, and insofar as clearing deficits are structural, they would not be remedied by financial devices. On the other hand, external convertibility requires substantial reserves and is more difficult to achieve the higher the degree of internal liberalization [68; 69]. Liberalization would result in lower inventories — inventories are notoriously high in the Yugoslav economy — which would mean a considerable saving in foreign exchange and working capital.

Later in the debate, professional opinion swung in the direction of external convertibility. Mrkušić argued that, in fact, Yugoslavia maintained external convertibility with the convertible currency countries. If Yugoslav traders pay foreign exporters in their own currency, this is the same as if they paid in an externally convertible dinar. The official proclamation of external convertibility would lead to greater financial discipline, to greater influence of the world market on the internal costs of production, and also to some foreign exchange economizing, because foreign exporters would not insist on converting dinar balances immediately into their own currency [70]. The Economic Institute in Zagreb pointed out that external convertibility would facilitate multilateralization of trade with the Comecon countries [42, p. 191].

As already noted, Yugoslavia belongs to neither of the trade areas in Europe and is politically uncommitted. As a result, it encountered considerable difficulties in trade with its neighbors. However, why not transform this position of weakness into a position of strength? A country that went through underdevelopment, central planning, and market organization and that is economically and politically uncommitted might perhaps become a desirable economic meeting place for the three different worlds. If so, external convertibility certainly would be one of the preconditions for making the mediating role of the Yugoslav market attractive for its partners from the West, the East, and the underdeveloped South [69, p. 82].

The reform of 1965 envisaged the establishment of currency convertibility by 1970. The preceding analysis shows that the goal could not be achieved. But it was not given up. In the ensuing debate, the following strategy for achieving the goal by phases seems to have been accepted: (1) start with elaborate control of imports; (2) encourage exports in order to accumulate foreign exchange reserves; (3) gradually liberalize the import regime; (4) establish external convertibility (convertibility for foreign residents); and, finally, (5) establish full convertibility.

The foreign trade reform of 1967 established the following six import categories. Under the liberalized imports regime (LB), commodities can be imported without any restriction. Conditionally liberalized import (LBO) entails a fixed obligation to purchase a specified volume of goods from the clearing currency area in order to acquire the right to free imports. Commodities included in the global foreign exchange quota (GDK) can be imported and paid for in foreign exchange only in amounts and kinds of currency allotted to firms by the government within the limits of established foreign exchange quotas. Under the commodity quota regime (RK), the government is authorized to fix a yearly import quota for a certain number of commodities. Similar treatment is implied under foreign exchange quotas (DK). Finally, import permits (D) apply to specified individual deals and represent the most restrictive category [82, pp. 58-59]. In 1969, the share of various categories in the total imports of commodities were as follows: LB, 20.8; LBO, 14.2; GDK, 44.8; RK, 11.0; DK, 1.9; and D, 7.3 percent [81, p. 45]. Soon these six basic categories were modified in various ways, and in 1970 Pertot could enumerate eight additional subcategories [86, pp. 293-97].

In order to encourage exports, Mrkušić suggests direct subsidies out of a special fund, tax reliefs, and a refund for customs duties paid for inputs used in export production [81, p. 87]. In 1968, a special Export Credit and Insurance Fund was established. The fund finances credits extended by authorized banks to firms for exports of equipment and ships and the construction of capital projects abroad, and insures their claims abroad against political risks [83, p. 63].

Liberalization of foreign trade proceeded through increases in the share of LB and LBO categories at the expense of restrictive forms of imports. In addition, a foreign exchange market, based on a limited flexibility of the exchange rate, was created. The market includes only commercial banks and the National Bank. Commercial banks keep deposits of residents, offer and take credits in foreign exchange, and buy and sell foreign exchange on account of their clients or on their own account. Current and capital transactions by nonresidents are also handled by this market, though without external convertibility. The National Bank intervenes when necessary in order to keep the exchange rates within the desired limits. The substantially greater sophistication of economic policy, as compared with the days of the DOM, make it possible for the foreign exchange market to function reasonably well.

One unexpected consequence of the 1965 reform was the massive emigration of labor to Western Europe and the consequent inflow of hard currency in the form of remittances to families that stayed at home. Soon remittances became by far the most important export industry, amounting to double the earnings of the tourist trade. Stagnant imports (−6 percent) and an export boom (17 percent) in 1972, together with remittances, led to the first substantial balance of payments surplus in 1973. Foreign exchange reserves were sharply increased. The country looked ready for the next phase, external convertibility. Instead, however, the energy crisis, coupled with an output boom, generated an enormous increase of imports — 74 percent in current prices in the first three quarters of 1974 — a deficit reappeared, the dinar was devalued, and convertibility was lost in the mist of a highly uncertain future.

In the context of liberalization of transactions with the outside world, another development ought to be mentioned. The country has always used large amounts of foreign capital to speed up its growth. Apart from a brief interlude with Soviet-Yugoslav mixed companies, this was exclusively loan capital. For a long time, loans were received only through official channels, through government agencies and the National Bank. In the period under consideration, commercial banks and individual firms acquired the right of access to the international capital market. Since 1967, however, direct foreign investment in the form of joint ventures has become possible. M. Sukijasović describes the motives for this decision as follows: "to find new ways to enable the home enterprises to gain and apply sooner modern techniques and technology; to take advantage of the impact of foreign firms in industrial and business engineering of home enterprises; to obtain easier access to the foreign markets thanks to the foreign partner's network; to acquire additional capital; and to increase the capacities and productivity of domestic enterprises not engaged in joint ventures" [84, p. 11].

The motives just enumerated make clear that banking, insurance, domestic transportation, trade, social services, and portfolio investment will be closed to foreign investment. Foreign firms may directly invest up to 49 percent of the capital value of a domestic firm. However, this percentage has more of a symbolic than a real meaning, for all aspects of management are regulated by a contract and all crucial decisions are made unanimously. All joint venture contracts must be approved by the appropriate ministry, which performs a preventive check to ensure that the contract conforms to law; is likely to increase output, productivity, and, in particular, exports; treats both partners equally; does not overvalue the patents, licenses, and technology contributed by the foregoing partner; and does not conflict with the interest of national security.

The impact of joint ventures has been rather limited so far. In the first five years, 1968-72, seventy-two contracts were signed. Foreign funds amounted to 19 percent of total investment in equity ventures, which represented only 4 percent of the total inflow of medium- and long-term capital [85, p. 734].

MONEY, BANKING, AND
PUBLIC FINANCE

VI

19. BANKING AND MONETARY POLICY

Much experimentation has been carried out in the Yugoslav economy. This is true for the monetary field more than for any other.

Banking can be organized in a centralized or decentralized fashion. Decentralization can be regional, functional, or both. Centralization can be absolute or partial. Thus there are five possible organizational solutions. All of them have been tried out in Yugoslavia at one time or another.

Banking for a Centrally Planned Economy

According to the Institute of Finance, in the socialist economy of 1949, money was a tool used by the state authorities to distribute social product in proportion to the labor of each working person, to establish economic ties among enterprises, and to exercise control over their activities. Money was also a means of accumulation and an instrument of control over plan fulfillment [1, p. 63]. The banking system was expected to provide money which had such properties.

From prewar times, Yugoslavia inherited a certain number of private and state banks. The former were eliminated by 1947. The latter were reorganized. The National Bank was a descendant of the Serbian National Bank created in 1883. The former State Mortgage Bank — the heir of a state bank set up in Serbia in 1862 (Uprava fondova) — continued to operate as the State Investment Bank. The Agricultural Bank of 1929 continued to operate in the same field. There was also a Handicraft Bank, and, in view of the ambitious industrialization programs, it appeared advisable to set up a separate Industrial Bank.

The war had not yet ended when the creation of regional banks began — six regional banks for the six states.

For a country aiming at central planning, all these banks did not represent a very purposeful arrangement. In September 1946, the banking system began to be consolidated. All existing banks were merged into the National Bank, which was entrusted with short-term transactions, and the State Investment Bank, which was to handle investments and foreign loans. Apart from dealing with short-term credit, the National Bank issued currency, performed general banking and agency services for the government, and served as a clearinghouse for the entire economy. In 1948, the two-bank system seemed overly centralized. Since local enterprises and agricultural cooperatives played special roles at that time, eighty-nine communal banks and six regional state banks for lending to agricultural cooperatives were formed. Communal banks were universal banks: they serviced local budgets, extended short- and long-term credits, collected savings, and controlled plan fulfillments of local enterprises. Banks charged a 1 percent interest rate, which was in fact a commission charge for their services. It was not deemed appropriate for a socialist system to charge interest as a price for capital.

Since it is much easier to control financial transactions conducted through bank accounts than those made in cash, as early as 1945 all enterprises and other nonprivate transactors were obliged to have drawing accounts with the bank. Soon about nine-tenths of payments were conducted without the use of cash. This was one of the lasting results of the early period of banking development. Payments through bank balances developed into a unique internal payment system, channeled through local offices of the National Bank. It embraced all banks, post offices, enterprises, government funds, and a considerable part of the private sector, and connected all money streams of the economy into a single consistent system [2, p. 366].

In many respects, the early Yugoslav monetary system was a replica of the Soviet model. This is particularly true for the three instruments of monetary control: credit planning, cash distribution, and the automatic collection of invoices.

Credit planning was the only instrument to service the administrative phase. Until 1950, credit planning simply meant summing up the credit needs of individual enterprises. This was done by the planning authorities. The bank was supposed to implement such plans in a routine way. Later, credit plans were transformed into credit balances, which meant that needs were balanced with means. Banks were made responsible for drawing up credit balances [3, p. 172]. The planned amount of credit for individual enterprises was obtained by dividing the output target into an individual capital-turnover coefficient and then subtracting the enterprise's working capital [2, p. 366].

The main purpose of cash distribution plans was to control receipts (mainly in retail trade, catering, and passenger transport) and expenditures made in cash (primarily for wages and payments to peasants) [4, pp. 145-46]. The cash plan was made for territorial units and for separate money streams, and so provided useful information about receipts and expenditures of the population and about various channels in which the money was circulating in the economy. But it was a rather rigid instrument with not much use outside central planning and was therefore abandoned in 1951.

In order to enhance financial discipline, enterprises were forbidden to grant trade credits to each other. The automatic collection of invoices served the same purpose. The bank would automatically credit the seller's account when goods were shipped and then charge the buyer's account. In this way, no mutual crediting could be practiced. Payments were carried out smoothly. If there was no money in the buyer's account, credit was automatically extended. This, of course, meant that credits would expand beyond the limits set by the credit plan. At first, such matters did not worry planners too much; physical targets and not money flows were important. Other consequences were more disquieting. The total volume of credits depended more on debtors than on banks. The necessary discipline was jeopardized. Sellers did not care about the solvency of their buyers, and also tended to pay insufficient attention to delivery terms, assortment, and quality of goods. Buyers did not mind accumulating excessive inventories. After a while, careless buyers had to be put on blacklists; their drawing accounts were blocked and many cases were brought before the courts. The automatic payments mechanism broke down and was replaced in 1951 by free contracts among the trading partners [5, p. 21].

Learning by Doing

What sort of banking system was appropriate for a self-management economy — centralized or decentralized? There was a lively discussion on that issue. E. Neuberger surveyed the principal arguments advanced in favor of one or the other alternative [6].

Whatever the merits of these arguments might have been per se, the government decided to play it safe. No one could be sure of the business behavior of labor-managed enterprises. It seemed advisable that decentralization in the market for goods and services be accompanied by strict centralization in the financial sphere. All other control instruments, remarked J. Pokorn, were to be replaced by bank control and supervision [7]. In March 1952, communal banks ceased to exist and other banks were merged with the National Bank into one single giant bank with 550 offices and 16,000 employees.

In order to make control as efficient as possible, the working capital of enterprises was transferred to the bank. Enterprises were to pay a reasonable interest rate, which was to induce them to economize with the credit money.

The short-term interest rate was differentiated according to turnover velocity of working capital and ranged from 2 percent for crude oil production and agriculture to 7 percent for electric power plants. This span was reduced to 5 to 7 percent in 1953. In 1954, it was again increased and the rates differentiated in a somewhat different fashion (for different kinds of credits). Experimentation with interest rates continued even later, and in 1956 there were twenty-five categories of active interest rates [5, p. 183].

So-called social accounting represented one lasting result of the 1952 reform. The bank established special accounts — at first thirteen of them — for all important transactions of each enterprise. All changes that took place in the current account of an enterprise were entered here. In this way, (1) the bank and the government had up-to-date information; (2) the bank was able to exert stringent control; it would stop any irregular payment, which was particularly important in relation to wages; and (3) the bank checked on the fulfillment of tax and other obligations of an enterprise to the state. The system was later simplified, the number of separate accounts was gradually reduced, and the bank began to rely more on quarterly accounting statements of the enterprises. A standard accounting scheme, obligatory for all enterprises, made this task a routine matter.(In 1959, social accounting, with its drawing accounts system for the entire economy, was separated from the National Bank and turned into an independent social service.) The work was computerized and the service became very efficient. A little later it was discovered that the monopoly of the Social Accounting Service on the payments traffic posed no obstacle to enterprises' keeping their financial resources with the banks of their own choice.

Today every nonprivate income earner has both a drawing account with the Social Accounting Service (and pays commission charges) and a deposit account with one of the banks (and receives interest on deposits).

The proper procedure to be used in extending short-term credits was one of the important problems the all-embracing National Bank had to solve. In those days of romantic beliefs in the possibility of inventing simple problem-solving devices — such as the rate of accumulation and funds — that would eliminate the arbitrariness of a bureaucratic apparatus, the bank hired a couple of mathematicians and asked them to invent appropriate formulas for credit extension. A booklet with several dozen such formulas was published in 1952 [8]. They were based on turnover coefficients of credits and ratios of sales to costs. Since parameters to be used in the formulas could be calculated only as some sort of averages, it was soon discovered that some enterprises got more credits than they needed, while others badly lacked the money to keep production going. Formulas were abandoned and in 1953 the amount of credit extended was related to the maximum quarterly credit used by the enterprise in the previous year. This practice favored last year's debtors and penalized good entrepreneurs and had to be abandoned. But the idea of some automatic credit-evaluating mechanism was not given up. In 1954 the bank experimented with credit auctions. M. Vučković explains that credit auctions were to be a kind of socialist credit market where the supply and demand of money would meet and determine the general conditions for credit extension [5, p. 38]. The bank expected that less profitable enterprises would refrain from asking for credit because they would not be able to bear high interest rates. It turned out that precisely the less profitable or unprofitable enterprises were prepared to offer the highest interest rates — up to 17 percent — because they considered credit the only available solution to their problems. The bank then set the marginal interest rate at 7.5 percent. But this was a negation of the whole idea of auctions. Soon credit was extended automatically to every enterprise that had satisfied the formal conditions of an auction. Since all automatic devices proved inefficient, in 1955 the bank fell back on the traditional banking practice of the individual evaluation of every credit request.

By 1954, two facts were established: (1) the New Economic System worked well as a whole, but (2) the centralized bank left much to be desired. As soon as that had become clear, regional and functional decentralization were initiated. One of the main justifications for decentralization was the socioeconomic incongruity between self-management in the commodity market and state monopoly in the financial market. Vučković approvingly quotes the Governor of the National Bank, who declared that in a decentralized banking system the credit function would be subject to the control of social self-government instead of bureaucratic management [5, p. 86]. Communal banks, with all their diverse activities, were reestablished. The banks were obliged to keep reserves of up to 30 percent of demand deposits and 100 percent of investment funds with the National Bank. In the next three years, three specialized federal banks were added: a Foreign Trade Bank, an Investment Bank, and an Agricultural Bank. The National Bank was relieved of investment and some other banking operations. Each bank was run by a managing board whose members were partly appointed by the authority that founded the bank and partly elected by the bank's personnel in the proportion of 2:1.

After all these changes had been made, it appeared appropriate to give working capital back to enterprises. This was done in 1956, and the system was stabilized for the time being. Working capital was not given back free of charge; enterprises were obliged to pay an interest rate of 6 percent.

Banking for a Self-Governing Economy

It was eight years before a formerly administratively run economy learned how to handle a few basic financial mechanisms. The task of creating an adequate institutional system in the financial sphere was yet to be accomplished. It took eight more years for an outline of such a system to become visible.

The deficiencies of the banking system as it developed until 1960 were described by V. Holjevac as follows [11]. The National Bank offices were inefficient and unimaginative, engaged in distributing the planned increase in credits and executing the decisions of the head office. Communal banks fell under the complete control of local authorities, which often made it impossible to conduct a sound business policy of profitable and safe investments. The federal government often directly interfered with the banking business by immobilizing certain kinds of deposits or running a deficit inconsistent with the social plan. To overcome these deficiencies, a series of reforms was undertaken. As in the post-1952 period, reforms were carried out in two-year intervals starting with 1961.

In 1961, communal banks became basic and universal credit

institutions. In order to eliminate the monopolistic influence of political authorities, a two-thirds majority of the members of the banks' managing boards were nominated by workers' councils of the enterprises located in the territory of the bank. Next, eight regional banks reappeared. They were to serve as mediators between communal banks — which were required to keep a 5 percent reserve with respective regional banks — and the National Bank. That was a rather unfortunate arrangement, since it caused the disintegration of the national credit market into six regional markets with different business conditions, and so on [17, p. 53]. This mistake was rectified four years later.

In 1962, an interesting new institution was created — the joint reserve funds of the enterprises. D. Dimitrijević describes joint reserves as a semifinancial intermediary. Joint reserves — created at communal and state levels — grant credits to those enterprises that have losses, are not competitive, have an unsound financial position, and are not eligible for regular bank credit [34, p. 19].

For more than a decade, Yugoslav banking practice — and monetary theory — had maintained a fundamental difference between fixed capital and working capital financing. This made sense in a centrally planned economy, but it led to mistaken policies in a market setting. It was now realized that working capital was not homogeneous: it consisted of a constant part, which could and should be financed as fixed capital, and a fluctuating part, which was a proper object of short-term credits. In 1961, enterprises consolidated the fixed capital and working capital funds into one single business fund. Thus, all liquid assets could be used both for current payments and for capital formation.[1] In order to increase the financial independence of enterprises, they were encouraged to finance the constant part of the working capital out of their own funds and to rely on bank credit for the fluctuating part only. But that was not enough for a full-fledged credit policy.

Policymakers had to solve the following problem: design a flexible credit policy with a minimum of administrative allocations

---

1. However, enterprises were still obliged to hold five separate accounts, apart from the drawing account, with the Social Accounting Service. These accounts — depreciation, undistributed profits, nonbusiness expenditures, and two types of reserves — were operated under special rules designed to induce enterprises to behave in a proper business fashion [14]. Separate accounts, of course, reduced the possibility of rational use of money, since it could not be freely transferred from one account to another. However, separate accounts have gradually been eliminated.

when there is no proper money and capital market. They decided to use so-called qualitative control, which implied regulating the demand for credit. The new policy was introduced in 1963, and one of its architects, N. Miljanić, Governor of the National Bank, gave a detailed account of it in a book published a year later [17]. According to Miljanić, final demand ought to be financed out of income produced. This implies that inventory formation should be financed out of accumulation. The governmental budget deficit could be used as a source of new money, but that is not desirable because, in the absence of a money market, the distribution of such money occurs in a haphazard way and cannot be controlled. Miljanić even insists that the federal budget should be balanced in any case [17, p. 31]. This contention, though clearly not defensible in theory, has some justification in practice in view of the sometimes less than responsible deficit financing of government agencies. The official document of the National Bank adds that in case of a recession it is preferable to increase (selectively) the money supply rather than to run a budgetary deficit [25, p. 28]. Since the liquidity trap is nonexistent in the Yugoslav economy, this is a valid statement.

New money ought to be used to finance primarily the circulation of commodities. Thus credit is given on the basis of some evidence (invoice, bill of exchange) that a commodity has been sold (by a producer) or bought (by a merchant). Credit cannot be given for sales to final buyers (government, investors, consumers). As exceptions to the rule, and on the basis of individual evaluation by the bank, credits can also be given for seasonal stocks and for stocks due to some circumstances beyond the enterprise's control. (In fact, credit for stocks, far from being an exception, almost reached the level of credits for commodity circulation [17, p. 72].) Apart from this first category of credits, which creates some sort of neutral money, credits can also play an active role in supporting production. Such are credits for specific ventures, primarily for exports, for agricultural production, and for construction of apartments for sale. Miljanić also noticed one difficulty with his system. Business operations require that an enterprise always have at its disposal a certain amount of money pure and simple. This money is a part of constant working capital, but, being money, should not be financed out of income. On the other hand, if it is financed by credits, they are clearly not short-term ones. Miljanić feels that revolving credits might do the job [17, p. 88].

This system lasted for four years and produced some good results. Enterprises knew in advance what conditions they must fulfill in order to obtain credit from the bank. Commercial banks were sure to get credits from the National Bank if they met the prescribed conditions. But the system was also deficient in many ways. B. Mijović, a Director in the National Bank, points out that qualitative control (conditions, purpose, duration, and kinds of credits) could not quite achieve the aims of quantitative regulation of the money supply. The National Bank had to generate a constant stream of detailed and extensive instructions, which became particularly cumbersome. Since not all practical cases could be envisaged and regulated in advance, the handling of borderline cases caused considerable difficulties. Frequent institutional changes elsewhere in the economy caused additional problems [18, pp. 73, 112]. By 1967, the credit system was ripe for a new reform. This time, supply of — and not demand for — credit was made a primary object of monetary control. Selective control was accommodated within a system of quantitative regulation.

The three types of credits — investment, commercial, and consumer — led to a law providing for the establishment of three types of banks: investment banks financing fixed and constant working capital; commercial banks extending short-term credit; and savings banks dealing with consumer credit. Table 27 summarizes the latest organizational changes [16, p. 78].

Organizational changes reflected very definite policy changes: (1) Federal, state, and communal banks disappeared. All banks can, in principle, conduct their transactions anywhere in the country. This deterritorialization policy came as a response to frequent complaints about parochialism and unsound political pressures of local and state authorities. (2) The market orientation of banks resulted in a concentration process that reduced the total number of banks to one-half in only three years. By the end of 1968, the number of banks was further reduced to 74. This number should

Table 27

Banks in Yugoslavia

November 1964		June 1967	
Type of bank	Number	Type of bank	Number
Communal banks	206	Commercial banks	61
State investment banks	8	Mixed banks	39
Specialized federal banks	3	Investment banks	11
Total	217	Total	111

be compared with the total of 700 private banks before the war. But the most important was (3) the change in setting up and running the banks. Here at last, a solution consistent with the organization of the rest of economy was found.

Banks are now established by enterprises and sociopolitical communities (federal, state, or local) as equal partners. In order to be independent business establishments, banks have their own capital, called the credit fund. The founders invest their capital in the credit fund of the bank and become shareholders. At least twenty-five founders are required for any bank, to preserve the essentially service function of the bank. The bank is managed by enterprises and sociopolitical communities in proportion to the amount of their capital invested in the credit fund. Shareholders are entitled to dividends depending on business success. These dividends cannot be distributed in wages, but can be used only for capital formation. To prevent monopolization, no single shareholder can have more than 10 percent of the total number of votes in a bank's assembly, regardless of the amount of capital invested. Also, no enterprise or sociopolitical community can be refused the right to invest in a bank and take part in its management. The assembly of a bank consists of investors and representatives of the bank's personnel. It appoints the executive committee, the director, and his deputy. The executive committee implements the bank's general business policy. The credit committee deals with individual requests for credit except in some special cases. In order to ensure an objective and expert business evaluation of requests, the credit committee is composed of the bank's own experts. The employees of a bank have their own self-management bodies, which deal with the distribution of personal income, use of various funds, personnel matters, and the like, and, through their representatives on the executive committee and in the assembly, participate in the management of the bank.

After a network of commercial banks had been established, the National Bank discontinued its direct business contacts with enterprises and became a central bank in the traditional sense.[2]

In its function of regulating the money supply, the National Bank had the following weapons at its disposal in 1961 [12, pp. 95-104]:

1) currency issue;
2) sale of foreign exchange;

---

2. Neuberger examined the role of central banking under three types of economic systems, the Yugoslav system before 1961 being one of them [9].

3) fixed terms for the extension of short-term credit by communal banks;

4) legally required reserves held by communal (later by commercial) banks with the National Bank; the upper limit was set at 35 percent of liquid deposits;

5) interest rate limits (in practice, 8-12 percent);

6) restrictions on the use of certain kinds of deposits; this instrument was often and indiscriminately used, which greatly annoyed the owners of funds; I. Perišin points out that in the period 1954-62 between 34 and 45 percent of total deposits were blocked in this way [13];

7) special credits extended by the National Bank to other banks; these credits were used to finance about one-half of all short-term credits extended by commercial banks to their clients;

8) consumer credit policy;

9) consultations and recommendations.

Compared with traditional banking, some items appear superfluous, but one important item is missing: there is no place for an open market policy, since there are (so far) no treasury bills. Instrument (8) is a substitute for that. By special credits, new money is created and the liquidity of commercial banks ensured. If a bank wants to reduce excessive liquidity (in order to avoid paying passive interest), it can do so by repaying its credit to the National Bank.

As already mentioned, the 1967 reform replaced credit demand control by credit supply control, and so functions of the National Bank had to be adjusted accordingly. Instruments (3) and (6) were abandoned and the existing amount of special credits could no longer be increased. Several new instruments were added:

10) rediscount credit, which is used as an instrument of both global and selective control; it amounts to about 12 percent of all commercial credits; in order to qualify for this type of credit, a commercial bank must fulfill two conditions: (a) its total indebtedness with the National Bank cannot be greater than its demand deposits, and (b) at least one-half of its short-term credits must consist of credits with repayment periods shorter than three months; condition (b) is a special type of liquidity reserve requirement designed for the Yugoslav environment, where there is enormous pressure to use short-term sources for investment loans;

11) discount rate;

12) credit for liquidity as a substitute for the call money market; it enables commercial banks to overcome temporary and unexpected drains of reserve money;

216

13) quantitative restriction of credit (credit ceiling) as an exceptional measure.

This is an impressive array of weapons, which, if inappropriately used, can cause considerable damage. In a later section we will see how this can happen.

In 1967, a daily market was set up within the Association of Banks for interbank borrowing of call money to cover a sudden drain of reserve money. Banks in need can obtain credit for a period not exceeding fifteen days [16, p. 81].

Let me also mention the practice of monetary planning. On the basis of reliable and up-to-date information provided by the Social Accounting Service, a sophisticated system of flow-of-funds accounts was designed. Since 1967, this system has also been used for annual and monthly monetary planning, thus replacing the old-fashioned credit balances. Its author, D. Dimitrijević, gave a technical description of the methods used in [26].

As one might have expected, institutional changes have not ceased with the reform of 1967. After constitutional amendments in 1971, a new reorganization of banking — the eighth, by N. Vučić's count [73, pp. 287-89] — became imminent. First of all, in the general mood of decentralization and "defederalization," the National Bank appeared much too central and too federal. Six states and two provinces acquired their own national banks and their own governors, eight altogether. The Council of Governors of the national banks became the supreme monetary authority. The Council — that is, the National Bank of Yugoslavia — determines the general rules of behavior and the global framework of monetary policy. This includes the issue of new money and its distribution among member banks, the determination of minimal reserves, minimal discount rates, maximal credit ceiling, and the like. State and provincial national banks shape and apply monetary instruments on their territories within the general, agreed-upon framework of monetary policy [72].

Under the 1967 reform, the credit fund of the bank represented its own capital. The shares in the fund were transferable. To facilitate transfers, issuance of certificates to the owners of the shares was introduced in 1969. These were the first equities in the system. Due to the processes described in the following sections, banks soon acquired considerable independent financial power, which contradicted the proclaimed goal that they be service organizations of productive firms. As a consequence, in 1972 credit funds were abolished, the minimum number of founders was increased to fifty, and the capital of banks was transferred to their founders. The credit policy of the bank is determined by the founders. This implies, comments Dimitrijević, that credit conditions are determined by the users of credits themselves. As a result, the bank will not allocate resources to the most productive uses in the economy, but will instead try to secure maximum credit at the most favorable conditions, including a lower interest rate, for its founders [75, p. 33]. In addition, although local governments cannot obtain more than 10 percent of the vote in the bank assemblies, their influence on business decisions is uncomfortably great. Thus, the credit market appears to be doubly compartmentalized — by clients and by regions.

In 1973, the number of available financial instruments was increased. Apart from bonds, which had already been used on two occasions, cashier's certificates for capital invested in special joint funds were added. Two such funds have been created by the firms so far: for export credits and for selling process equipment and electrical equipment on the domestic market. The capital certificates are similar to conventional shares. In the first two years of their existence, the impact of the new financial instruments has been insignificant.

Investment Financing

The amount of professional literature on investment financing varies in inverse proportion to the number of complaints against the state of affairs in this field. It is difficult to figure out why this is so. Perhaps it is because of the fact that investment financing is, in a sense, a borderline case: neither monetary theorists nor fiscal policy experts nor (predominantly physical) planners feel competent to deal with it. In any case, investment financing has been one of the weakest links in economic policy for a long time, yet no serious study of its problems has been undertaken so far. Thus, I will confine this exposition to a description of actual development.

Capital formation may be financed by fiscal means, that is, out of taxation, out of the enterprises' own funds, by bank loans, or through securities of various kinds. This is roughly the order in which the various kinds of investment financing have been tried out in Yugoslavia.

Early in 1945, the government created the Fund for Reconstruction, whose resources consisted of confiscated war profits[3] and proceeds from the sale of goods supplied by the UN Relief and Rehabilitation Administration. Very soon loans given by the fund were written off and capital formation was financed in the budgetary fashion typical of a centrally planned economy. Investment resources were allocated by the plan and given to enterprises from the budget free of charge. Enterprises could not sell capital goods; they could only transfer them to other enterprises after obtaining permission to do so. Since the state was the only owner of capital and prices did not matter much anyway, this arrangement was consistent with the rest of the system.

The crucial year of 1952 inaugurated important changes. The federal budget as a source of investment finance was replaced by the Fund for Basic Capital Development. Investment resources were still allocated without repayment obligations, but the creation of the fund led to a division of the budget into two separate parts: one related to administrative expenses and the other consisted of various investment and interventionist funds. This was to become a permanent feature of the Yugoslav budget.

In 1952, the federal government concentrated just about all investment resources in its fund. This served to gain time for the preparation of a more thoroughgoing reform. As early as the next year, funds for crediting investment activities were formed. Enterprises established their own investment funds, financed out of profits left to them by the plan. Both measures led to a considerable decentralization of capital formation financing. The system assumed its more permanent shape in 1954, when social investment funds (SIFs) were created at all levels — federal, state, district, and communal. From that time until the latest reforms, social investment funds granted loans to business enterprises, while capital formation in the nonbusiness sector (schools, hospitals, government offices, etc.) continued to be financed out of the government budget. In 1955, special housing funds were introduced. They were financed by compulsory contributions of firms. The creation of social investment funds — which tended to multiply as time went by — had an interesting behavioral consequence. Since all levels of the government were under constant heavy pressure to invest, and funds were separated from the budget, their resources tended to be inflated beyond anything envisaged by the social plan. In the period 1955-60, the

---

3. In a similar setting after the First World War, the government had great difficulties in introducing the tax on war profits, and once the required law was promulgated, it could not be implemented [35, pp. 168-82].

volume of investment surpassed the target established in the social plan by 20 percent [19, p. 2157].

The reform of 1954 introduced two other important innovations. One consisted of the transfer of capital assets to enterprises. For the privilege of using social capital, they had to pay an interest rate of 6 percent; the rate was lowered to 4 percent in 1965, and in 1971 was finally abolished. Interest had to be paid on capital used regardless of the source of its finance. The proceeds from this interest, as well as the repayment of the loans granted, represented resources of the General Investment Fund operated by the federal government. The interest rate on social capital was differentiated according to the goals of price policy and the capital intensity of particular industry groups. It ranged from close to zero for agriculture to 1 percent for electric power generation and coal production, 2 percent for transportation, 4 percent for ferrous metallurgy, and 6 percent for most other industries. In this way, the interest burden, as a percentage of net product, was more evenly distributed among various industry groups. The average rate of interest was 2.8 percent in 1961 and 1.3 percent in 1966 in terms of capital, and 3.8 and 2.4 percent, respectively, in terms of net products [20, p. 23].

The second innovation is related to investment auctions. There are four types of investment allocation decisions: (1) the level of total investment; (2) the allocation of investment funds among sectors of the economy; (3) the allocation among firms within a sector; and (4) the technological variants within a firm [21, p. 103]. The last decision is made by the enterprise; the first two are determined by the plan. After priorities have been determined and investment allocated to various industry groups, the allocation among the enterprises may be carried out by auctions. This is an old textbook idea. In various texts on socialist economics with a neoclassical background, one can find statements that run roughly as follows: "In principle, the applicants would be list according to the level of the rate of interest they offered and if two offered the same rate, the one who offered the shorter period for repayment of the loan would be given preference. The bank would go down the list until the amount allocated for this auction, or category within the auction, was exhausted, and the rate of interest offered by the first intramarginal applicant would become the one that everyone paid." In fact, this is not an invented quotation, but Neuberger's description of actual investment auctions in Yugoslavia [21, p. 93]. In theory, one could, of course, improve this scheme in various ways. One could apply price discrimination in order to siphon out all nonlabor income contained in the difference between the offered and paid interest rates, or one could replace point offers by schedule offers. In practice, the experiment did not achieve great success. It was soon discovered that the two price criteria — the interest rate and the repayment period — were insufficient. Thus, other criteria were added: the percentage share of participation with the bidder's own resources (differentiated according to industries and ranging from zero for electric power to 80 percent in manufacturing), the shortest period of construction, the lowest cost per unit of output, and regional effects [2, p. 372; 62, p. 220]. The main defects of auctions appeared to be the following ones. It takes time and is very costly to prepare an application for credit. Auctions are held at widely spaced times which may not correspond with the enterprise's need for investment funds. As in the case of credit auctions, enterprises were ready to offer high rates of interest only to secure the loan. They did not worry too much about future repayments because the tradition of free social capital was still very much alive and it seemed obvious that a plant of any size cannot be closed down "just because the loan cannot be paid." Thus, the authorities in charge of social investment funds had to examine every case very thoroughly, as they would have done anyway, even without auctions. According to Neuberger's estimates, at most one-third of all investments at any given time were allocated through auctions. In such circumstances, auctions gradually degenerated into an old-fashioned administrative distribution of investment from government funds.

Auctions failed. The criteria used for investment allocations from social investment funds had never been very transparent — another reason for the lack of analytical literature — and had always been greatly influenced by political considerations. As a result, "political factories" appeared. All important investment projects were somehow multiplied by six, one for each state. Besides, social investment funds absorbed two-thirds of total investment resources, and — owing to participation requirements — directly controlled an even larger share of total investment. Inefficiency and bureaucratic control were not quite compatible with the self-management aspirations of the economy. Enterprises pressed for an increase in their share in investment finance. The data on actual development in characteristic years are given in Table 28.

A considerable share of investment money in the social investment fund was obtained through taxation. When in 1962 these

Table 28

Composition of Investment in Fixed Capital by Source of Finance (Excluding Private Investment) (in percent)

	1948	1951	1952	1953	1954	1955	1960	1962	1964	1966	1968	1971
Social funds and budgets	99	98	98	87	74	64	52	59	36	16	16	15
Federation	60	50	95	71	50	47	37	30	7	6	9	8
States	27	41	2	11	12	9	7	9	8	3	3	3
Communes and districts	12	7	1	5	12	8	18	20	21	7	4	4
Work organizations	1	2	2	13	26	35	37	38	32	46	37	34
Business	1	2	2	13	26	27	31	30	26	39	31	27
Nonbusiness	–	–	–	–	–	8	6	8	6	7	6	7
Banks	–	–	–	–	–	1	1	3	32	39	47	51

Sources: 1948-55: Yugoslav Survey, 15(1963), p. 2167; 1960-71: Statistički bilten SDK, 3(1969), pp. 68-69; 8(1972), pp. 68-69.

"contributions to social investment funds" were raised by 50 percent [15] a general outcry was raised against the "expropriation." It was requested that "state capital" be abolished. Two years later, the contributions to SIFs were abolished, and funds were transferred to bank credit funds. That is why bank investment loans increased so sharply in 1964. The starting principle of the reform of 1965 was to leave a larger share of the enterprises' savings at their disposal and consequently to restrict the role of sociopolitical communities in investment decisions [22, p. 3222].

The pendulum was pushed a little too far in the decentralization direction, for it was requested that even large capital-intensive projects (power generation, communications) be financed out of capital concentrated in banks.

The role of the Federation in investment was reduced to the operation of the Fund for Undeveloped Regions that would distribute annually to undeveloped regions close to 2 percent of national income as investment funds. State and communal funds also diminished considerably. But the share of enterprises, with the exception of a short-lived postreform increase, remained stagnant. As Table 28 shows, what actually happened was that the Federation and the bank simply changed places in investment financing.

Under conditions of chronic excess demand for investment resources, banks could easily assume a dominant role. The sum of the regular and penalty rates of interest could be as high as 18 percent. The first recession — which in fact followed the reform — was bound to reduce the investment funds of enterprises and make enterprises more dependent on banks. D. Vojnić points out that, in 1968, the repayments of bank loans amounted to 111 percent of net profits of enterprises [23, p. 89].

With almost one-half of investment resources under their control, banks established themselves as a dominant force in the investment market. What should be done to safeguard the independence of enterprises? The answer is by no means clear. The present discussion has concentrated on possible improvements of the capital market. In 1963, government bonds became negotiable. In 1968, the first enterprise bonds appeared. Bank shares were invented in 1969 and then abolished. The present author suggested that participating debentures be introduced [24]. The securities market could supply at least part of the capital outside the bankers' control. Pooling of resources and joint ventures are encouraged. After the social investment funds had been abolished, interest on social capital became a mere capital tax that flowed into the government budget. That was resented and the tax was abolished in 1971. It is now being suggested that this interest be reintroduced and that it be given to enterprises as resources earmarked for investment (i.e., it would be treated similarly to depreciation funds). It would not be surprising if soon another reform in this field were carried out. After a money market has been to a certain extent adequately organized, its twin, the capital market, surely cannot lag behind for very long.

Another possibility for reducing the power of the banks is to increase the self-financing of investment by firms. To achieve this, since 1972 social compacts have regulated the allocation of the firm's earnings between the wage funds and internal investment funds. The principle was adopted that firms with earnings per worker above the average would allocate increasingly larger percentages of their income to internal funds.

This brings us to the problem of the investment behavior of a labor-managed firm. The literature in this area is almost nonexistent. The first theoretical attempt was made by Svetozar Pejović. He observed an interesting consequence of the existence of interest rates on private savings. A rational worker, faced with the alternative of investing in his firm (and thereby increasing his wages in the following years) or opening a private savings account (and earning interest while also increasing his private wealth) will opt for the former if the marginal efficiency of investment is sufficiently higher than the savings account interest rate. At 5 percent interest rate, this implies a marginal efficiency of investment of 23 percent, 19 percent, 13 percent, or 9 percent corresponding to expectations of staying with the firm for five, six, ten, or fifteen years. If bank credits are available and there is a decreasing marginal efficiency schedule of investment, a sufficiently large loan may reduce marginal efficiency below the point where collective saving is preferable to private saving and thus destroy self-financing of investment altogether [76]. No empirical testing of this theory has been undertaken. Three facts may be mentioned. Considerable pressure exists to reduce collective saving. Table 28 illustrates the point. Since 1964, personal savings have increased substantially (from 10 percent to 36 percent of gross national saving in 1972 [75, p. 28]). Due to inflation, the interest rate, both for business loans and on savings accounts, has been negative since 1971.

Anti-Inflationary or (Anti-)Anticyclical Monetary Policy

In a centrally planned economy, market disequilibria result

in physical shortages; in a market economy, they are reflected in inflation. The age-old discussion about the real causes of inflation was resurrected among Yugoslav economists, after 1961, in particular.

Monetary theorists, not unexpectedly, tended to see the source of all troubles in an uncontrolled expansion of the money supply. M. Čirović argued that the increase in commodity prices represented the way in which the economy adapted itself to the excessive expansion of credit and money supply [27, p. 183]. Similarly, M. Vučković believed that inflation was essentially a result of excess demand. Since new money brings new demand unaccompanied by supply, a market disequilibrium arises and generates increases in prices. The excessive expansion of short-term credits is a consequence of the following deplorable practices: the use (irregular of course) of short-term credit for long-term investments, for nonsalable stocks, to cover losses, to finance budget deficits, and to finance taxes at all levels of government [28, pp. 128-29]. The last-mentioned practice is probably also one of the Yugoslav inventions in the field. Owing to fairly complete budgetary decentralization, local governments are very keen on squeezing every possible dinar out of "their" enterprises. In the early days of the New Economic System, they could do that by tailoring taxes so as to leave the coffers of the enterprises empty. This phenomenon was described by Miljanić and Vučković as early as 1956 [29; 3]. Thus, in 1954, in one single year, communes managed to increase their budgetary revenues by 98 percent [3, p. 173]. In order to comply with these patriotic requests, enterprises would have to increase prices or ask for credits or both. Credits were readily granted because paying taxes on time had always been considered a first priority. After the budget system had been somewhat more efficiently designed, the arbitrariness in taxation was reduced; but whenever they were in need, communes would simply delay payments for goods and services they bought. The states and the Federation as well have been guilty of this practice until this very day. It is not surprising, therefore, that the business community does not trust its governments very much and tries to get rid of any "bureaucratic" control.

Now, although it is true that credit was excessive and the money supply inconsistent with stable prices, it does not necessarily follow that prices were the consequence and credit the cause in the inflationary process. This hypothesis was tested at the Institute of Economic Sciences, and it turned out that there was either no correlation between credit and prices or a slight <u>negative</u> correlation: higher credits — lower prices. This paradox will become understandable in a moment.

Prices are determined predominantly by changes in wages, and so most of the time inflation is a cost-push inflation. As already mentioned (section 16), wages appear to be a function of capital intensity, technological rent, and institutional monopoly (banks, insurance companies). Wage increases in privileged work organizations initiate wage increases throughout the economy, and whenever prices cannot bear a cost increase, they are revised upward. Bajt adds that the high degree of price control increases the pressure of excess demand on the free section of the market, which then generates price increases, and that inefficient investment planning produces an inadequate structure of output, which, in a semiclosed economy, makes it difficult to match demand [30; 61].

Business cycles complicate matters even further. Prices are formed in a rather peculiar way in Yugoslavia. Depreciation and interest on social capital represent fixed elements. Wages, as everywhere, are inflexible downward. For reasons explained in the next chapter, all taxes are tied up with wages and vary in proportion to wages. Since tax payments enjoy high priority, it may — and did — happen that the total amount of taxes collected increases in the trough of a depression. Finally, repayments of loans represent an additional fixed element. Thus, as soon as there is a slight retardation of production, the enterprise finds it impossible to cover costs and has to run losses — or increase prices.

In a downswing, a labor-managed enterprise will not dismiss workers. Thus, production will be continued and inventories accumulated. Inventory accumulation is financed out of profits and credits. When these two sources are exhausted, involuntary trade credits and price increases will replace them. As far as inflationary pressure is concerned, we may expect price increases in the downswing and stable prices in the upswing. Chart 1 (page 53) confirms such an expectation.

The analysis just sketched — a result of research by the Institute of Economic Sciences — was unknown at the time monetary reforms were designed and implemented. The traditional view that inflation means "too much money chasing too few goods" gained wide acceptance. All one had to do, it was thought, was to curtail the supply of money and the economy would be stabilized. Stabilization was envisaged exclusively as price stabilization. In the program of the 1965 reform, employment targets were even not mentioned. Foreign exchange reform, membership in GATT, and cooperation with the IMF were interpreted as an international obligation to keep the dinar stable. Stability of the dinar was to be maintained at all costs — a task that even a Tory government would nowadays be reluctant to undertake, but that was cheerfully attempted in an economy innocently unaware of what it might mean. Tight money policy was to be the only device for achieving price stability. There were some doubts about the wisdom of such a policy, but critics were frowned upon and the policy was implemented. This proved to be fatal. Since prices vary inversely to the cycle, an anti-inflationary monetary policy meant an anti-anticyclical policy, a policy of continuous and direct destabilization.

The vicissitudes of monetary policy in the last eight years have been analyzed by Holjevac [11] and Perišin [32], since recently the Governor of the National Bank. In the text that follows, I will draw mainly on their work and on the research conducted at the Institute of Economic Sciences.

In 1960, the cycle reached the upper turning point (see Chart 1). That passed unnoticed, but price increases were observed. The analytical device used in such situations consisted of a comparison of "commodity funds" (social product in real terms) and "purchasing funds" (personal and government consumption and investment in money terms), made possible by good and up-to-date statistics. The difference between the two was interpreted as excessive money supply. In 1960, the difference was considerable and called for monetary restrictions. In addition, in 1961, during the recession, a monetary reform was undertaken with the purpose of instilling business discipline. Enterprises were forced to increase the share of their own funds in total working capital at their disposal. This share was indeed raised from 7.8 percent in 1960 to 22.4 percent in 1961; the operation was financed out of savings, which meant less investment [15]. Recession deepened, retail prices continued to rise at a rate of 6-9 percent, inventories accumulated at a rate of 20-25 percent a year, and monetary authorities decided to tighten up the policy. As a result, one enterprise after another found it impossible to settle its debts, and mutual indebtedness was expanding at a rate of about 50 percent a year. The federal government ran out of money and obtained a substantial credit with the National Bank; also, the "moneylessness" — a new term coined for the occasion — had to be cured by some credit expansion. All this, of course, ruined the credit balances. The year ended with money supply increased at a rate more than twice as high as the one envisaged. Holjevac complained about the absence of monetary discipline and the fact that the National Bank lost control over credit expansion [11, p. 36]. But the cycle was reversed and the rate of growth accelerated.

The upswing continued through 1963. Given all that excessive (from the viewpoint of monetary planners) money in the economy, prices were remarkably stable; industrial producer prices rose by 1 percent, retail prices by 4 percent. By the end of that year, the upswing developed into a boom, industrial output was expanding at a rate of 15-20 percent a year, and the balance of payments deficit was increasing. Several months later, the cycle reached the upper turning point, and in the second half of 1964 the recession was already in full swing. All the symptoms of the 1961 recession were repeated, and so was the monetary policy. In the second half of 1964 and the beginning of 1965, reserve requirements were raised to the legal limit of 35 percent, enterprises were forced to use savings for increases in working capital, investment banks had to use one-quarter of their loans for working capital financing, and consumer credits were reduced. All this, together with the upheavals caused by the price reform, reduced aggregate demand and output growth from about 15 percent in 1964 to about 4 percent by the end of 1965. Since the tax reform left the federal government without money, it had to resort to substantial deficit financing, which once again upset monetary planning. But the downswing was arrested for a period of four quarters, and all signs normally present at an upward reversal of the cycle became apparent. This time, however, the National Bank had formidable monetary weapons at its disposal and it decided to use them to combat "excessive" liquidity.

For reasons not explained in the documents, the National Bank established the rule that the liquidity reserves of commercial banks held as balances with the National Bank should amount to no more than 6 percent of monetary demand deposits [32, p. 515]. These reserves ran around 10 percent in the second half of 1966. As "purchasing funds" were appreciably higher than "commodity funds" — which is reflected in price increases — it seemed obvious that there was too much money in the economy. The National Bank reduced its special credits to commercial banks and put an absolute limit on their credit operations. Consumer credits were further reduced. In 1967, exports were retarded, and so it was decided to depress internal demand even more in order to achieve an export drive. As might have been expected, this did not help exports — in fact, their rate of growth was soon reduced below zero in spite of selective export credits — but liquidity reserves were brought down to 5 percent, even lower than planned.

As a result of this anti-inflationary policy, output growth was reduced to −2 percent, which had not happened since the Cominform days. The present author estimated losses due to the mistaken monetary policy at 11 percent of social product. Perišin found that gross savings had been reduced from 43 percent of GNP in 1964 to 30 percent in 1967 [32, p. 517]. Unemployment was increasing rapidly. But price stability was not achieved (see Table 26).

The new system of regulating the money supply proved to be very efficient in reducing money supply to any desired level. This conclusion follows from the foregoing description of its practical operation, but it can also be illustrated by a series of indexes. If we compute ratios of money supply per 100 dinars of transactions (expressed as a sum of gross national product and the output of intermediate goods), we get the following data [33, p. 63]:

1957	15.3	1963	19.4
1958	15.3	1964	18.3
1959	14.5	1965	14.9
1960	15.1	1966	12.3
1961	15.3	1967	11.4
1962	18.7	1968	13.1

In three years following 1964, the relative money supply was reduced to less than one-half of its original level. One might be tempted to think that this simply meant a doubling of the transactions velocity of money. But that is not so; the lack of banking credits was compensated by involuntary trade credits. The latter amounted to 69 percent of short-term bank credits in 1964 and 138 percent in 1967, and surpassed bank credits almost two times by the middle of 1969.

One other fact is worth noting. Chart 1 shows that boom periods of business cycles occurred in 1960 and 1963 and recession periods in 1961 and 1967. A glance at the table above suffices to show the extent to which monetary policy was cyclically synchronized: there was an abundant money supply in the boom and tight money policy in the recession. Consequently, monetary policy has been an important destabilizing factor preventing the economy from exploiting its growing potentials.

The second half of 1967 brought the revival, and the acceleration of growth continued through 1968 into 1969. Prices were stabilized for a while, inventories reduced, exports soared in 1969, and monetary policy had a relatively easy job to support these favorable trends. Yet business trends soon were reversed again. The illiquidity crisis reappeared. In 1971 and 1973, the National Bank undertook to convert the short-term credits for working capital into long-term ones. That left the quantity of money unchanged but relieved firms of the burden of immediate repayments. Further retardation of growth required new monetary injections; all credit plans were revised and by 1974 inflation was raging at rates above 20 percent.

The financial system, as it has evolved so far, has certain peculiarities. Ivan Ribnikar observes that the value of the monetary multiplier is only unity. Since the National Bank increases the quantity of primary money largely by discounting, special credits to commercial banks require high obligatory reserves (30 percent), and the share of currency is high, the volume of primary money has to be increased almost as much as the total quantity of money. Ribnikar suggests that the indebtedness of commercial banks be reduced and the issue of new money be channeled through credits to the federal government [31]. This would reduce the scope of central bank interventions and might improve the financial position of firms (since the taxes necessary for financing government activities would be reduced).

Dimitrijević and Macesich, on the other hand, argue that monetary policy in Yugoslavia can control the supply of funds more efficiently than in Western market economies because banks are the main suppliers of funds, so all that is necessary is to control the major part of supply of funds [74, p. 136]. The authors note that the Yugoslav financial transmission mechanism "is based mainly on money-real goods portfolio adjustments of individual balance sheets, excluding financial assets as a significant choice for holding assets instead of money...as a result...effects of changes in money supply are shorter-lagged and more directly related to changes in expenditures for goods and services..." [74, p. 187].

Monetary policy alone has a restricted field of application. And its combination with fiscal policy is hampered by an inadequate financial market. "The federal government cannot borrow on the market," observe Dimitrijević and Macesich. "Its only source of borrowing is the central bank. This has at least two consequences that hamper the use of fiscal policy. First, fiscal surplus-deficit necessarily leads to changes of high-powered money in the same amount, so that expenditure effects of fiscal deficit-surplus are necessarily accompanied by monetary effects. Second, lack of an efficient financial market makes it very difficult for individual enterprises to borrow on the market. . . . It is for this reason that discount policy includes a broad system of selective channels for discounting, which work as a substitute for inadequate borrowing facilities in the market. This means, however, that high-powered money cannot be created in large amounts by granting credit to the federal government. The major part of creation of high-powered money has to be left to selective discounts. As a consequence, there is relatively little room left for the government financing required by the fiscal policy action" [74, p. 138].

Fiscal policy itself is the subject of the next section.

20. PUBLIC FINANCE AND FISCAL POLICY

Budget for a Centrally Planned Economy

In the first two years after the war, the new state tried to make the best of the inherited financial system. Taxation was improved in two ways. Before the war, a sales tax levied on consumer goods was a major source of government budgetary revenue. That represented a great burden for the poorer groups of the population. Next, income tax progression was mild (up to 32 percent) and there were several separate income taxes for various sources of income. Thus, persons with several sources of income — that is, the richer ones — could easily evade paying high taxes. It was only natural that the new revolutionary government would make the necessary corrections. The sales tax was reduced (from 62.8 percent of government budgetary revenues in 1939-40 to 46.5 percent in 1946), and separate income taxes were replaced by a single tax applied to all personal income at increased rates [1, p. 25]. Uneven taxation soon reappeared, however, and even in 1969 B. Jelčić complained that the differential tax burden for the same personal income of different taxpayers meant the negation of principles proclaimed and guaranteed by law [66, p. 159].

When central planning was inaugurated in 1947, the financial system of the country had to be changed radically. In the old system, the government budget used to finance the activities of public administration and some social services. That corresponded to the administrative character of the old state. The new socialist state, as described by the Institute of Finance [1, p. 16], acts as an organizer of the entire economy. The targets are elaborated annually in the economic plan and the budget ought to reflect them financially. Each planning organ has its own budget, which is a constituent part of the overall budget. The sum of all financial plans of all ministries — that is, of all industries — represents an annex to the budget. Thus, the budget becomes the financial plan of the entire economy [1, p. 11; 36, p. 170]. The budget amount to 64 to 83 percent of national income [37, p. 126]. About one-half of budgetary revenues were spent on investments.

R. Radovanović describes four principles on which such a budget was based: (1) All resources at the disposal of a political-territorial unit (municipality, district, county, province, state, federation) are centralized in the budget of its government. (2) All social activities are financed from the budget. As far as business firms are concerned, only net revenues are entered into the budget. (3) The budgets of all political-territorial units are concentrated in the federal budget to ensure central direction in carrying out the most important tasks. This is the famous principle of budgetary monism. (4) As a result of (3), funds are allocated among various bodies in accordance with their recognized needs and irrespective of their budgetary potentials. Lower bodies are obliged to implement general policy and higher bodies are expected to provide the necessary resources. This had at least one negative consequence. Lower organs were not stimulated to economize with their funds. Instead of trying to expand production in their territories, they were busy increasing their budget expenditures and exerting pressure on higher bodies to find the necessary resources [38, p. 1112].

In such a system, taxes are just a technical means for channeling gross profits into the budget [39, p. 29]. The price of a product consists of the cost of production, profit, and the turnover tax. Profit is generally a small item and is mostly left to the enterprise. If individual planned profit is higher than the average, there is extra profit, half of which must be paid into the budget of the higher administrative organ. A planned loss is covered from the higher budget. If achieved profit is higher than planned profit, half of the difference is left to the enterprise as an incentive. Turnover tax is just a balancing item in an administratively set price. Since it is charged on all commodities and is paid as soon as a commodity is shipped, it is also used as an indicator of how the implementation of the plan is proceeding.

In order to accommodate productivity changes in such a rigid price structure, the "decrease in full cost of production" was explicitly planned as a separate item. This decrease is partly paid into the budget, and so a rather unusual new type of tax was created. Finally, various types of prices, discussed in section 16, generated so-called commercial profit, which was mostly absorbed by the budget.

In 1949, the four items enumerated above amounted to (in billions of dinars): turnover tax, 66.6; share of profits, 4.6; decrease in cost of production, 3.8; and share of commercial profits, 13.1 [39, p. 96]. Turnover tax, of course, represented the bulk of budgetary revenues.

The major proportion of budget revenues came from the business sector. Taxes paid by the population were steadily decreasing in importance, from 22.4 percent of all revenues in 1946 to 9.7 percent in 1952. As a consequence, taxation of the population was governed by extrafiscal considerations. In 1950, the tax on income earned in the state sector was abolished. (It was to be reintroduced only in 1960.) This did not matter much, since wage and salary differentials were greatly reduced and income distribution was extremely egalitarian. But income taxes were retained for the private sector and the progression was rather stiff. For peasants, the tax rates went up to 70 percent in 1947 and up to 90 percent in 1948, as compared with the flat rate of 3 percent for members of peasant work cooperatives (cooperatives organized similarly to state firms) [1, p. 34]. This tax policy was inspired by the idea of the class struggle and was aimed at inducing peasants to join cooperatives.

The policy of stiff taxation of peasants and artisans was continued later as well and for the same reasons. In agriculture, it was discontinued after the second agrarian reform in 1953, which reduced the maximum size of agricultural estates to 25 acres and thus eliminated any possibility of capitalist development. In 1954, taxation on the basis of cadastral revenue was introduced, and rates were lowered. Both proved to be stimulating. It is interesting to note that Radovanović described the tax on cadastral revenue as an instrument designed to replace compulsory deliveries while making sure that a minimum output would be produced [42, p. 91]. There was no possibility of capitalist development in handicrafts either, for artisans could employ five workers at most. However, public opinion held that there was something vicious about private business. Tax rates were substantially reduced only in 1963 [62, p. 33]. The policy of containment continued until the ownership discussions in 1967 analyzed in section 15. In the meantime, the number of artisan shops was substantially reduced, which caused economic difficulties.

Taxation Experiments

After the French Revolution in 1789, remarked J. Lovčević, the Constituent Assembly abandoned taxes in favor of contributions. After the Yugoslav Revolution, a law on taxes passed in 1946 declared that a tax was "a contribution . . . given to the state for economic development, cultural advancement . . . and for the maintenance of the state apparatus" [40, p. 34]. In spite of all the protests of the public finance experts, the term stuck.[4] Since 1952, enterprises have been paying contributions (turnover tax representing an exception) and individuals, taxes. Contributions somehow emanated from social property, taxes from private property. Since the 1965 tax reform, contributions have become synonymous for direct taxes or taxes levied on labor income, and the term "tax" is used to denote various forms of turnover tax or property tax. The terminological confusion did not matter very much. But lack of professional competence in designing an appropriate taxation system did matter. In the period 1952-65, the tax system was changed five times with obvious consequences as far as the efficiency of conducting business was concerned.

In 1952-53, the system of AF rates — whose rationale was discussed in section 11 — predetermined the taxation system. The social contribution was paid to the budget out of accumulation and funds obtained through applying a rate prescribed by the social plan to the net product of an enterprise. It contained social insurance payments, was proportional to the wage bill, and was paid at the flat rate of 45 percent. Wage bills above the prescribed standard were taxed at steeply increasing rates. A tax on extra profits was envisaged by law but never applied due to technical difficulties [39, p. 97]. Turnover tax was greatly reduced and amounted to 9 to 14 percent of budgetary revenues [41, p. 14]. Its task was to absorb monopoly profit and to influence price formation [42, p. 62].

---

4. Fiscal theory distinguishes taxes, contributions, and stamp duties. A tax is a compulsory payment for, in principle, no specific service. A contribution represents a compulsory payment for a specific service and in principle covers the cost. Stamp duty is a payment for a specific service at the initiative of the payer, but it bears no necessary relation to the cost.

The system of AF rates helped to eliminate administrative ties between enterprises and planning authorities, but it soon degenerated into administrative determination of AF rates for each individual enterprise. It had to be replaced by a system that worked more in a market fashion. How to design such a system was not clear. It seemed advisable to make use of the experience of traditional market economies. Instead of net product, profit was the base of taxation for the next four years (1954-57). Wages became part of the costs of production. Profit was taxed at a flat 50 percent rate. The other half of gross profit was used for contributions to social investment funds, supplements to basic wages, enterprise funds, and some other purposes. Wages from profits were linked with contributions to local budgets, which amounted to a kind of progressive payroll taxation. A tax on monopoly profit was envisaged but never applied because it proved impossible to establish which part of the income resulted exclusively from the work of the collective. The share of the enterprise (wages and undistributed profits) gradually increased to one-third of net product generated (net product included turnover tax) [39, p. 99].

In this period, two interesting new taxes were introduced. Mines, hydroelectric power stations, and some other firms were to pay rent. Artisans and peasants were obliged to pay tax on hired labor. The latter tax was insignificant in quantitative terms (because only one-eighth of the artisans and almost no one among peasants hired labor), but it served as a reminder that hiring labor meant exploitation.

To consider wages as part of the cost of production was deemed inappropriate for a self-management system. Thus, the new system, inaugurated in 1958, was based on the distribution of total enterprise income. That was a switch back from profit to net product (reduced for turnover tax and some other items). There was also a terminological change: "wages" and "salaries" were replaced by "personal income." With many changes, the system lasted until 1964.

The major tax, surpassed only after 1961 by the turnover tax, was the contribution from income. The rates rose progressively to 80 percent. In 1961, tax progression was replaced by a flat rate of 15 percent and a surtax of 25 percent. In the meantime, another development took place. It appeared reasonable to link collective consumption and public services to the level of personal incomes earned in any particular territory. For this purpose, contributions to budgets were made out of the wage bill. In 1958, these contributions were progressive; in 1959, a flat rate of 11 percent was charged; the rate was increased to 15 percent in 1963. In 1964, some tax rates were reduced, and mining taxes and contributions to social investment funds were abolished. The abolition of progressive rates for the wage bill led to a reintroduction of the progressive personal income tax [39, p. 207]. This indicated that the economic functions of the payroll tax and personal income tax, as discussed below, had been confused. The share of the enterprise in its net product increased to about one-half.

In order to increase this share still further, the last reform of 1965 abolished all contributions from enterprise income. The share in net product jumped to about two-thirds. Since then, enterprise taxation has rested exclusively on payroll taxes. If we count social insurance contributions, labor has been made about 60 percent more expensive than necessary. This has serious consequences. Before 1960, taxation created capital-saving inducements [43]. In a labor surplus economy, that was rational. Since 1964, taxes have stimulated labor-saving practices. Enterprises did in fact react: coal was being replaced by oil, cotton growing and cattle raising by wheat cultivation, and so on, and thousands of workers became redundant. Further, flat rates introduced an awkward rigidity and tended to intensify cycles. Finally, the abolition of progressive payroll taxation after 1958 and the lifting of wage control in 1961 meant that two important checks on inflationary pressures were eliminated. We have already discussed the consequences.

Taxation experiments clearly have not been completed. What can be said about how an appropriate taxation system ought to be designed? On various occasions, the Institute of Economic Sciences has made suggestions in this regard, and they may be summed up as follows. The equalization of personal income distribution can be achieved by the familiar progressive personal income tax. There is no need to tax profits, even less to tax them progressively, since capital is socially owned. But it is necessary to tax payrolls and to make the tax progress. To do this, wages should be standardized by applying accounting wages for certain categories of skill. (The skill rating should not of course be left to enterprises themselves, just as school diplomas are not issued by pupils themselves.) When faced with the alternative of either losing a greater part of the "excess wage fund" through taxes or using that money for development purposes, the work collective will often opt for the latter. This will check wage increases in the most profitable enterprises — which have continually been generating wage pushes — and expand their investment, increasing the supply of their products relative to demand and lowering prices. Labor should be made as cheap as possible (for the enterprise, of course, not for the workers) in order to stimulate labor-intensive production. If some taxes still prove necessary, they may be levied on the enterprise income at a flat rate. Such "contributions from income" may be considered as a self-management counterpart to the familiar value-added tax.

While direct taxes have received little attention in professional economic literature, turnover tax has been extensively discussed. And with good reason. It survived all the tax reforms as one of the principal taxes. Since 1954, the share of turnover tax in total budget revenues has oscillated between 29 and 43 percent [44, p. 28]. By 1964, six kinds of turnover tax were in operation [45]. Producers' turnover tax was inherited from the days of central planning. It was levied on some 250 products at rates varying between 2 and 81 percent; the tax was contained in producers' prices, represented a part of the enterprises' gross receipts, and was collected at the time the invoice was issued. It was collected easily and quickly — even before bills were paid — and was favored by the government. It was also used as an instrument of price policy. In order to provide independent sources for communal budgets, a communal sales tax was introduced in 1956. In 1961, due to the abolition of progression in enterprise income taxation, the government ran short of money and introduced the 1 percent general turnover tax. This was a multistage tax and was intended to reduce the number of middlemen between producers and final consumers; however, apparently no effect of this kind was achieved [62, p. 47]. There was then also a purchase tax on specific products, a service sales tax, and duty on real estate and other transfers.

Producers' turnover tax has been severely criticized. Both the government and the enterprises tended to abuse it as a price formation device. In twelve years, its tariff was changed almost one hundred times [46, p. 4]. The handling of the tax required a large amount of working capital on the part of the enterprise. It tended to distort prices, and so did the multistage general turnover tax. In the case of exports, tax deductions had to be computed and made. For all these reasons, the two kinds of turnover tax were abolished and in 1965 were replaced by a sales tax levied on consumer goods in retail trade, which was added to retail prices, charged directly to buyers, and collected when the commodity was sold. But a retail trade sales tax cannot be changed often and cannot be differentiated for many products. Thus its use as a price formation instrument is rather limited. It is now primarily a device for collecting budget revenue.

Budgets for a Self-Governing Economy

The more all-embracing a budget is, the more consistent it is with a centrally planned economy. Ideally, all financial transactions of such an economy should be regulated by the budget. It is the other way around in a self-governing economy. Here the budget ought to be restricted to as small a section of the economy as possible in order not to interfere with the economic activities of work collectives. Ideally, the budget should cover only activities of various state agencies. In this respect, the 1952 reform initiated three important developments. They were related to the organization of the nonmarket sector of the economy, to the creation of various social funds, and to the decentralization of budgetary revenues and expenditures.

The Yugoslav tradition had made a sharp division between enterprises [poduzeća] and institutions [ustanove]. The former were business establishments; the latter were financed from the budget and corresponded roughly to nonprofit institutions in the United States and elsewhere. Since the latter depended for their revenues on the budget — that is, on the government administration — it was clear that self-management had little chance of developing. Thus institutions that (a) performed public services and (b) could be financed partly or wholly by selling their services were separated in a special group of "institutions with independent finance." (The law of 1959 changed this condition into "institutions organized according to the principles of social self-government." The institutions were renamed "independent institutions." In 1965, they obtained the status of work organizations with the same self-management rights as enterprises.)

Gradually it became evident that there were two fundamentally different types of public services: one (government administration, judiciary, police, defense) rendered various administrative services to society; the other (education, science, medical care, etc.) increased the welfare of the members of society. It seemed appropriate to finance the former from the budget ("public expenditure") and to organize them in a more or less traditional fashion, but the latter ("collective consumption") required a different approach. M. Hanžeković suggested that taxes be used to finance the former and contributions the latter [44, p. 17].

Next, while there was to be a free market for the short-run operations of enterprises, it appeared advisable to retain substantial central control in the field of capital formation. But capital financing was to be on a credit basis, and budgetary financing implied grants without repayments. Thus, investment resources were separated from the budget and concentrated in investment loan funds. The budget continued to finance investment projects in the nonmarket sector (schools, hospitals, etc.).

In 1952, social insurance had also been separated from the budget. This decision was motivated by the fact that social insurance could be efficiently operated as an independent social service under a social self-government regime. The latter meant that the governing bodies were composed of representatives of various social interests (physicians, social workers, citizens, government representatives).

Very soon, various funds (for housing, for the advancement of agriculture and forestry, for roads, for cultural activities, for education, etc.) proliferated. Most of these funds had their own independent management bodies and obtained their resources from special contributions or from budgets. Hanžeković suggested the following threefold classification [44, p. 13]: (1) funds for capital formation (SIFs) or for financing public services; (2) funds for financing without repayment obligation or for granting credit; (3) funds with self-government bodies or without. Definite trends have appeared in further development. Loanable funds were mostly transferred to the banks. Funds without independent management bodies are used as instruments (often temporary) of budgetary financing for special purposes. The third category, permanent funds with independent self-government, represents an innovation.

The social insurance fund set an example. A decade later, this example was followed by education. At first, T. Konevski remarked, it was just a transmission mechanism in budgetary financing [47, p. 163]. But in 1967, education communities were formed to operate the funds. Assemblies at communal and state levels vote money to be allocated to education funds. Education communities — self-government bodies composed of representatives of schools, outstanding figures in cultural life, and representatives of government agencies — distribute the money by negotiating the services to be rendered by various educational establishments. In 1969, research communities were formed. They operate funds for research work created in 1960. Interest communities are described as the quasi-market sector in section 6. Since the adoption of the 1974 Constitution, interest communities have gradually taken over the financing of various social services.

Hanžeković points out that in 1965 funds absorbed 8.8 percent and institutions 14.2 percent of national income, which should be compared with total budgetary expenditures that amounted to 20.1 percent of national income [44, p. 14]. Institutions obtain about one-third of their income from selling their services to direct buyers (to the market); 50 to 60 percent of their revenues come from various funds (quasi-market); and only one-tenth derives from budgetary subsidies. Such a structure of revenues enabled the nonmarket institutions (not nonprofit, for they do make profits) to gain a considerable degree of independence. Also, they established closer contacts with the buyers of their services and with the rest of the economy. Is there, one might ask, any economic activity in which the archeology department of a university, a museum, or an art gallery can engage? Yes, there is, though perhaps not directly. Tourist agencies and hotels may be — and in fact are — interested in financing the development of an archeological site, a local museum, or an art gallery. Sometimes these are rather roundabout ways for achieving certain goals, but if they eliminate government control and increase independence, the price may not be too high. Yet there are other costs involved. Konevski points out some of them [47, pp. 128-65]. To administer a fund, an administrative apparatus has to be set up. Unlike business enterprises in the market, a school or a hospital is in an inferior position when it negotiates contracts with the funds. Commercialism may and does have detrimental effects in such fields as culture, education, science, or medical care. The consumer is often victimized. Since it is too early to evaluate the operation of the system, one can only invoke the wisdom of the ancient Greeks concerning the organization of human affairs: right proportions, no extremes.

The creation of funds and the establishment of self-financed institutions represent two aspects of decentralization. As a consequence, the share of budgetary revenues in national income was reduced from one-third in 1952 to one-fifth in 1967. The third aspect of decentralization was related to the division of revenues among budgets of various sociopolitical units. The Federation was gradually transferring its responsibilities for various social services to states and communes. As a result, the share of federal expenditures in total budgetary expenditures dropped from 74 percent in 1952 to 53 percent in 1968. The trends have been reversed as compared with what has happened elsewhere.[5]

The division of budget revenues among various budgets is a somewhat complicated technical problem. In the period 1952-65, no less than five laws tried to solve it, and with only limited success. In theory, there are two possibilities: a separation of revenues and joint revenues. Both have been tried out at one time or another.

After 1952, the budget monism of a centrally planned economy was replaced by budget pluralism better suited to a self-governing economy. The former budgetary system was based on participation in joint revenues, with the higher governmental bodies determining the conditions of participation. If lower budgetary units were to be made more independent in the development of revenue sources on their own territories, a system based on the separation of revenue sources seemed more appropriate. Thus, sources of revenue were allocated to budgets at various levels. Only the Federation was entitled to introduce new taxes, but, if introduced, taxes had to be immediately allocated to specific budgets or funds. In principle, every unit was to cover expenditures from its own revenues. This principle was not fully implemented, but there was a great change as compared with the former practice. In two characteristic years, states and communes obtained their revenues in the following ways [49, p. 445]:

	1948	1954
Own revenues	53.7%	72.5%
Participation in joint revenues	43.3	22.5
Federal subsidies	3.0	5.0

With many changes, this system lasted for eight years (1952-59). It had two main shortcomings, as described by R. Radovanović [38, p. 1115] and K. Bogoev [48, pp. 188-90]. Sources allocated to lower units were not sufficient to meet the recognized needs. Deficits were substantial and were covered by sharing in revenues and by subsidies. These were discussed anew every year, which made lower units very dependent on higher authorities. Next, the lack of objective allocation criteria generated a bargaining process.

---

5. In the United States, the share of federal revenues in total budgetary revenues increased from 42 percent in 1890 to 75 percent in 1954; in Switzerland, federal expenditures amounted to one-half of cantonal expenditures in 1913 and to 111 percent in 1958 [48, p. 10].

For both reasons, the system failed to provide stability and incentives.

In the period 1960-64, the budgetary system was again based on participation. Separate sources were allocated only to the Federation (they covered 90 percent of its revenues) and to communes (about 20 percent of their revenues). States and districts had no separate sources. The participation of all units was determined by federal and state laws. The higher units could not arbitrarily select more favorable sources for themselves. In order to eliminate another possible cause of arbitrariness, participation rates were not differentiated according to sources as before, but one single participation rate was applied to all sources of revenue. Participation rates were increased for less developed units, and if this was not sufficient, subsidies were granted. Increased shares and subsidies were to be determined on the basis of the funds needed for carrying out "mandatory tasks and services." However, since objective criteria were not established, the familiar arbitrariness crept into the process. In 1960, only 9 percent of all communes, and in the following year only 3.6 percent, were able to cover their needs in the regular way [48, p. 205]. About one-half of all communes had to rely on both increased participation shares and subsidies. What was intended to be a corrective device turned out to be the main instrument for balancing the budgets of lower units.

The 1965 tax reform introduced the separation principle once again. The sources are allocated as follows. Taxes on personal income and sales taxes may be introduced by all sociopolitical communities. Apart from that, taxes on property (and some other taxes) belong to communes, estate duties to states, and customs duties to the Federation. Communes and states are empowered to decide independently what kinds of revenue to introduce for their territories and to fix the tax rates. There are two safeguards. The federal government can fix temporarily the limits for the tax rates set by the states and communes. Communes and states are legally obliged to cooperate with one another in fixing the level of their revenues in order to assure citizens equal treatment. States and provinces are entitled to federal subsidies provided their per capita revenue is below the Yugoslav average and they have exhausted all possibilities for collecting revenue through taxation of personal income in conformity with the economic potential of their population [50].

This time, the criterion for subsidies was defined somewhat

more precisely. But it has also been criticized. Hanžeković argues that approximately equal budgetary revenue per capita cannot be an appropriate criterion. Instead, appropriately defined necessary and justified expenditure should provide a basis for allocations [44, p. 7]. In fact, this seems to be the problem of the Yugoslav budget system. Yugoslav territories are extremely unevenly developed. Per capita income is 5.4 times higher in the state of Slovenia than in the autonomous province of Kosovo. Communal budgetary revenues are, of course, even more unequal: in 1965, the most developed commune in Slovenia obtained per capita revenue almost 16 times higher than the least developed commune in Kosovo. Such extreme differences must ruin all schemes in which allocation criteria are not precisely defined. Konevski complains that in the new system more than one-half of communes in Serbia have to rely on subsidies, which is inconsistent with the philosophy of self-government [47, p. 116].

In 1968, the government asked a research institute to study the problem. A group under the chairmanship of P. Sicherl prepared a voluminous report [51]. Sicherl finds that, although differences between the developed and the undeveloped regions in per capita income are extreme, differences in nonagricultural income per worker are small. He uses a special statistical method developed by his colleague B. Ivanović [52] to establish that the spread between developed and underdeveloped regions is appreciably greater in the economic sphere than in the sphere of social services and living standard. In a later article, Sicherl argues that it is easier to reduce the spread in the latter sphere (in terms of flows of services) than in per capita national income [53]. As a basis for subsidy computations, Sicherl takes accounting budgetary revenue, which he defines as revenue obtained by applying the average Yugoslav tax rates to actual tax sources in the region. The dilemma of whether policy should be based on the equalization of needs or revenues is resolved in favor of revenues, on the grounds that not only is it difficult to determine needs in an objective way but it is also inconsistent with the philosophy of decentralized decision making. There follows a long and involved discussion of the most appropriate method of determining standard revenue. The difference between the standard and the accounting revenue is to be covered by federal subsidy. Sicherl's report has been discussed in government and parliamentary committees but has not produced practical results as yet.

Constitutional amendments and the Constitution of 1974 preserved

the taxation principles and trends as developed after 1965 except
in one important aspect: the Federation lost the power to determine
taxes. That is done by the states for their own territories or by an
explicit agreement of all states when the entire national territory
is concerned.

Pero Jurković characterizes the existing tax system in the following way [77, pp. 516-18]. First of all, it is oriented primarily
toward the collection of revenues, while allocational, distributive,
stabilizing, and development functions are neglected. Next, taxes
are levied on factors of production and not on business results. As
a consequence, taxes do not provide elastic cushions in recessions
and booms and generally result in swollen government revenues.
Third, the use of particular tax revenues is rigidly determined in
advance. For instance, in 1970, 6000 various special funds existed
[78, p. 171]. This makes an efficient fiscal policy next to impossible.

The share of taxes and social insurance contributions in gross
national product (SNA definition) in the period 1966-72 varied between 31 and 35 percent. This is less than in Scandinavian countries, the United Kingdom, France, or the Netherlands.

Communal Economy

In daily life, every person appears in a double capacity: as a
producer and as a citizen. Thus, direct democracy will also have
two aspects: one relating to the work place, the other to the territory where citizens live. As members of work collectives, people
engage in self-management. As inhabitants of towns and villages,
they manage their affairs by establishing local self-government.
The territorial association that corresponds to the collective at
the work place is the commune.

There has been a strong tradition of local government in Yugoslavia since the days of the National Liberation War. People's
liberation committees, as local government bodies, worked with
great independence, initiative, and resourcefulness to supply the
partisan army and organize daily life in the liberated territories.
It is hardly a matter of chance that the first people's committee
and the first committee of workers' management appeared simultaneously in the fall of 1941 in the mining town of Krupanj. People's committees continued to exist after the war, but then as components of a rigidly centralized system. The system was based on
the principle of democratic centralism, which meant that higher
bodies could abrogate decisions of people's committees.

This practice was radically changed in the fateful year of 1952. The principle of democratic centralism was replaced by the principle of the control of the legality of acts [54, p. 24]. District people's committees became organs of self-government and communal people's committees organs of local government. District committees had assemblies with two houses: one composed of political representatives, the other of representatives of producers. The next crucial step was taken three years later. The 1955 law on local self-government proclaimed that the commune was "the basic political-territorial organization of self-government by the working people and the basic socioeconomic community of the population on their territory." The Constitution of 1963 changed the phrasing slightly to make the commune "the basic sociopolitical community." The development of the communal system has been greatly influenced by the historical example set in 1871 by the Paris Commune, "that finally discovered political form in which the emancipation of labor can be carried out" (Marx). It is useful to note, as D. Milivojević points out, that the commune has not been conceived as just a form of otherwise familiar local government. It is a community of those living, working, and producing, satisfying their basic needs, and realizing their civil and self-governing rights in a particular territory [55, p. 8]. For a while, districts retained certain coordinating functions and then gradually withered away.

Since the commune is a territorial association, one of the first problems to be solved was the determination of the size of the territory. The solution was found by practical experimentation over the period of a decade. A hierarchy of governmental levels was consistent with central planning. There were three levels below the level of the state: county [oblast], district [kotar], and local committee [mjesni narodni odbor]. In 1951, counties disappeared. The orientation toward a market economy made excessive administrative fragmentation (there were more than 7000 local committees) unnecessary, so in 1952 the number of local committees was halved and committees were replaced by communes. In order to bring local government closer to citizens, the commune was made the basic self-government unit in 1955. Since, however, the commune was expected to exercise a wide variety of functions, its territory had to be increased. Table 29 depicts the process of territorial transformation. Each new law on territorial changes was announced as the last and the definite one, as E. Pusić has commented [71, p. 245].

Communal territory was growing larger and larger, and by 1967

Table 29

Number of Territorial Units of Local Government (at year-end)

	1948	1952	1955	1967
Local committees/communities	7967	—	—	4968[a]
Communes	—	4052	1479	501
Districts	427	351	107	—

Sources: SZS, Jugoslavija 1945-54, pp. 35-36; SGJ-1968, p. 62; Yugoslav Survey, 1965, p. 3296.
    a. 1965.

the average population size of the commune, at 40,000, had almost reached the population size of the district at the beginning of the process of territorial transformation (48,000 in 1952). The district became superfluous and disappeared. The larger commune was more efficient, but less self-governing. For this reason, the new Constitution of 1963 provided for the creation of local communities. These were to be self-governing communities of citizens in rural and urban localities concerned with all activities connected with the satisfaction of the needs of citizens and their families. J. Djuričić describes three functions of a local community: it is (a) a form of self-government, including traditional political activities; (b) a unit of town planning; and (c) an organization that takes care of some social services, public utilities, and so on [56]. Pusić is rather skeptical about the ability of local communities to contribute in any important way to self-government. In his view, their activities are too restricted to be particularly attractive to the citizens, and in a modern urban setting territorial closeness per se generates no specially active social ties [63, p. 243]. There are 27,706 localities in Yugoslavia, and by 1965 statutes of communes provided for the creation of 4968 local communities. By the end of 1972, almost 9000 local communities were in existence. The organizational circle seems to have been closed: communes have replaced districts and local communities have replaced local committees. But considerable social experience has been accumulated in the process.

Apart from exercising the functions of traditional local government, which includes local politics, public utilities, education, social welfare, and so on, a commune is also responsible for other aspects of local life. Miljković explains this in detail. The commune is expected to harmonize individual and social interests. It is responsible for social property, both that under its own control

and that "belonging" to enterprises. It takes care of economic development and cultural advancement. It coordinates all economic,
social, and political activities in its territory, prepares a social
plan, and makes it possible for citizens to participate in the process of social decision making [57; 66]. But communal self-
government is a contradictory institution, remarked Djordjević;
it carries within it forces of unification and disintegration [54,
p. 202]. Both forces will soon make themselves felt.

The 1955 law was preceded by extensive discussions about the
functions of the commune. In a paper presented at the annual meeting of Serbian economists in 1954, J. Davičo maintained — and those
present agreed — that a labor-managed enterprise had no incentive
to embark upon substantial capital formation. In his opinion, large
investment would imply creation of a new enterprise which would
be equally labor managed and so could not be dominated. For this
reason, Davičo argued that the commune was "the natural investor
in our circumstances" [58, p. 192]. As Table 28 shows, communes
indeed became large investors. In 1964, when a maximum was
reached, 25 percent of all investment in fixed capital was financed
by communes (and districts). Since 1959, communes have been
entitled to initiate the setting up of all kinds of enterprises, to
bring about mergers, or to carry out liquidations [48, p. 129]. However, the last economic reform put an almost exclusive reliance on
enterprises as far as capital formation was concerned, and by 1968
the communal share in investments dwindled to 4 percent. But
other economic functions of the commune were left intact. In cases
of the failure of an enterprise, the commune shares a good deal of
the financial responsibility involved. The commune also gives guarantees for credits and loans granted by the banks to enterprises located on its territory.

For people accustomed to central planning — that is, to administrative methods in running an economy — it was difficult to imagine
a really free market. They were determined to get rid of governmental controls. It seemed obvious that the best way to achieve
that was to replace it by communal control. The self-governing
commune would tell enterprises what to do and how to behave. In
1954 and 1955, communes were empowered to determine the needs
of enterprises and to distribute their profits after federal taxation.
Since they were entitled to determine their shares in profits, and
since they were independent in budget expenditures, communes
taxed the incomes of enterprises more than the latter could bear.
The consequence was a general price rise as shown in Table 26

and Chart 1. In 1956, taxation rights of the communes again came under regulation by federal laws [59, pp. 113-16; 48, p. 166].

Gradually, the romantic views of conflict-free communities — local or otherwise — had to be revised. Hopes have been directed toward an impersonal market mechanism. Expectations have again been a little unwarranted, I am sorry to say as an economist. But at least people have been willing to learn from experience. Enterprises gained a large degree of independence and crossed communal boundaries. Communal banks, which kept appearing in the period 1948-64, became just commercial banks. The approach to communal economy, self-government, and life became far more sophisticated. The actual economic, social, and political importance of communes has not decreased, though lately states show a tendency to encroach upon communal finance.

In an excellent study, K. Bogoev surveys the development of communal finance [48]. In this context, one difficult fiscal problem — adequate finance for administrative and, in particular, social services — may be singled out for closer scrutiny. Bogoev and Petrović point out that the 1957 resolution of the Federal Assembly on public expenditure and collective consumption (which together comprise "general consumption" as distinct from privately financed consumption in Yugoslav terminology) demanded that such expenditure be tied to the economic potentials of the area in question [48, p. 179; 65, p. 57]. Later, the new Constitution insisted on the principle of work performed as one of the taxation criteria to be applied to revenues of sociopolitical units. Tax laws interpreted these two principles to mean that taxes should be collected in proportion to personal income. For this reason, the proportional payroll tax gained in importance until, after 1964, it became the only tax paid by the enterprises. Since collective consumption is a kind of personal consumption collectively financed, it seemed just and proper to link it to personal incomes earned in a particular territory. The payroll tax was made even more attractive when it was arranged that it be paid into the budget of the commune where people lived and not where they worked or where the head office of the enterprise was located. It is only recently that the shortcomings of the payroll tax and the fallacy in the reasoning by which it was introduced have begun to be discussed.

Let me close this section with a brief review of the main activities of a commune. What communes do is best seen from a breakdown of budgetary expenditures, as shown in Table 30.

Table 30

Budget Expenditure in 1966 (in percent)

	Federation	States and provinces	Communes
Total expenditure effected	45.8	19.4	34.8
Education	0.1	21.5	78.4
Science and culture	5.3	58.1	36.6
Social welfare and medical care	52.0	11.6	36.4
Public utilities	—	16.2	83.8
Public administration	16.7	40.0	43.3
National defense	99.7	—	0.3
Infrastructural investment	5.3	38.8	55.9

Source: [50, p. 71].

Public utilities, education, infrastructural investment, and public administration are activities controlled by the commune more than by either republics or the Federation. Bogoev points out that the communal share in total budgetary expenditures is one of the highest in the world (29 to 35 percent, or 50 percent excluding defense, in Yugoslavia, as against 30 percent in West Germany, 25 percent in Switzerland, 22 percent in Austria, and 20 percent, or 35 percent excluding defense, in the United States) [48, p. 329]. Whether this share has reached the upper limit remains to be seen.

Fiscal Policy

I add this section for the sake of completeness. But it might just as well have been left out. Strange as it may sound, there is no fiscal policy in Yugoslavia. In fact, this is quite consistent with the belief in the absence of business cycles — or ignorance of their presence.

Fiscal policy can affect aggregate demand by means of the revenue or the expenditure side of the budget. The revenue side — taxation — has been recognized as a legitimate tool of fiscal policy in theory and is sometimes used in practice. Producers' turnover tax has been used occasionally to influence the general level of prices in order to absorb excessive purchasing power. In general, however, the numerous tax changes have been made in order to influence individual prices or to increase the discretionary power of enterprises over their incomes and have not been intended to affect aggregate demand. To a certain extent, selective turnover tax reductions have occasionally had price-stabilizing effects.

The federal government occasionally ran a substantial deficit in recession years, as for instance in 1962 and 1965. But that was purely accidental, a consequence of the combined effects of tax reforms and the lack of revenues. Textbooks on public finance, invariably written by persons with training in law, keep on reminding students of the time-honored principle of sound finance — the balanced budget. And since governments on all levels were not too scrupulous in their spending practices, insisting on balancing the budget was quite justified. Bogoev points out that the budget has always been balanced when presented to the Federal Assembly for acceptance and that deficits would appear in implementation. Deficits have amounted to 10 to 15 percent of the federal budget and up to 5 percent of state and communal budgets, but they have been much larger for extrabudgetary expenditures (investment, social insurance) [60, p. 159].

The first public debate about fiscal policy took place in 1967. At an economic conference in Ljubljana, K. Bogoev [61], M. Hanžeković [62], and B. Jelčić [66] discussed the absence of fiscal policy in Yugoslavia and made various suggestions. Bogoev quotes the resolution of the Federal Assembly on economic policy in 1967, which stated that there was excess demand and that not only did all budgets have to be balanced but reserves had to be accumulated. As Chart 1 shows, Yugoslavia experienced an unusual depression in 1967. Bogoev also points out that proportional tax rates levied on payrolls have cycle-intensifying effects and that the small amount of transfer expenditures (unemployment compensation, debt repayment, subsidies) limits the possibilities for an effective anticyclical policy. In the postwar period, the federal government raised three internal loans (for the First Five-Year Plan, to counteract the effects of the Cominform economic boycott, and to finance the rebuilding of Skopje, destroyed by an earthquake). The sole purpose of these loans was to transform a part of personal consumption into investment. Bogoev believes that the rigidity of the existing fiscal pluralism may be softened and an effective anticyclical use made of appropriately designed federal budgetary subsidies to other budgets.

B. Šoškić is the only other economist to make written contributions related to fiscal policy prior to 1970 [63]. Šoškić was interested primarily in the expansionary effects of public works. In his view, the most appropriate objects of increased public financing are housing and communal construction, road construction, land reclamation and irrigation projects, and power generation projects. Such investment projects are desirable also because of their very low import content, as was pointed out by the Institute of Economic Studies. Šoškić added that they were very labor intensive as well, which is of great importance for a labor surplus economy [67].

In 1973, a young Slovenian economist named Marko Kranjec undertook to examine the effects of fiscal policy after the 1965 reform. He found that tax revenues systematically changed in the opposite direction from economic activity, thus contributing to contraction of aggregate demand in recessions and to expansion of demand in booms. He estimated that this strange fiscal policy reinforced business oscillations between 66 and 99 percent compared with what would have happened without any change in taxes [79].

SELF-GOVERNMENT, MARKET, AND SOCIALISM

Limitations of space preclude the examination of various important social and political issues. But there is one permanent theme of Yugoslav social science discussion that cannot be neglected: the interrelationship between socialism, self-government, and market. Recent discussions of this problem will be surveyed in this concluding chapter.

I have already examined (section 1) the familiar contention that socialism and markets ("commodity production") are incompatible. This was the basis of Paul Sweezy's criticism of Yugoslav economic policy as a "gradual transition from socialism to capitalism" [1]. Sweezy argues that the market restricts socialist relations and transforms social ownership into a sort of collective ownership. Material incentives and market orientation necessarily generate a profiteering mentality. The evaluation of social usefulness by profit is characteristic of a capitalist system. Gadgetry and acquisitiveness replace socialist values. This sort of criticism is fairly common. J. Djordjević argues in reply that such undesirable social phenomena are the result of industrial civilization and not only the consequence of the market. The abolition of the market means a return to etatism and state property. Self-government implies free disposal of earned income and, more generally, business autonomy, which in turn implies markets. If this is not understood, the alternative is an old one: the eschatological idea of state rule and the reeducation of man. "Man would be placed under the tutelage of the state (or party, or some other mechanism) to be prepared and educated, so that one day he may become an adult socialist subject" [2, p. 96].

Yugoslav economists are quite unanimous in believing that the market ought to be maximally exploited as a device of economic organization. Philosophers, however, have their doubts. M. Marković, a leading philosopher actively interested in economic affairs, believes that initial forms of workers' self-management cannot be achieved without material incentives, which imply market competition. But if exclusive reliance on money relations were to become a permanent feature of the society, self-management might gradually degenerate into a sort of capitalist cooperative. If the results of work were permanently evaluated in terms of income, and if the desire to earn as much money as possible were to become a permanent and basic interest of a worker, the product would be a type of personality basically no different from that produced by a capitalist society [3, p. 70].

Referring to Marx, some of my philosopher colleagues have declared that socialist commodity production is a contradictio in adjecto. In Marx's sense, commodity production implies market relationships, which result in "commodity fetishism" and various alienation phenomena. I have tried to clarify matters in the following way. The familiar statement that commodity production generates capitalism ought to be reversed. Commodity production existed under slavery, feudalism, and capitalism as well as under etatism. It clearly did not determine all these socioeconomic systems; on the contrary, it was determined by some more fundamental social relationships and was shaped by respective social systems. Thus, for instance, capitalism resulted from private ownership, etatism from state ownership. Since there are so many types of commodity production, it need not be surprising if we also find socialist commodity production. The elimination of private ownership does not necessarily produce socialism, although it may restrict the role of the market considerably. If private ownership is replaced by state ownership, capitalism is replaced by etatism and commodity fetishism by office fetishism. In both cases, relations among people are reified, social inequality preserved, class exploitation continued, and essentially human existence made impossible. In socialism, social ownership makes social capital equally accessible to anybody, while authoritarianism of a privately managed or a state-managed firm is replaced by self-management. In this context, the market and planning are not goals but means. If a working collective is to be really autonomous in economic decision making, the market is indispensable. But planning contradicts the business autonomy of an enterprise, and so the choice is between planning and the market — says a time-honored fallacy. In fact, social planning, far from restricting the autonomy of enterprises, enlarges it for at least three reasons: (1) it reduces uncertainty, which is the basic restriction on free decision making; (2) it increases the rate of growth, the market expands, and so the number of available alternatives increases; (3) it equalizes business conditions and thus makes the success of a producer less dependent on external conditions that he cannot control and that are economically and socially irrational [4].

The nature of the relationship between the market and the plan is a frequently discussed subject. Plan and market have traditionally been contrasted as two separate mechanisms (see section 2). But some economists try to develop a monistic approach. V. Bakarić argues that there can be no contrasting, that the law of value reigns supreme and that planning is just one element in it, although the most important one [5, p. 52]. This statement seems to be the reverse of what I said in the preceding paragraph and in section 2. But the contradiction is more apparent than real. What Bakarić tries to do is to combat the voluntarism of etatist planning and to show that there is an objectively given framework within which planners are obliged to move. I. Maksimović understood this statement to mean too much laissez-faire for his taste. He criticizes the inconsistencies of the officially proclaimed economic policy and warns that an insufficiently controlled market causes damage to individuals (negation of distribution according to work), to enterprises (different business conditions in various industries), as well as to the society at large (less than optimal production). All this tends to generate an ideology which maintains that socialism is not economically superior to organized capitalism, and that inequality and exploitation are products of human nature and cannot be eliminated [6].

D. Mišić sees the shortcomings of self-management as it exists today in Yugoslavia to lie primarily in the fact that it is confined to the enterprise. Investment resources are not allocated rationally; in the present situation, self-management and planning contradict each other; the socialist distribution principle is negated; and there is a tendency for group ownership to arise. As a result, a laissez-faire approach is extolled. Mišić suggests that the self-management structure be completed upward. He believes that integration processes, which we discussed in section 14, are neither fast enough nor quite appropriate. Mišić pleads for an integral system of self-management in which coordinating self-management bodies would be created on the level of industries and also regionally. Membership in such associations would be obligatory [7]. Mišić's system resembles the system of higher business associations that existed in the two-year transitional period 1951-52. A few years after self-management became operative, the present author suggested a somewhat different approach. A careful study of the economics of the oil industry showed that there was very little to be gained by competition and a lot to be achieved by a coordinated policy based on independent and competent research. I suggested that industries possessing similar characteristics establish common but independent economic-technological research bureaus. The bureaus would prepare alternatives for major policy decisions. The most acceptable alternative, perhaps modified in the process, would be chosen by the representatives of enterprises through some sort of self-management mechanism. The industrial research bureaus would also serve as development planning institutions and, as such, would cooperate with territorial planning bureaus [8, ch. 24].

Self-management in enterprises is just one element in an integral system of social self-government. E. Pusić points out that such a system has three basic components: territorial (various levels of government), functional (enterprises and institutions, that is, work organizations), and social (cultural, religious, and other associations of individuals). Pusić is mostly concerned with the first component. He is thus first among Yugoslav authors to study systematically the problem of the withering away of the state — generally considered utopian outside Yugoslavia. The state will wither away when government over individuals is replaced by the management of things. Engels took this famous phrase from Saint-Simon. The latter, as well as other writers of his time, maintained that public administration was exclusively an instrument of power but that it was otherwise unimportant for the life of a nation. Marx and Engels agreed with the first part of the statement, but regarded public administration as very important. Later a significant duality appeared: public administration was no more exclusively an instrument of power, but was also entrusted with various socially necessary activities. Education, medical care, social welfare, and so on, differ basically from defense, police, and judiciary. The monopoly of physical power might occasionally be useful, but it is not at all necessary where social services are concerned. In socialism, public administration without state political power becomes the question of the day. In other words, systematic planning and coordination of social services no longer presupposes the existence of a commanding center such as is embodied in political power [9]. The interest communities and the quasi-market, discussed in section 6, represent an attempt to move in this direction.

Self-government is not a purely economic phenomenon. While economists are, naturally enough, interested primarily in economic aspects, other social scientists explore additional dimensions. Lj. Tadić, the political scientist, points out that Yugoslav self-governing socialism is confined largely to the economic sphere. It has been developed on the microlevel without a corresponding reflection on the macrolevel — the level of the global society [10, p. 55]. S. Stojanović, the philosopher, maintains that without faster political democratization it is impossible to create self-government on higher levels of social organization [10, p. 34]. R. Supek, the sociologist, explains that political pluralism does not mean a multi-party system, which can also be bureaucratized. In a self-government setting, political pluralism means direct control of various centers of power. How this is to be achieved is an open problem. Supek expects a certain duality of power to develop at first, a combination of classical representative democracy and self-government.

Evidently, self-government is not a closed and complete system. Many questions are still open, many problems unresolved. The Yugoslav social laboratory is bound to be active for some time to come.

REFERENCES

CHAPTER 1

1. Informativni priručnik o Jugoslaviji. Belgrade, October 1948.
2. Bićanić, R. Ekonomska politika Jugoslavije. Zagreb, 1962.
3. Milić, R. Ekonomika FNRJ. Belgrade, 1951.
4. Dobrinčić, M., et al. Privredni sistem FNRJ. Zagreb, 1951.
5. Kidrič, B. "Kvalitet robno-novčanih odnosa u FNRJ." Komunist, 1, 1949, 33-51.
6. Kidrič, B. Privredni problemi FNRJ. Belgrade, 1950.
7. Horvat, B. Ogled o jugoslavenskom društvu. Zagreb, 1969. English ed.: An Essay on Yugoslav Society. White Plains, N.Y., 1969.
8. Kidrič, B. "Teze o ekonomici prelaznog perioda u našoj zemlji." Komunist, 6, 1950, 1-20.
9. Novak, M. Uvod u političku ekonomiju socijalizma. Zagreb, 1955.
10. Pašić, N. Javne korporacije u Velikoj Britaniji i drugim zapadnim zemljama. Belgrade, 1957.
11. Dragičević, A. Potreban rad i višak rada. Zagreb, 1957.
12. Kovač, P., and Miljević, D. Samoupravljanje proizvodjača u privredi. Belgrade, 1958.
13. Stanovčić, V., and Stojanović, A. (eds.). Birokracija i tehnokracija. Book I. Belgrade, 1966.
14. Stanovčić, V. Birokracija i tehnokracija. Book II. Belgrade, 1966.
15. Pečujlić, M. Klase i savremeno društvo. Belgrade, 1967.
16. Stojanović, S. "Etatistički mit socijalizma." Praxis, 1967, 30-38.
17. Horvat, B. Note on the Rate of Growth of the Yugoslav Economy. Belgrade, 1963.
18. Popov, Z. "Osvrt na kretanje privrednog razvoja u svetu." Economic Analysis, 1968, 353-65.
19. Schumpeter, J. A. Capitalism, Socialism and Democracy. New York, 1950.
20. Savezni zavod za statistiku. Jugoslavija 1945-1964. Belgrade, 1965.
21. Vidaković, Ž. Promene u strukturi jugoslavenskog društva i Savez Komunista. Belgrade, 1967.
22. Vučković, M. V. Naš novi planski i finansijski sistem. Belgrade, 1952.
23. Horvat, B. "Još jedan prilog pitanju prelaznog perioda." Ekonomist, 5-6, 1951, 45-56.
24. Perović, M. "Još o prelaznom periodu." Ekonomski pregled, 1953, 29-42.

References

25. Horvat, B. Towards a Theory of Planned Economy. Belgrade, 1964; Serbo-Croatian ed., 1961.
26. Polemics. Dragičević, A., Stampar, S., Horvat, B. Naše teme. 1962, 872-94, 1318-33, 1487-1523; 1963, 99-100.
27. Mandel, E. "Yugoslav Economic Theory." Monthly Review, 11, 1967, 40-49.
28. Ward, B. "Marxism-Horvatism: A Yugoslav Theory of Socialism." American Economic Review, 1967, 509-23.
29. Popović, M. "O sistemu ekonomske i socijalističke demokratije u Jugoslaviji." Komunist, 3-4, 1952, 1-14.
30. Kardelj, E., et al. Razvoj privrede FNRJ. Belgrade, 1956.
31. Program Saveza Komunista Jugoslavije. Belgrade, 1958.
32. Kardelj, E. "Basic Principles of the New Constitution." Yugoslav Survey, 11, 1962, 1529-56.
33. Bilandžić, D. Management of Yugoslav Economy. Belgrade, 1967.
34. Savezna skupština. Osnovni problemi daljneg razvoja privrednog sistema. Belgrade, 1964.
35. Savezna skupština. Privredna reforma. Belgrade, 1965.
36. Horvat, B. (ed.). Uzroci i karakteristike privrednih kretanja u 1961. i 1962. godini. Belgrade, 1962.
37. Dabčević, S., et al. O nekim problemima privrednog sistema. Zagreb, 1962. Reprinted in Ekonomski pregled, 3, 51, 1963.
38. Savjetovanje jugoslavenskih ekonomista, Zagreb 17-19 januara 1963. "Aktuelni problemi privrednog razvoja i privrednog sistema Jugoslavije." Ekonomist, 1, 1963.
39. Bićanić, R. "Economics of Socialism in a Developed Country." Foreign Affairs, 1966, 633-50.
40. Džeba, K., and Beslać, M. Privredna reforma. Zagreb, 1965.
41. Horvat, B. Samoupravlenie, centralizm i planovanie. Belgrade, 1964.
42. Savetovanje jugoslovenskih ekonomista, Ljubljana, 9-11. marta 1967. "O uslovima stabilizacije jugoslavenske privrede." Ekonomist, 1-4, 1966; 1-2, 1967.
43. Institut ekonomskih nauka. Nauka i ekonomska politika. Belgrade, 1968.
44. Institut ekonomskih nauka. Sumarna analiza privrednih kretanja i prijedlozi za ekonomsku politiku. Belgrade, 1968.
45. Institut ekonomskih nauka. Ocjena ekonomske situacije i predvidjanja daljeg razvoja. Belgrade, 1969.
46. Horvat, B. Ekonomska nauka i narodna privreda. Zagreb, 1968.
47. Sirotković, J. Planiranje proširene reprodukcije u socijalizmu. Zagreb, 1951.
48. Lavrač, I. "Konkurencija i stimulacija u našem privrednom sistemu." Ekonomist, 1958, 601-19.
49. Novak, M. "O prelaznom periodu." Ekonomski pregled, 1952, 203-13.
50. Korač, M. "Prilog pitanju o prelaznom periodu." Ekonomist, 3-4, 1951, 37-46.
51. Uvalić, R. "Zakon vrednosti i njegovo korišćenje u planiranju narodne privrede." Ekonomist, 1, 1948, 20-27.
52. Kraigher, S. "O politični ekonomiji v prehodnom razdoblju." Ekonomska revija, 1-2, 1950, 9-46.
53. Uvalić, R. "O nekim principima našeg privrednog sistema i problemi njihove primene." Ekonomist, 3, 1954, 5-17.

54. Maksimović, I. Teorije socijalizma u gradjanskoj ekonomskoj nauci. Belgrade, 1958.
55. Černe, F. Planiranje in tržni mehanizem v ekonomski teoriji socijalizma. Ljubljana, 1960.
56. Jelić, B. "Neki aspekti dejstva plana i tržišta u našoj privredi." Ekonomist, 1958, 183-201.
57. Uvalić, R. "Funkcije tržišta i plana u socijalističkoj privredi." Ekonomist, 1962, 205-19.
58. Bićanić, R. "Centralističko, decentralističko ili policentričko planiranje." Ekonomist, 1963, 456-69.
59. Šefer, B. Ekonomski razvoj Jugoslavije i privredna reforma. Belgrade, 1968.
60. "Diskusija ekonomista o prednacrtu ustava." Ekonomist, 1962, 439-517.
61. Rajković, V. "Ocjena ostvarivanja privredne reforme i aktuelni problemi." In Aktuelni problemi ekonomske politike Jugoslavije, 1969/1970, Zagreb, pp. 21-48.
62. Bakarić, V. Aktuelni problemi sadašnje etape revolucije. Zagreb, 1967.
63. Russett, B. M. World Handbook of Political and Social Indicators. New Haven, Conn., 1964.
64. "Platform for the Preparation of Positions and Decisions of the Tenth Congress of the League of Communists of Yugoslavia." Yugoslav Survey, 3, 1973, 1-140.
65. Černe, F. "Ohridski problemi v luči majhne ankete in njene analize." Ekonomska revija, 1971, 5-17.
66. Horvat, B., et al. Ekonomske funkcije federacije. Belgrade: Institut ekonomskih nauka, 1971. Translated as "Economic Functions of the Federation." Eastern European Economics, 2, 1972-73, 3-46.
67. Horvat, B. "Nacionalizam i nacija." Gledišta, 5-6, 1971. Translated as "Nationalism and Nationality." International Journal of Politics, 1, 1972, 19-46.
68. Bošković, B., et al. Privredni sistem SFRJ. Belgrade: Institut za ekonomiku investicija, 1973.
69. Kardelj, E. "Principal Causes and Trends of Constitutional Changes." Socialist Thought and Practice, 54, 1973, 3-56. See also the first two parts of Kardelj's article in the same journal, 52 and 53, 1973.
70. Madžar, Lj. "Problemi i perspektive razvoja jugoslovenske privrede." Ekonomska misao, 1, 1974, 9-36.
71. Čobeljić, M. "O raskoraku izmedju razvojne politike i privrednog sistema." Ekonomska misao, 1, 1974, 63-70.
72. Institut društvenih nauka. Privredni sistem SFRJ. Belgrade, 1973.
73. Horvat, B. An Essay on Jugoslav Society. White Plains, N.Y., 1969.
74. "Ocena sadašnjeg momenta i daljeg razvoja." Borba, March 9, 1969, p. 2.
75. Jašić, Z. "Federativno uredjenje Jugoslavije i koordinaci ja u vodjenju ekonomske politike." Ekonomski pregled, 3-4, 1973, 99-114.
76. Cvjetičanin, V. "Prilog analizi samoupravljanja." Naše teme, 1971, 484-88.
77. Šuvar, S. Samoupravljanje i druge alternative. Zagreb, 1972.

References

CHAPTER 2

1. Čalić, D. Metodologija planiranja proizvodnje. Belgrade, 1948.
2. Kidrič, B. Sabrana dela. Book III. Belgrade, 1960.
3. Begović, V. "Dvije i po godine Petogodišnjeg plana." Komunist, 5, 1949, 82-101.
4. "Izvještaji savezne planske komisije." Informativni priručnik o Jugoslaviji.
5. Vučković, M. Naš novi planski i financijski sistem. Belgrade, 1952.
6. Jelić, B. "Characteristics of the Yugoslav Economic Planning System." Socialist Thought and Practice, 1, 1961, 58-81.
7. Popović, M. Društveno ekonomski sistem. Belgrade, 1964.
8. Lovrenović, S. Ekonomska politika Jugoslavije. Sarajevo, 1963.
9. Sirotković, J. Problemi privrednog planiranja u Jugoslaviji. Zagreb, 1961.
10. Dabčević-Kučar, S. "Decentralized Socialist Planning: Yugoslavia." In E. E. Hagen (ed.), Planning Economic Development. Homewood, Ill., 1963.
11. Jelić, B. Sistem planiranja u Jugoslavenskoj privredi. Belgrade, 1962.
12. Čobeljić, N., and Stojanović, R. Teorija investicionih ciklusa u socija-lističkoj privredi. Belgrade, 1966.
13. "Resolution of the Federal Assembly on the Guidelines for Drawing Up Yugoslavia's Social Plan for the 1964-1970 Period." Yugoslav Survey, 1964, 2703-16.
14. Čobeljić, N. "O raskoraku između razvojne politike i privrednog sistema." Ekonomska misao, 1, 1974, 63-70.
15. Bajt, A. "Fluctuations in Growth Rates in Post War Socialist Economies." International Economic Seminar — CESES. Balatonfüred, 1969.
16. Horvat, B. "Tehnički progres u Jugoslaviji." Ekonomska analiza, 1969, 29-57.
17. Horvat, B. Privredni ciklusi u Jugoslaviji. Belgrade, 1969. English ed.: Business Cycles in Yugoslavia. White Plains, N.Y., 1970.
18. Šefer, B. "Problemi i politika razvoja lične i društvene potrošnje." In J. Sirotković (ed.), Suvremeni problemi jugoslavenske privrede i ekonomska politika. Zagreb, 1965.
19. Djordjević, J. "Teorijska i ustavna pitanja planiranja u Jugoslaviji." In Usmeravanje društvenog razvoja u socijalizmu. Belgrade, 1965.
20. Čobeljić, N. Politika i metodi privrednog razvoja Jugoslavije. Belgrade, 1959.
21. Marschak, T. A. "Centralized Versus Decentralized Resource Allocation: The Yugoslav Laboratory." Quarterly Journal of Economics, 1968, 561-87.
22. Bićanić, R. "The Threshold of Economic Growth." Kyklos, 1962, 7-28.
23. Bjelogrlić, D. "O nekim problemima društvenog usmeravanja privrede." In Usmeravanje društvenog razvoja u socijalizmu. Belgrade, 1965.
24. Savezna skupština. Osnove sistema društvenog planiranja. Belgrade, 1966.
25. Sirotković, J. Planiranje u sistemu samoupravljanja. Zagreb, 1966.
26. Mesarić, M. Planiranje privrednog razvoja. Zagreb, 1967.
27. Jugoslavenski institut za ekonomska istraživanja. Sumarna analiza privred-nih kretanja i prijedlozi za ekonomsku politiku. Belgrade, 1968.
28. Mesarić, M. "Uloga planiranja u jugoslavenskom privrednom modelu." Ekonomist, 1969, 403-26.
29. Horvat, B. "Planning in Yugoslavia." In Faber, M., and Seers, D. (eds.), The Crisis in Planning. Vol. II. London, 1972.
30. Cole, G. D. H. Guild Socialism Re-Stated. London, 1920.

References

31. Horvat, B. An Essay on Yugoslav Society. White Plains, N.Y., 1969.
32. Bićanić, R. "O monocentričnom i policentričnom planiranju." Ekonomski pregled, 1963, 469-528.
33. Bićanić, R. Problems of Planning: East and West. The Hague, 1967.
34. Horvat, B. "The Optimum Rate of Investment." Economic Journal, 1958, 747-67.
35. Horvat, B. "The Optimum Rate of Investment Reconsidered." Economic Journal, 1965, 572-76.
36. Sekulić, M. Primjena strukturnih modela u planiranju privrednog razvoja. Zagreb, 1968.
37. Horvat, B. Primjena medjusektorske analize u planskom bilanciranju privrede. Belgrade, 1969.
38. Horvat, B. "A Restatement of a Simple Planning Model with Some Examples from Yugoslav Economy." Sankhyā, Series B, 1960, 29-48.
39. Nikolić, D. (ed.). Elementi metodologije planiranja dugoročnog privrednog razvoja. Belgrade, 1964.
40. Horvat, B. "An Integrated System of Social Accounts for an Economy of the Yugoslav Type." Review of Income and Wealth, 1968, 19-36.
41. Horvat, B., et al. Integrisani sistem društvenog računovodstva za jugoslovensku privredu. Belgrade, 1969.
42. Bićanić, R. "Economic Growth Under Centralized and Decentralized Planning: Yugoslavia — A Case Study." Economic Development and Cultural Change, 1957, 63-74.
43. Čobeljić, N. "Tri osnovna problema u teoriji razvoja nedovoljno razvijenih zemalja." Ekonomist, 1959, 225-53.
44. Stojanović, R. "Stopa rasta socijalističke privrede." In R. Stojanović (ed.), Savremeni problemi privrednog razvoja u socijalizmu. Belgrade, 1960.
45. Bajt, A. "Optimalna veličina investicija iz nacionalnog dohotka." Ekonomist, 1958, 79-91.
46. Bajt, A. "Stopa rasta u nacrtu perspektivnog plana." Ekonomist, 1963, 584-91.
47. Černe, F. "O stabilizaciji in nihanjih v gospodarstvu." Ekonomska revija, 1967, 212-29.
48. Bajt, A. "Privredna kretanja i ekonomska politika u 1969. i 1970. godini." In Aktuelni problemi ekonomske politike Jugoslavije 1969/1970. Zagreb, 1969, pp. 5-17.
49. Horvat, B. "Kratkoročna nestabilnost i dugoročne tendencije razvoja jugoslovenske privrede." Ekonomist, 1-2, 1974, 51-71.
50. Vukčević, R. "Srednjoročni planovi i rezultati u razvoju." Ekonomska misao, 4, 1973, 41-57.
51. Bićanić, R. Economic Policy in Socialist Yugoslavia. Cambridge, Mass.: Cambridge University Press, 1972.
52. Bajt, A. "Potrošna funkcija jugoslovenske privrede." Ekonomist, 1, 1971, 7-26.
53. Mihailović, K., and Berković, E. Razvoj i životni standard regiona Jugoslavije. Belgrade: Ekonomski institut, 1970.
54. Srebrić, B. "Policy, Methods and Basic Results of Developing the Underdeveloped Areas in Yugoslavia." Ekonomist (English issue), 1969.
55. Mladenović, M. "Sistem dopunskog finansiranja razvoja privredno nedovoljno razvijenih republika i autonomnih pokrajina." Finansije, 3-4, 1972.

References

56. Kidrič, B. "O nekim problemima naše industrijalizacije." In Privredni problemi FNRJ. Belgrade: Kultura, 1950.
57. Mihailović, K. Regionalni razvoj socijalističkih zemalja. Belgrade: Uporedna studija, SANU, 1972.
58. Kubović, B. "O privrednoj snazi naših kotara i gradova." Ekonomski pregled, 7, 1954.
59. Kubović, B. "Regionalni razvoj u društvenom planu perspektivnog privrednog razvoja Jugoslavije." Ekonomski pregled, 12, 1957.
60. Ivanović, B. Diskriminaciona analiza sa primenom u ekonomskim istraživanjima. Belgrade: Naučna knjiga, 1963.
61. Lang, R., and Gorupić, D. "Neka pitanja analize stepena i mogućnosti racionalnog privrednog razvoja." Ekonomski pregled, 8-9, 1956.
62. Krešić, I. "Značaj transportnih troškova u pitanju industrijskog smeštaja." Ekonomski pregled, 8, 1956.
63. Gorupić, D. "Prilog metodi ekonomske analize i izbora lokacija industrijskih objekata." Ekonomski pregled, 11, 1956.
64. Srebrić, D. "Neki načelni problemi lokacije industrije." Ekonomist, 1-2, 1957.
65. Mihailović, K. "Regionalni aspekt privrednog razvoja." Problemi regionalnog privrednog razvoja. Belgrade: Ekonomska biblioteka, 1962.
66. Stojanović, R. "O potrebi potpunijeg uključivanja regionalnog aspekta pri planiranju dugoročnog privrednog razvoja." Problemi regionalnog privrednog razvoja. Belgrade: Ekonomska biblioteka, 1962.
67. Kubović, B. "Regionalni privredni razvoj i samoupravljanje." Problemi regionalnog privrednog razvoja. Belgrade: Ekonomska biblioteka, 1962.
68. Čolanović, D. "Organizacija industrijalizacije nerazvijenih područja." Problemi regionalnog privrednog razvoja. Belgrade: Ekonomska biblioteka, 1962.
69. Mladenović, N. "Regionalni razvoj i ekonomska rejonizacija." In Problemi regionalnog privrednog razvoja. Belgrade: Ekonomska biblioteka, 1962.
70. Vinski, I. "Regionalna distribucija nacionalnog bogatstva u Jugoslaviji." Problemi regionalnog privrednog razvoja. Belgrade: Ekonomska biblioteka, 1962.
71. Horvat, B. "Medjuregionalna medjusektorska analiza." Problemi regionalnog privrednog razvoja. Belgrade: Ekonomska biblioteka, 1962.
72. Mihailović, K. Nerazvijena područja Jugoslavije. Belgrade: Aktuelna pitanja, Ekonomski institut, Belgrade, 1970.
73. Vukčović, R. "Brži razvoj privredno nedovoljno razvijenih područja kao uslov stabilizacije jugoslovenske privrede." Ekonomist, 1-4, 1966.
74. Horvat, B. "Struktura privrede i investicije." Ekonomist, 1-2, 1967.
75. Bazler, M. "Analiza stepena razvijenosti jugoslovenskih područja." Ekonomska analiza, 1-2, 1967.
76. Sicherl, P. "Analiza nekih elemenata za ocenu stepena razvijenosti republika i pokrajina." Ekonomska analiza, 1-2, 1969.
77. Kubović, B. Regionalni aspekt privrednog razvitka Jugoslavije. Zagreb: Biblioteka ekonomskog pregleda, 1961.
78. Bogoev, K. "Politika bržeg razvoja nerazvijenih republika i pokrajina." Ekonomist, 2-3, 1970.
79. Sicherl, P. "Regional Aspects of Yugoslav Economic Development and Planning." Separat 74, JIEI. Belgrade, 1969.

80. Deveti Kongres SKJ. Belgrade: Kultura, 1969.
81. Pešaković, M. "Medjurepublički ekonomski odnosi." Finansije, 3-4, 1971.
82. "Diskusija povodom knjige dr Koste Mihailovića." Ekonomska misao, 2, 1970.
83. Goljanin, M. "Regionalni aspekt kreditno-monetarne politike." Ekonomska misao, 4, 1970.
84. Hadžiomerović, H. "Pristup pitanju integracije jugoslovenske privrede." Ekonomist, 2, 1969.
85. Rakić, V. "Integracija jugoslovenske privrede." Ekonomist, 2, 1969.
86. Horvat, B. "Integriranost jugoslovenske privrede i samoupravno planiranje." Ekonomist, 2, 1969.
87. Savetovanje o temi. "Jedinstveno tržište, nacionalne ekonomije i jugoslovenska privreda." Gledišta, 3, 1971.
88. Čobeljić, N. Privreda Jugoslavije (Rast, struktura i funkcionisanje). Book II. Belgrade: Savremena administracija, 1974.

CHAPTER 3

1. Stipetić, V. Poljoprivreda i privredni razvoj. Zagreb: Informator, 1969.
2. Stipetić, V. "Ekonomika poljoprivrede i ribarstva." In J. Sirotković and V. Stipetić, Ekonomika Jugoslavije. Separate part. Zagreb: Informator, 1971.
3. Savezna narodna skupština. Stanje poljoprivrede i zadrugarstva i perspektive njihovog razvoja. Belgrade: Kultura, 1957.
4. Drače, Dž. "Development of Agriculture, 1945-1970." Yugoslav Survey, 4, 1970, 13-40.
5. Janjetović, M. "Proizvodnja i produktivnost u društvenom sektoru." Socijalizam, 12, 1965, 1549-62.
6. Tomin, M. "Agrarna politika i individualno gazdinstvo." Socijalizam, 12, 1965, 1563-79.
7. Marković, P. "Merenje produktivnosti u poljoprivredi." Ekonomika poljoprivrede, 5, 1964, 3-20.
8. M. Trkulja i suradnici. Politika dugoročnog razvoja poljoprivrede. Novi Sad: Zavod za ekonomiku poljoprivrede, 1970.
9. Bićanić, R. "Zaokreti u ekonomskom razvoju i agrarna politika." Ekonomski pregled, 11-12, 1965, 737-58.
10. Marković, P. "Napuštanje individualnog poljoprivrednog gazdinstva." Naše teme, 6, 1965, 828-34.
11. Šuvar, S. "Eksodus seoske omladine." Naše teme, 6, 1965, 835-52.
12. Prva konferencija SKJ. "Rezolucija o razvoju socijalističkog odnosa u poljoprivredi i na selu i zadaci Saveza komunista Jugoslavije." Jugoslovenski pregled, 10, 1970, 359-66.
13. Drugo plenarno zasedanje CK SKJ. "Rezolucija o osnovnim zadacima partije u oblasti socijalističkog preobražja sela i unapredjenja poljoprivredne proizvodnje." Komunist, 2, 1949, 2-15.
14. Kardelj, E. "Zadaci naše politike na selu." Komunist, 2, 1949, 39-68.
15. Kardelj, E. "Komunistička partija Jugoslavije u borbi za novu Jugoslaviju, za narodnu vlast i socijalizam." In V kongres Komunističke partije Jugoslavije. Belgrade: Kultura, 1949, pp. 307-414.
16. Livada, S. "Osnovne strukture i pokretljivost seoskog i poljoprivrednog

References

stanovništva u Jugoslaviji." Sociologija sela, 29-30, 1970, 76-91.

17. Tomašević, J. Peasants, Politics and Economic Change in Yugoslavia. Stanford: Stanford University Press, 1955.

18. Erić, M. Agrarna reforma u Jugoslaviji 1918-1941. god. Sarajevo: V. Masleša, 1958.

19. Stipetić, V. "Agrarna reforma i kolonizacija u FNRJ godine 1945-1948." Rad JAZU br. 300. Zagreb, 1954, pp. 431-72.

20. Mirković, M. Ekonomika agrara FNRJ. Zagreb: NZH, 1950.

21. Vukčević, D. "The Legal Status of Private Agricultural Land." Yugoslav Survey, 1, 1968, 13-22.

22. Marković, P. Strukturne promene na selu kao rezultat ekonomskog razvitka. Belgrade: Zadružna knjiga, 1963.

23. Bogdanović, M. Ekonomika poljoprivrede Jugoslavije. Belgrade: Savremena administracija, 1967.

24. Puljiz, V. "Mješovita gospodarstva u socijalno-ekonomskoj strukturi našeg sela." Sociologija sela, 29-30, 1970, 92-104.

25. Krašovec, S. "Budućnost mješovitih gospodarstava." Sociologija sela, 7-8, 1965, 5-23.

26. Livada, S. "Mješovita gospodarstva u Jugoslaviji." Sociologija sela, 7-8, 1965, 25-43.

27. Livada, S. "Staračka poljoprivredna domaćinstva." Sociologija sela, 13-14, 1966, 3-15.

28. Magdalenić, I. "Neke razlike izmedju staračkih domaćinstava i poljoprivrednih domaćinstava koja imaju radno sposobne članove." Sociologija sela, 27-29, 1970, 27-36.

29. Bićanić, R. "Agrarna prenapučenost." Sociologija sela, 2, 1963, 3-21.

30. Bićanić, R. "Pregled teorija o agrarnoj prenapučenosti." Sociologija sela, 23-24, 1969, 5-21.

31. Klauzer, I. "Viškovi radne snage u poljoprivredi Jugoslavije." Sociologija sela, 7-8, 1965, 101-14.

32. Ružić, Z. "Viškovi radne snage na individualnim poljoprivrednim gazdinstvima u SR Hrvatskoj." Sociologija sela, 4, 1964, 39-46.

33. Čobeljić, N., and Mihajlović, K. "Pitanje agrarne prenaseljenosti u Srbiji." Ekonomist, 1, 1953.

34. Figenwald, V. Viškovi poljoprivrednog stanovništva u SR Hrvatskoj. Zagreb, 1964.

35. Puljiz, V. "Iseljavanje stanovništva iz sela i poljoprivrede." Sociologija sela, 27-28, 1970, 14-25.

36. Vasić, V. Putevi razvitka socijalizma u poljoprivredi Jugoslavije. Belgrade: Rad, 1960.

37. Burzevski, V. Rezerve poljoprivredne radne snage na individualnim gazdinstvima Jugoslavije. Skopje: Zajednica naučnoistraživačkih ustanova za ekonomiku poljoprivrede, 1964.

38. Kostić, C. Seljaci industrijski radnici. Belgrade: Rad, 1955.

39. Begović, V. Put socijalističkog preobraćaja poljoprivrede pod rukovodstvom KPJ. Zagreb: Mala ek. biblioteka br. 14, Naprijed, 1948.

40. Božić, Lj. Agrarna politika. Sarajevo: V. Masleša, 1960.

41. Bakarić, V. O poljoprivredi i problemima sela. Belgrade: Kultura, 1960.

42. Sinanović, S. "Državne poljoprivredne-mašinske stanice na početku godine 1949." Poljoprivreda, 1, 1949.

43. Todorović, M. "O radnoj zadruzi." Komunist, 1-2, 1952, 68-94.

References

44. Kardelj, E. "Zemljoradničko zadrugarstvo u planskoj privredi." Komunist, 3, 1947, 34-84.
45. Kidrič, B. "O izgradnji socijalističke ekonomike Federativne Narodne Republike Jugoslavije." In V Kongres KPJ. Zagreb: Kultura, 1948.
46. Vučković, M. Zadrugarstvo. Zagreb: Zadružna štampa, 1957.
47. Vasić, V. Putevi razvitka socijalizma u poljoprivredi Jugoslavije. Belgrade: Rad, 1960.
48. Todorović, M. "O prelaznim oblicima zemljoradničkih zadruga." Komunist, 3, 1949, 119-30.
49. Todorović, M. "O radnoj zadruzi." Komunist, 1-2, 1952, 68-94.
50. Stojanović, R. Poljoprivreda u socijalizmu. Belgrade: Rad, 1954.
51. Horvat, B. Neka pitanja iz ekonomike baranjskog agrara. Zagreb: Ekonomski fakultet, 1950.
52. Kautsky, K. Agrarno pitanje. Belgrade: Kultura, 1953.
53. Engels, F. "Seljačko pitanje u Francuskoj i Njemačkoj." In K. Marx and F. Engels, Izabrana djela. Vol. II. Zagreb: Kultura, 1950.
54. Lenin, V. I. "Prvobitni projekt teza o agrarnom pitanju." Izabrana djela. Vol. II, Book 2. Zagreb: Kultura, 1950.
55. Horvat, B. Ekonomska analiza I. Proizvodnja i tehnološki progres. Belgrade: Oeconomica, 1972.
56. Stipetić, V. Stočarstvo. Belgrade: Jugoslavija, 1969.
57. Stipetić, V. Jugoslovensko tržište poljoprivrednih proizvoda. Belgrade: Zadružna knjiga, 1964.
58. Bakarić, V. Problemi zemljišne rente u prelaznoj etapi. Zagreb: Kultura, 1950.
59. Stojanović, R. Agrarno pitanje prema marksističkim teoretičarima. Belgrade: Zadružna knjiga, 1955.
60. Stipetić, V. Kretanje i tendencije u razvitku poljoprivredne proizvodnje na području NR Hrvatske. Zagreb: JAZU, 1959.
61. Marx, K. "Inauguralna adresa medjunarodnog radničkog udruženja." In K. Marx and F. Engels, Izabrana djela. Vol. I. Zagreb: Kultura, 1949.
62. Engels, F. "O stambenom pitanju." In K. Marx and F. Engels, Izabrana djela. Vol. I.
63. Milosavljević, B. Podruštvljenje u poljoprivredi i kolektivizacija kao metod njenog socijalističkog preobražaja. Belgrade: Institut za ekonomiku poljoprivrede, 1962.
64. Oboljenskij, K. R. "Krupna poljoprivredna proizvodnja i njeni problemi." Ekonomika poljoprivrede, 9, 1964, 63-70.
65. Hasanagić, H. "Agrarno i seljačko pitanje." In Problemi poljoprivrede u Jugoslaviji. Belgrade: Nolit, 1956.
66. Vukčević, D. J. Zemljišni odnosi i kooperacija. Belgrade: Institut društvenih nauka, 1964.
67. Program Saveza komunista Jugoslavije. Belgrade: Kultura, 1958.
68. Kardelj, E. Problemi socijalističke politike na selu. Belgrade: Kultura, 1958.
69. Starc, A. "Kooperacija društvene privrede s individualnim poljoprivrednim proizvodjačima." Sociologija sela, 29-30, 1970, 57-75.
70. Blagojević, O. "Problemi individualnih proizvodjača." Ekonomika poljoprivrede, 4, 1964, 3-38.
71. Glavni savez zemljoradničkih zadruga Jugoslavije. Razvitak i problemi kooperacije zemljoradničkih zadruga i individualnih proizvodjača. Bel-

References

grade: Savezna privredna komora, 1964.

72. Vučković, M. Radničko samoupravljanje u zemljoradničkom zadrugarstvu, Belgrade: Zadružna knjiga, 1961.

73. Vučković, M. "Bitne karakteristike i značaj Osnovnog zakona o poljo-privrednim zadrugama." Ekonomika poljoprivrede, 11, 1965, 763-69.

74. Šekularac, B. "Samoupravljanje u zemljoradnickom zadrugama." Ekono-mika poljoprivrede, 2, 1965, 83-93.

75. Ingolič, S. "O nekim problemima i zadacima u ostvarivanju politike razvo-ja poljoprivredne proizvodnje i društvenih odnosa." Ekonomika poljo-privrede, 7-8, 1965, 483-92.

76. Marković, P. "Agrarna politika Jugoslavije i rezultat u proizvodnji." Sociologija sela, 29-30, 1970, 17-33.

77. Šuvar, S. "Osnovne karakteristike i uvjeti procesa podruštvljavanja zemlje u Jugoslaviji." Sociologija sela, 11-12, 1966, 3-80.

78. Leković, M. "Neki problemi društvenog sektora poljoprivrede." Ekono-mika poljoprivrede, 12, 1969, 835-50.

79. Šuvar, S. "Kulturne promene u selima Jugoslavije." Sociologija sela, 29-30, 1970, 117-29.

80. Marković, P. "Problemi poljoprivrede u dokumentima SKJ i Ustavu SFRJ." Ekonomika poljoprivrede, 7, 1966, 491-500.

81. Pavlović, U. "Traktori na individualnim poljoprivrednim gazdinstvima." Ekonomika poljoprivrede, 6, 1972, 15-24.

82. Sivčev, S. "Opremanje individualnih poljoprivrednih gazdinstava SR Srbije traktorima." Ekonomika poljoprivrede, 3, 1971, 125-34.

83. Dimković, B. "Traktor u privatnom vlasnistvu." Ekonomika poljoprivrede, 3, 1967, 169-76.

84. Komisija za agrarnu politiku Predsedništva SKJ. Agrarna politika i zadaci Saveza komunista Jugoslavije. Belgrade, 1970.

85. Institut za ekonomiku poljoprivrede-Beograd. "Uslovi privredjivanja poljoprivrede u toku sprovodjenja reforme u SR Srbije." Ekonomika poljo-privrede, 1-2, 1969, 23-47.

86. Odbor za zadrugarstvo SPK. "Zaklučci i predlozi." Ekonomika poljo-privrede, 1-2, 1968, 3-8.

87. Sivčev, S. "Osnovne karakteristike dosadašnjeg razvoja kooperacija." Ekonomika poljoprivrede, 5, 1972, 3-14.

88. Pokrajinsko izvršno veće Vojvodine. "Odraz aktuelnih problema poljo-privrede na položaj poljoprivrede i privrede u AP Vojvodina." Ekonomika poljoprivrede, 1-2, 1969, 55-74.

89. Tadić, D. "Cena poljoprivrednog zemljišta u 1965. godini." Ekonomika poljoprivrede, 6, 1966, 453-61.

90. Radovanović, B. "Individualno poljoprivredno gazdinstvo i njegovo opre-manje krupnim mašinama." Ekonomika poljoprivrede, 6, 1966, 425-31.

91. Popović, S. "Individualno gazdinstvo u integracionim procesima poljo-privrede Jugoslavije." Ekonomika poljoprivrede, 11-12, 1971, 739-54.

92. Mitić, S. "Uzroci smanjivanja uticaja okrupnjene zadruge na društveno ejonomske odnose na selu." Ekonomika poljoprivrede, 8, 1966, 571-84.

93. Radovanović, B. "Neki aspekti daljeg razvitka poljoprivredne zadruge." Ekonomika poljoprivrede, 6, 1969, 369-78.

94. Kovačević, M. "Uvodno izlaganje." Ekonomika poljoprivrede, 9, 1967, 615-26.

95. Milenković, P. "Idejni projekt nove organizacije zemljoradničke zadruge." Ekonomika poljoprivrede, 7-8, 1970, 537-47.

96. Odbor za zadrugarstvo SPK. "Zaključci i predlozi." Ekonomika poljo-
    privrede, 1-2, 1968, 3-8.
97. Filipović, S. "Aktuelna pitanja kooperacije u poljoprivredi Vojvodine."
    Ekonomika poljoprivrede, 9, 1967, 635-59.
98. Stipetić, V. "Opandanje zemljišne rente u savremenoj kapitalističkoj
    poljoprivredi." Ekonomist, 4, 1959, 415-45.
99. Stipetić, V. "Radna i agrarna prenapučenost." Ekonomika poljoprivrede,
    4, 1967, 243-60.
100. Levstik, J. "Seljaci-radnici kod nas." Ekonomika poljoprivrede, 11,
    1966, 817-30.
101. Livada, S. "Promjene socijalno-ekonomske strukture poljoprivrede i sela
    u svijetlu novijih podataka." Sociologija sela, 26, 1969, 3-11.
102. Simić, J. "Vidovi i faktori promena u strukturi dohotka domaćinstava na
    individualnim poljoprivrednim gazdinstvima." Ekonomika poljoprivrede,
    5, 1970, 321-46.
103. Petrović, M. "Raspodela dohotka seoskih domaćinstava Jugoslavije."
    Ekonomika poljoprivrede, 7-8, 1970, 553-56.
104. Komar, S. "Neki problemi sela i seljačkih gazdinstava." Socijalizam,
    5, 1962, 17-79.
105. Drače, Dž. "Poljoprivreda 1961-1971." Jugoslavenski pregled, 3, 1972,
    93-104.
106. Perišić, M. "Neka pitanja proizvodnosti rada u gajenju glavnih ratarskih
    kultura na ispitivanim društvenim poljoprovrednim gazdinstvima Jugo-
    slavije." Ekonomika poljoprivrede, 9, 1970, 667-80.
107. Horvat, B. "Renta kao element teorije cena planske privrede." Ekono-
    mist, 4, 1959, 398-414.
108. Bergmann, T. "Porodično gospodarstvo: problematika i razvojne tendenci-
    je." Sociologija sela, 27-28, 1970, 68-81.
109. Dimković, B. "Kooperacija kao funkcija socijalističkog preobražaja poljo-
    privrede i sela." Ekonomika poljoprivrede, 11, 1968, 491-502.
110. Milenković, P. "Neki ekonomski pokazatelji poslovanja zemljoradničkih
    zadruga Vojvodine." Ekonomika poljoprivrede, 11, 1967, 899-916.
111. Mutapović, D. "O zadrugarstvu." Problemi poljoprivrede u Jugoslaviji.
    Belgrade: Nolit, 1956.
112. Čukanović, S. Zemljoradničko zadrugarstvo u agrarnoj politici Jugo-
    slavije. Zrenjanin: NIP Mala poljopriv. biblioteka, 1971.
113. Bićanić, R. "Lack of Institutional Flexibility in Agriculture." Proceed-
    ings of the Tenth International Conference of Agricultural Economists.
    New York: Oxford University Press, 1960, pp. 157-78.
114. Georgescu-Roegen, N. "Economic Theory and Agrarian Economics." In
    Oxford Economic Papers, 1960, pp. 1-40.
115. Brown, L. R. Seeds of Change. New York: Praeger, 1970.
116. Šuvar, S. "Neki aspekti konfliktnih odnosa selo-grad u našem društvu."
    Sociologija sela, 35-36, 1972, 3-16.
117. Tričković, V., and Ostraćanin, M. (eds.). Nauka i tehnologija u privrednom
    razvoju Jugoslavije. Book II. Belgrade: Institut ekonomiskih nauka, 1971.
118. Pjanić, Z., et al. Specifična cena proizvodnje i stvarne cene u privredi.
    Belgrade: Institut društvenih nauka, 1971.
119. Statistički bilten 655. Belgrade: Savezni zavod za statistiku, 1973.
120. Župančić, M. Vjesnik, June 29, 1972.

References

CHAPTER 4

1. Fiamengo, A. "Samoupravljanje i socijalizam." In V. Janičijević (ed.), Društveno samoupravljanje u Jugoslaviji. Belgrade, 1965, 11-38.
2. Horvat, B. An Essay on Yugoslav Society. White Plains, N.Y., 1969.
3. Tanić, Ž. (ed.). Radničko samoupravljanje; razvoj i problemi. Belgrade, 1963.
4. Ward, B. "Workers' Management in Yugoslavia." Journal of Political Economy, 1957, 373-86.
5. Horvat, B., and Rašković, V. "Workers' Management in Yugoslavia: A Comment." Journal of Political Economy, 1959, 194-98.
6. International Labour Office. Workers' Management in Yugoslavia. Geneva, 1962.
7. Novak, M. Organizacija poduzeća u socijalizmu. Zagreb, 1967.
8. Gorupić, D. "Razvoj samoupravnih društvenih odnosa i samoupravno odlučivanje u privredi." Ekonomski pregled, 1969, 1-26.
9. Županov, J. O problemima upravljanja i rukovodjenja u radnoj organizaciji. Zagreb, 1967.
10. Gorupić, D. "Tendencije u razvoju radničkog samoupravljanja u Jugoslaviji." Ekonomist, 1967, 593-638.
11. Institut ekonomskih nauka. Sumarna analiza privrednih kretanja i prijedlozi za ekonomsku politiku. Belgrade, 1968.
12. Kovačević, M. "Enterprise Rules and Regulations." Yugoslav Survey, 1969, 1-8.
13. Županov, J. "Radni kolektiv i ekonomska jedinica u svjetlu organizacione teorije." Ekonomski pregled, 1962, 143-69.
14. Vučković, M. Naš novi planski i finansiski sistem. Belgrade, 1952.
15. Dautović, M. "Economic Integration." Yugoslav Survey, 1968, 75-82.
16. Miljević, Dj. Privredni sistem Jugoslavije. Belgrade, 1965.
17. Friedmann, W., and Mates, L. (eds.). Joint Business Ventures of Yugoslav Enterprises and Foreign Firms. Belgrade, 1968.
18. Sukijasović, M., and Vujačić, Dj. Industrial Cooperation and Joint Investment Ventures between Yugoslav and Foreign Firms. Belgrade, 1968.
19. Ward, B. "The Firm in Illyria: Market Syndicalism." American Economic Review, 1958, 566-89.
20. Domar, E. "The Soviet Collective Farm." American Economic Review, 1966, 734-57.
21. Dubravčić, D. Ponašanje samoupravnog poduzeća kod izbora kombinacije proizvodnih faktora. Zagreb, 1967.
22. Dubravčić, D. "Prilog zasnivanju teorije jugoslavenskog poduzeća: Mogućnosti uopćavanja modela." Ekonomska analiza, 1968, 120-27.
23. Horvat, B. "Prilog zasnivanju teorije jugoslavenskog poduzeća." Ekonomska analiza, 1967, 7-28.
24. Horvat, B. Towards a Theory of Planned Economy. Belgrade, 1964.
25. Županov, J. "Proizvodžač i riziko -- Neki socijalno-psihološki aspekti kolektivnog poduzetništva." Ekonomist, 1967, 389-408.
26. Djordjević, J. "A Contribution to the Theory of Social Property." Socialist Thought and Practice, 24, 1966, 73-110.
27. Toroman, M. "Oblici društvene svojine." Paper presented at the Symposium on Social Ownership, Serbian Academy of Science and Art, Belgrade, September 20-22, 1965.

References

28. Gams, A. "Društvena svojina i društveno usmeravanje." In Usmeravanje društvenog razvoja u socijalizmu. Belgrade, 1965, 50-67.
29. Bajt, A. "Društvena svojina-kolektivna i individualna." Gledišta, 1968, 531-44.
30. Pejovich, S. The Market-Planned Economy of Yugoslavia. Minneapolis, 1966.
31. Marx, K. Rani radovi. Zagreb, 1953.
32. Rašković, V. "Osnovni idejni i politički problemi ličnog rada u sistemu društvenog samoupravljanja." In Privatni rad: Za ili protiv. Belgrade, 1967.
33. Bilandžić, D. "Odnosi izmedju samoupravljanja i rukovodjenja u poduzeću." In Savremeno rukovodjenje i samoupravljanje. Belgrade, 1969, pp. 67-96.
34. Dirlam, J. "Problems of Market Power and Public Policy in Yugoslavia." In U.S. Senate, Subcommittee on Antitrust and Monopoly of the Committee on the Judiciary, 90th Congress, 2nd Session, Economic Concentration. Part 7. Washington, 1968, pp. 3758-85.
35. Drutter, I. "Uticaj koncentracije ponude na cijene i poslovni uspjeh privrednih organizacija." Ekonomist, 1964, 697-700.
36. Wachtel, H. M. Workers' Management and Workers' Wages in Yugoslavia. Ithaca, N.Y., 1973.
37. Drutter, I. "Tržišni aspekti koncentraci je." In Ekonomski institut, Ekonomske studije 3. Zagreb, 1965.
38. Miletić, M. "Da li je upravni odbor prevazidjen." Direktor, 9, 1969, 56-60.
39. Lemân, G. Ungelöste Fragen in jugoslawischen System der Arbeiterselbstverwaltung. Cologne, 1969.
40. Lemân, G. Stellung und Aufgabung der ökonomischen Einheiten in den jugoslawischen Unternehmungen. Berlin, 1967.
41. Horvat, B. "Critical Notes on the Theory of the Labour-Managed Firm and Some Macroeconomic Implications." Economic Analysis, 1972, 288-93.
42. Adizes, I. Industrial Democracy: Yugoslav Style. New York, 1971.
43. Novak, M. "Osnovna organizacija udruženog rada kao temeljna organizacija samoupravne privrede." Ekonomist, 1973, 7-21.
44. Kratina, H. "The Legal Status of the Enterprise Director Within the Self-Management System." Yugoslav Survey, 4, 1968, 53-60.
45. Jovanov, N. "The Organization of Workers' Self-Management in the Bor Mines and Smelting Works." Yugoslav Survey, 2, 1971, 21-32.
46. Šuvar, S. Samoupravljanje i druge alternative. Zagreb, 1972.
47. Vejnović, M. "Struktura utjecaja u samoupravnoj radnoj organizaciji." Naše teme, 1974, 993-1017.
48. Jerovšek, J. "Utjecaj obrazovanja na strukturu radne organizacije." Naše teme, 1974, 1038-48.
49. Jovanov, N. "Stvarno stanje samoupravljanja i položaj direktora u raspodeli društvene moći." Ekonomski pregled, 1973, 535-60.
50. Paj, I. "Uloga kolegijalnih izvršnih organa u procesu samoupravnog odlučivanja." Ekonomski pregled, 1971, 511-31.
51. Ivanišević, S., Pavić, Ž., and Ramljak, M. Samoupravljanje. Zagreb, 1974.
52. Maksimović, I. Teorijske osnove društvene svojine. Belgrade, 1974.
53. Dirlam, J., and Plummer, J. An Introduction to the Yugoslav Economy. Columbus, Ohio, 1972.

References

CHAPTER 5

1. Radulović, M. "Sistem i politika cijena u Jugoslaviji." Unpublished doctoral dissertation, Titograd, 1968.
2. Kidrić, B. Privredni problemi FNRJ. Belgrade, 1948.
3. Šefer, B. "Tržište u posleratnom periodu." In Razvoj privrede FNRJ. Belgrade, 1956.
4. Dobrinčić, M., et al. Privredni sistem FNRJ. Zagreb, 1951.
5. Čobeljić, N., Mihajlović, K., and Djurović, S. "Problem našeg tržišta s naročitim osvrtom na tržište poljoprivrednih proizvoda." Ekonomist, 3-4, 1954, 31-70.
6. Vuković, D. "Price Formation and Social Price Control." Yugoslav Survey, 1968, 51-58.
7. Drutter, I. "Sistem cijena i tržišnih odnosa." In Poduzeće u reformi. Zagreb, 1968.
8. Institut ekonomskih nauka. Ocjena ekonomske situacije i predvidanja daljneg razvoja. Belgrade, 1969.
9. Institut ekonomskih nauka. Sumarna analiza privrednih kretanja i prijedlozi za ekonomsku politiku. Belgrade, 1968.
10. Pertot, V. "Stabilizacija u uslovima disparitetnih odnosa troškova proizvodnje." Ekonomist, 1966, 216-44.
11. Horvat, B. Towards a Theory of Planned Economy. Belgrade, 1964.
12. Kidrič, B. "Teze o ekonomici prelaznog perioda u našoj zemlji." Komunist, 1950, 1-20.
13. Kidrič, B. "O nekim teoretskim pitanjima privrednog sistema." Komunist, 1952, 41-67.
14. Todorović, M. Oslobodjenje rada. Belgrade, 1965.
15. Institut društvenih nauka. Koncepcija i verifikacija specifične cene proizvodnje u jugoslavenskoj privredi 1964. i 1965. Belgrade, 1968. Specifična cena proizvodnje i stvarne cene u privredi Jugoslavije 1964-68. Belgrade, 1971.
16. Savjetovanje jugoslovenskih ekonomista. "Problemi teorije i politike cena." Ekonomist, 1964, 499-792.
17. Mesarić, M. "Prilog diskusiji o obliku gravitacione cijene u socijalističkoj privredi." Ekonomski pregled, 1965, 607-34.
18. Tomić, T. "Dosadašnji razvoj raspodele ličnih dohodaka u SFRJ." In Obračun i raspodela osobnih dohodaka u radnim organizacijama. Zagreb, 1968, pp. 3-22.
19. Berković, E. "Differentiation of Personal Incomes." Yugoslav Survey, 1969, 81-90.
20. Janković, N. "Lični dohoci kao faktor podizanja životnog standarda." In Obračun i raspodela osobnih dohodaka u radnim organizacijama. Zagreb, 1968, pp. 155-68.
21. Lipovec, F. "Razvoj profitne mere v sistemu samouprave delovnih kolektivov." Ekonomska revija, 1954, 141-51.
22. Pejovich, S. The Market-planned Economy of Yugoslavia. Minneapolis, 1966.
23. Horvat, B. "Tehnički progres u Jugoslaviji." Ekonomska analiza, 1969, 29-57.
24. Popov, S. "Kretanje produktivnosti rada i ličnih dohodaka u pojedinim granama u periodu od 1952 do 1966. godine." In Obračun i raspodela osobnih

dohodaka u radnim organizacijama. Zabreb, 1968, pp. 613-33.

25. Wachtel, H. M. Workers' Management and Workers' Wages in Yugoslavia. Ithaca, N.Y., 1973.

26. Korač, M. Analiza ekonomskog položaja privrednih grupacija na bazi zakona vrijednosti. Zagreb, 1968.

27. Horvat, B. "Raspodela prema radu medu kolektivima." Naša stvarnost, 1962, 52-66.

28. Šefer, B. "Rasponi ličnih dohodaka, njihovo formiranje i tendencije." In Obračun i raspodela osobnih dohodaka u radnim organizacijama. Zagreb, 1968, 421-38.

29. Bakarić, V. Problemi zemljišne rente u prelaznoj etapi. Zagreb, 1950.

30. Horvat, B. "O problemu rudničke rente." Ekonomski pregled, 1953, 253-57.

31. Bajt, A. "Osebni dohodki in delovna storilnost." Ekonomska revija, 1956, 97-134.

32. Gorupić, D., and Perišin, I. "Proširena reprodukcija i njeno financiranje." Ekonomski pregled, 1965, 109-30.

33. Gorupić, D. "Samoupravno poduzeće i privredna reforma." In Poduzeće u reformi. Zagreb, 1968, pp. 3-26.

34. Lavrač, I. "Cena upotrebne vrednosti kapitala." Ekonomska misao, 1968, 407-23.

35. Popović, S. "Merenje dohotka i njegova raspodela." Ekonomska misao, 1968, 424-36.

36. Černe, F. "Poskus ekonomsko-logičnega testiranja sedem hipotez iz teorije dohodka." Ekonomska revija, 1967, 12-29.

37. Samardžija, M. "Metodološke i društvene osnove teorije raspodele do-hodka." Gledišta, 1968, 124-49, 293-304.

38. Bajt, A. "Faktori dohotka i osnovne ekonomske zakonitosti u njegovoj raspodjeli u socijalističkoj tržišnoj privredi." Ekonomist, 1967, 347-87.

39. Bajt, A. Raspodela nacionalnog dohotka i sistem ličnih dohodaka u našoj privredi. Belgrade, 1962.

40. Jurković, P. "Suština i značaj promjena u sistemu utvrdivanja i raspodjele dohotka." Ekonomski pregled, 1969, 27-52.

41. Milenković, V. "Spoljna trgovina." In Razvoj privrede FNRJ. Belgrade, 1956, pp. 399-419.

42. Fabinc, I., et al. "Problemi ekonomskih odnosa s inozemstvom." In Poduzeće u reformi. Zagreb, 1968, pp. 133-216.

43. Čehovin, D. Ekonomski odnosi Jugoslavije s inostranstvom. Belgrade, 1960.

44. Serdar, S. Da li FNR Jugoslavija postaje agrarnouvozna i industrijski izvozna zemlja. Zagreb, 1953.

45. Mrkušić, Ž. Medunarodna trgovina i trgovinska politika. Belgrade, 1963.

46. Žiberna, M. "Neki problemi ekonomskih odnosa s evropskom ekonomskom zajednicom." Medunarodni problemi, 1969, 51-66.

47. Mitić, P. "Ekonomske integracije, svjetsko tržište i Jugoslavija." Gledišta, 1969, 1073-86.

48. Pelicon, I. "Sumarna ocena i neki problemi privredne suradnje SFRJ sa zemljama u razvoju u 1966-1967. godini." In Privredni odnosi Jugoslavije sa zemljama u razvoju. Ljubljana, 1968, pp. 1-23.

49. Uvalić, R. "Trojna ekonomska suradnja Jugoslavije, Indije i UAR-a." In Privredni odnosi Jugoslavije sa zemljama u razvoju. Ljubljana, 1968, pp. 128-46.

References

50. Bilandžić, D. Management of Yugoslav Economy (1945-1966). Belgrade, 1967.
51. Mihajlović, P., and Tanović, S. "Veza jugoslovenskog izvoza s konjukturom u svetu." Ekonomist, 1959, 45-79.
52. Pertot, V. Yugoslav Foreign Trade. Belgrade, 1960.
53. Obradović, S. Uvod u analizu spoljne trgovine. Belgrade, 1962.
54. Popović, M. "O ekonomskim odnosima izmedju socijalističkih država." Komunist, 4, 1949, 89-146.
55. Guzina, V. "Medunarodni zajmovi i socijalistička izgradnja." Komunist, 6, 1950, 21-79.
56. Avramović, D. "Funkcija deviznog kursa u socijalističkoj privredi." Ekonomist, 3, 1952, 3-31.
57. Meichsner, V. "Intervalutarni kurs i cene." Ekonomski anali, 3, 1956, 186-204.
58. Frković, M. "Disparitet spoljnotrgovinskih kurseva u našoj privredi." Ekonomist, 1957, 79-97.
59. Institut za spoljnu trgovinu. Analiza devizne reforme iz 1961. Belgrade, 1964.
60. Anakiovski, D. "Foreign Trade in the Yugoslav Reform." Yugoslav Survey, 3, 1969, 71-84.
61. Domandžić, A. "Customs Tariff." Yugoslav Survey, 24, 1966, 3485-88.
62. Savezna skupština. Devizni i spoljnotrgovinski režim. Belgrade, 1966.
63. Kovač, O. "Uzroci i posljedice strukturne neravnoteže u platnom bilansu Jugoslavije." Mimeographed study, Institut ekonomskih nauka. Belgrade, 1966.
64. Fabinc, I. "Uloga carinske politike u zemljama u razvoju." Medjunarodni problemi, 4, 1963, 37-39.
65. Fabinc, I. "Elementi programa zaštite jugoslavenske privrede." Ekonomist, 1968, 41-60.
66. Dujšin, U. "Determinante izbora izmedu fiksnog i fleksibilnog kursa kod nas." Ekonomist, 1968, 592-98.
67. Čičin-Šain, A. "Fiksni ili fleksibilni kursovi." Ekonomist, 1968, 642-48.
68. Čičin-Šain, A. Devizni režim i konvertibilnost dinara. Zagreb, 1967.
69. Čičin-Šain, A. "Problemi konvertibilnosti dinara." Ekonomist, 1968, 79-102.
70. Mrkušić, Ž. Spoljnoekonomska politika Trećeg svijeta. Belgrade, 1974.
71. Madžar, Lj. "Jedna empirijska analiza stabilnosti spoljnotrgovinskih tokova." Ekonomist, 1968, 580-87.
72. Macesich, G. Yugoslavia. The Theory and Practice of Development Planning. Charlottesville, 1964.
73. Mrkušić, Ž. "Problemi prilagođavanja deviznog kursa." Ekonomska misao, 1969, 133-41.
74. Mrkušić, Ž. "Neka pitanja na alternativu: prilagođavanje deviznog kursa — direktna kontrola." Ekonomist, 1967, 89-102.
75. Rašković, V. Društveno samoupravljanje i raspodela prema radu u Jugoslaviji. Belgrade, 1967.
76. Šefer, B. Ekonomski razvoj Jugoslavije i privredna reforma. Belgrade, 1969.
77. Černe, F. Tržište i cijene. Zagreb, 1966.
78. Govedarica, S. "Price System and Policy." Yugoslav Survey, 3, 1972, 15-28.

79. Popov, S., and Jovićić, M. Uticaj ličnih dohodaka na kretanja cena. Belgrade: Institut ekonomskih nauka, 1971.
80. Šefer, B. Socijalni razvoj u samoupravnom društvu. Belgrade, 1971.
81. Mrkušić, Ž. Teorijska osnova deviznog sistema. Belgrade, 1972.
82. Savičević, M. "Protective Tariffs and Other Measures of Protection of the National Economy." Yugoslav Survey, 1, 1970, 55-62.
83. Baum, S. "Crediting Exports of Capital Goods." Yugoslav Survey, 1, 1970, 63-68.
84. Sukijasović, M. Yugoslav Foreign Investment Legislation at Work: Experiences So Far. Belgrade, 1970.
85. Nichols, P. J. "Western Investment in Eastern Europe: The Yugoslav Example." In Reorientation and Commercial Relations of the Economies of Eastern Europe. A compendium of papers submitted to the Joint Economic Committee of the United States Congress. Washington, 1974, pp. 725-43.
86. Pertot, V. Ekonomika medjunarodne razmjene Jugoslavije. Zagreb, 1971.
87. Dirlam, J. B., and Plummer, J. L. An Introduction to the Yugoslav Economy. Columbus, Ohio, 1973.

CHAPTER 6

1. Finansiski institut. Finansiski sistem FNR Jugoslavije. Belgrade, 1949.
2. Vučković, M. "The Recent Development of the Money and Banking System of Yugoslavia." Journal of Political Economy, 1963, 363-77.
3. Vučković, M. "Preduzeće i kredit." Ekonomski anali, 1956, 166-85.
4. Stevanović, R. M. Novčani i kreditni sistem. Belgrade, 1954.
5. Vučković, M. Kreditni sistem u FNRJ. Belgrade, 1957.
6. Neuberger, E. "Centralization vs. Decentralization: The Case of Yugoslav Banking." American Slavic and East European Review, 1959, 361-73.
7. Pokorn, J. "Razvoj našeg finansiskog sistema." Financije, 1956, 1-10.
8. Miljanić, N., et al. Kreditni i finansiski sistem u Jugoslaviji. Belgrade, 1956.
9. Neuberger, E. "The Role of Central Banking under Various Economic Systems." In C. J. Friedrich and S. E. Harris (eds.), Public Policy. Cambridge, Mass., 1958, pp. 227-54.
10. Jelčić, B. "Poreski instrumenti kao instrument ekonomske politike." Ekonomist, 1967, 50-63.
11. Holjevac, V. "Kreditno-monetarni problemi." Mimeographed study, Ekonomski institut, Zabreb, 1967.
12. Golijanin, M. "Credit and Money Control." Yugoslav Survey, 1967, 93-104.
13. Perišin, I. "Stabilizacija i monetarno-kreditna politika." Ekonomist, 1967, 103-20.
14. Miljanić, N. "Reguliranje monetarnog volumena u SFR Jugoslaviji." Univerzitet danas, 9-10, 1966.
15. Vuksanović, R. "Credit and Money." Yugoslav Survey, 1966, 3461-74.
16. Basaraba, P. "Changes in the Organization and Management of Banks." Yugoslav Survey, 4, 1967, 77-81.
17. Miljanić, N. Novac i kredit. Zagreb, 1964.
18. Mijović, B. Novčana i kreditna politika. Belgrade, 1967.
19. Vasić, F. "Investment in the Post-War Period." Yugoslav Survey, 15, 1963, 2153-72.

References

20. Trklja, M. "Kamata na fondove u privredi." Mimeographed study, Ekonomski institut. Zagreb, 1968.
21. Neuberger, E. "The Yugoslav Investment Auctions." Quarterly Journal of Economics, 1959, 88-115.
22. Jovanović, B. "Reform of the Credit and Banking System." Yugoslav Survey, 22, 1965, 3216-36.
23. Vojnić, D. "Investiciona politika i sistem proširene reprodukcije." In Aktuelni problemi ekonomske politike Jugoslavije 1969/1970. Zagreb, 1969, pp. 75-92.
24. Horvat, B. "Jugoslavenski sistem samoupravljanja in uvoz tujega kapitala." Ekonomska revija, 1967, 406-17.
25. Narodna banka Jugoslavije. "Novčano-kreditna politika i stabilnost dinara." Mimeographed. Belgrade, 1965.
26. Dimitrijević, D. "The Use of Flow-of-Funds Accounts in Monetary Planning in Yugoslavia." Review of Income and Wealth, 1968, 101-16.
27. Čirović, M. Novac i kredit. Belgrade, 1966.
28. Vučković, M. "Dosadašnja inflaciona kretanja u Jugoslaviji." Ekonomist, 1967, 121-40.
29. Miljanić, N. "Prilog izučavanju problematike novca." Ekonomski pregled, 1956, 12-24.
30. Bajt, A. "Izvori inflacije u razdoblju posle reforme." Ekonomist, 1967, 141-46.
31. Ribnikar, I. "Emisija primarnega denarja." Ekonomska revija, 1973, 21-31.
32. Perišin, I. "Antiinflatorna politika Jugoslavije poslije reforme." Ekonomski pregled, 1969, 497-530.
33. Perišin, I. Monetarno-kreditna politika. Zagreb, 1968.
34. Dimitrijević, D. "The Financial Structure in a Changing Economy: The Case of Yugoslavia." Florida State University Slavic Papers, 1968, 1-22.
35. Milojević, D. M. Neposredni porezi Srbije i Kraljevine Srba, Hrvata i Slovenaca. Belgrade, 1925.
36. Matejić, M. Javne finansije. Belgrade, 1958.
37. Perić, A. Finansijska teorija i politika. Belgrade, 1964.
38. Radovanović, R. "Budgetary System and Budget Expenditure." Yugoslav Survey, 1962, 1111-22.
39. Tišma, T. Javne finansije. Zagreb, 1964.
40. Milatović, S. M. Poreski sistem. Belgrade, 1967.
41. Jelčić, B. "Problemi društvenih financija (prihoda)." Mimeographed study, Ekonomski institut. Zagreb, 1967.
42. Radovanović, R. Poreski sistem FNRJ. Belgrade, 1953.
43. Pejovich, S. "Taxes and Pattern of Economic Growth: The Case of Yugoslavia." Cahiers de l'ISEA, 1964, 227-35.
44. Hanžeković, M. "Problemi društvenih financija." Mimeographed study, Ekonomski institut. Belgrade, 1967.
45. Lazarević, B. "Turnover Tax." Yugoslav Survey, 1965, 3311-20.
46. Jelčić, B. "Ekonomski učinci oporezivanja prometa proizvoda." Mimeographed study, Ekonomski institut. Zagreb, 1967.
47. Konevski, T. Fundamentalnost i razvojne smernice novog sistema finansiranja društveno-političkih zajednica. Belgrade, 1968.
48. Bogoev, K. Lokalne finansije. Belgrade, 1964.
49. Radovanović, R. "Budžet u toku proteklih deset godina." In Razvoj

privrede FNRJ. Belgrade, 1956, pp. 443-51.

50. Turčinović, S. "Financing Socio-Political Units." Yugoslav Survey, 1968, 59-74.

51. Sicherl, P., et al. "Izučavanje problema dopunskih sredstava republikama na trajnijoj osnovi." Mimeographed study, Institut ekonomskih nauka. Belgrade, 1968.

52. Ivanović, B. Primena metoda I-odstupanja u problemima odredjivanja ekonomske razvijenosti. Institut ekonomskih nauka, Reprint No. 13. Belgrade, 1964.

53. Sicherl, P. "Analiza nekih elemanata za ocenu stepena razvijenosti republika i pokrajina." Ekonomska analiza, 1969, 5-28.

54. Djordjević, J. Sistem lokalne samouprave u Jugoslaviji. Belgrade, 1957.

55. Milivojević, D. The Yugoslav Commune. Belgrade, 1965.

56. Djuričić, J. "Local Communities." Yugoslav Survey, 1965, 3287-300.

57. Miljković, D. "Komuna i društvena reprodukcija." In Privredni sistem i ekonomska politika Jugoslavije. Belgrade, 1961.

58. Davičo, J. "Privredni problemi komune." Ekonomist, 3-4, 1954, 185-95; discussion, pp. 195-208.

59. Radovanović, R. Oporezivanje dohotka privrednih poduzeća. Belgrade, 1956.

60. Bogoev, K. "Opšti prikaz fiskalnog sistema i fiskalne politike Jugoslavije." Univerzitet danas, 9-10, 1968, 149-63.

61. Bogoev, K. "Stabilizaciona fiskalna politika." Ekonomist, 1967, 1-28.

62. Hanžeković, M. "Djelovanje porezne i monetarno-kreditne politike na stabilizaciju jugoslavenske privrede." Ekonomist, 1967, 29-49.

63. Šoškić, B. "Rast proizvodnje i zaposlenosti i mere ekonomske politike." Ekonomist, 1969, 143-55.

64. Petrović, M. Formiranje prihoda društveno-političkih zajednica u SR Srbiji i njihova raspodela izmedju republika, pokrajina i opština. Belgrade, 1968.

65. Košir, M. The Kranj Commune. Belgrade, 1966.

66. Jelčić, B. "Poreska i budžetska politika." In Aktuelni problemi ekonomske politike Jugoslavije 1969/1970. Zagreb, 1969.

67. Šoškić, B. "Povećanje zaposlenosti u našem sistemu tržišne privrede." Ekonomska misao, 1969, 79-92.

68. Bajt, A. "Yugoslav Economic Reforms, Monetary and Production Mechanism." Economics of Planning, 1967, 201-18.

69. Papić, A. "Investment Financing in Yugoslavia." Annals of Collective Economy, 1969, 208-31.

70. Djordjević, J. "The Communal System in Yugoslavia." Annals of Collective Economy, 1959, 169-207.

71. Pusić, E. Samoupravljanje. Zagreb, 1968.

72. Stranjak, A. "Monetarno regulisanje u multilateralnom sistemu centralne banke." Ekonomist, 1973, 239-50.

73. Vučić, N. "Änderungen in jugoslawischen Banksystem." Österreichisches Bank-Archiv, 1972, 287-300.

74. Dimitrijević, D., and Macesich, G. Money and Finance in Contemporary Yugoslavia. New York, 1963.

75. Dimitrijević, D. "Mehanizam finansiranje jugoslovenske privrede." Ekonomska misao, 1973, 25-45.

76. Pejovich, S. "A Note on Bank Credit and the Investment Behaviour of the

References

Firm in Socialism." In H. Raupach (ed.), Jahrbuch der Wirtschaft Osteuropas. Munich, 1974.

77. Jurković, P. "Sistem poreza i doprinosa." Ekonomski pregled, 1972, 513-40.
78. Kranjec, M. "Planiranje in fiskalna politika." Ekonomska revija, 1973, 161-74.
79. Kranjec, M. "Analiza nekaterih učinkov jugoslavanske fiskalne politike v luči novejših konceptov ekonomske teorije." Ekonomska analiza, 1973, 165-88.

CHAPTER 7

1. Sweezy, P. "The Transition from Socialism to Capitalism?" Monthly Review, 1964, 569-90.
2. Djordjević, J. "A Contribution to the Theory of Social Property." Socialist Thought and Practice, 24, 1966, 73-110.
3. Marković, M. "Socijalizam i samoupravljanje." In Smisao i perspektive socijalizma. Zagreb, 1965, pp. 54-71.
4. Horvat, B. "Socijalistička robna proizvodnja." Gledišta, 1968, 1321-30.
5. Bakarić, V. Aktuelni problemi izgradnje našeg privrednog sistema. Zagreb, 1963.
6. Maksimović, I. "Razmišljanja o nekim teoretskim i idejnim pitanjima robne proizvodnje povodom našeg privrednog sistema." Ekonomist, 209-26.
7. Mišić, D. "Sistem integralnog samoupravljanja u jugoslovenskoj privredi." Ekonomist, 1965, 289-312.
8. Horvat, B. Ekonomika jugoslavenske naftne privrede. Belgrade, 1962.
9. Pusić, E. Samoupravljanje. Zagreb, 1968.
10. Simpozij jugoslavensko-čehoslovačkih filosofa. "Savremeni trenutak socijalizma." Filosofija, 2, 1969, 1-98.

INDEX

Index

Index

ABOUT THE AUTHOR

Branko Horvat is Professor of Economics at the Institute of Economic Sciences in Belgrade. He has served as a member of the Federal Planning Board and participated in various economic committees of the Yugoslav federal government. Among the many books he has written are Business Cycles in Yugoslavia and Towards a Theory of Planned Economy. With Mihailo Marković and Rudi Supek he edited Self-governing Socialism, a reader in two volumes. All of these titles are published by International Arts and Sciences Press.

C